The work of Jacqu[es] D[errida] [   ] [   ] In this book
Robert Smith offers both [   ] [   ] an investigation
of current theories of autobiography. Smith argues that for Derrida autobiography is
not so much subjective self-revelation as relation to the other, not so much a general
condition of thought as a general condition of writing – what Derrida calls the
'autobiography of the writing' – which mocks any self-centred finitude of living and
dying. In this context, and using literary–critical, philosophical and psychoanalytical
sources, Smith thinks through Derrida's texts in a new, but distinctly Derridean way,
and finds new perspectives to analyse the work of classical writers including Hegel,
Nietzsche, Kierkegaard, Freud and de Man.

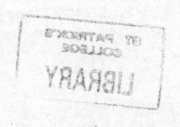

❖❖❖

Derrida and autobiography

Literature, Culture, Theory

❖❖

General editors

RICHARD MACKSEY, *The Johns Hopkins University*
and MICHAEL SPRINKER, *State University of New York at Stony Brook*

The Cambridge *Literature, Culture, Theory* series is dedicated to theoretical studies in the human sciences that have literature and culture as their object of enquiry. Acknowledging the contemporary expansion of cultural studies and the redefinitions of literature that this has entailed, the series includes not only original works of literary theory but also monographs and essay collections on topics and seminal figures from the long history of theoretical speculation on the arts and human communication generally. The concept of theory embraced in the series is broad, including not only the classical disciplines of poetics and rhetoric, but also those of aesthetics, linguistics, psychoanalysis, semiotics and other cognate sciences that have inflected the systematic study of literature during the past half century.

Derrida and autobiography

❖❖

ROBERT SMITH

All Souls College, Oxford

CAMBRIDGE
UNIVERSITY PRESS

Published by the Press Syndicate of the University of Cambridge
The Pitt Building, Trumpington Street, Cambridge, CB2 1RP
40 West 20th Street, New York, NY 10011-4211, USA
10 Stamford Road, Oakleigh, Melbourne 3166, Australia

First published 1995

Printed in Great Britain at the University Press, Cambridge

A catalogue record for this book is available from the British Library

Library of Congress cataloguing in publication data

Smith, Robert, 1965–
Derrida and autobiography / Robert Smith.
p.   cm. – (Literature, culture, theory; 16)
Includes index.
ISBN 0 521 46005 0 (hardback) – ISBN 0 521 46581 8 (paperback)
1. Derrida, Jacques. 2. Autobiography. I. Title. II. Series.
B2430.D484S55   1995
194 – dc20   94 33870   CIP

ISBN 0 521 46005 0 hardback
ISBN 0 521 46581 8 paperback

Contents

Preface

The family theatre organises this theory of judgment whose schema is already fixed for the whole future of Hegelian logic. It is dominated by the Johannine values of life (*zoe*) and light (*phos*), that is, truth. (*G*, 89a/*Gl*, 76a)

This is very much a family book, a book where family values come and take over the theory traced within it. But the family values are not easy to establish and overspill the containing of them by, say, a politics of the right such as is rampant in this part of Europe (and elsewhere) at the time of writing. For a start, what seemed to be a stable and even perpetual conjunction of life and light, of *zoe* and of *phos* in its clarity, what was clear about that unity came to be added to in a way that is still ongoing, in the form of the remains that Derrida refers to: in the figure of Esther. Her appearance, though delayed, should have been accounted for from the start. That is why 'The book of Esther' precedes the sections, 'Clarifying autobiography' and 'The book of Zoë'. The extended family, however, far from attaining a new stability thereby, only prompted all the more strongly the force of what Derrida calls the 'mark' to threaten it at its edges, sometimes even from within. With Esther arrived this disruptive mark.

For now this book attempts to frame this energy in a kind of still life. This theoretical perspect hopes to trap in its vision and bring home to itself the homely, habitual things of a still life that figures their domestication. At the same time it wants to welcome the outsider marked by foreignness, Derrida of course but others too.

I have tried to write according to what Derrida calls 'the extreme tension of a polyphony'. That is, I have tried to put into practice the tonal variety that takes what is theoretical in Derrida beyond theory. Thus, there are both more and less academic registers. Without this risk, *Derrida and autobiography* would have appeared deaf to its own statements.

Abbreviations

Page references to French publications by Derrida, followed by the relevant reference to their English translations where available; to Derrida texts available in English but not in French; to English 'anthologies' of Derrida texts; and to bilingual editions of his work, are included in the main text and abbreviated as shown below. All other references appear in the notes.

A   with Pierre-Jean Labarrière, *Altérités*. Paris: Osiris, 1986.

ADF   *L'archéologie du frivole: lire Condillac*. Paris: Denoël/Gonthier, 1976.

AOF   *The archeology of the frivolous: reading Condillac*, trans. John P. Leavey, Jr. Lincoln and London: University of Nebraska Press (Bison Book), 1987.

AL   *Acts of literature*, ed. Derek Attridge. New York and London: Routledge, 1992.

AL'O 'Avoir l'oreille de la philosophie', *La quinzaine littéraire*, 152 (16–30 November 1972), 13–16.

B   'Biodegradables: seven diary fragments', trans. Peggy Kamuf, *Critical inquiry*, 15 (Summer 1989), 812–73.

C   *Cinders/Feu la cendre*, trans. Ned Lukacher. Lincoln and London: University of Nebraska Press, 1991.

CN   'In discussion with Christopher Norris', in eds. Andreas Papadakis, Catherine Cooke and Andrew Benjamin, *Deconstruction* (Omnibus Volume). London: Academy Editions, 1989, pp. 71–5.

DD   *Dialogue and deconstruction: the Gadamer-Derrida encounter*, eds. Diane P. Michelfelder and Richard E. Palmer. Albany: State University of New York Press, 1989.

Des   'Desistance', trans. Christopher Fynsk, introduction to Philippe Lacoue-Labarthe, *Typography: mimesis, philosophy, politics*, ed. and trans. Christopher Fynsk. Cambridge, Mass.: Harvard University Press, 1989, pp. 1–42.

DLG   *De la grammatologie.* Paris: Minuit, 1967.

OG   *Of grammatology*, trans. Gayatri Chakravorty Spivak. Baltimore: Johns Hopkins University Press, 1976, 6th printing, 1984.

DLT1   *Donner le temps 1: la fausse monnaie.* Paris: Galilée, 1991.

GT1   *Given time 1: counterfeit money*, trans. Peggy Kamuf. Chicago and London: The University of Chicago Press, 1992.

DO   'Deconstruction and the other', in Richard Kearney, *Dialogues with contemporary Continental thinkers: the phenomenological heritage.* Manchester: Manchester University Press, 1984, pp. 105–26.

DR   *A Derrida reader: between the blinds*, ed. Peggy Kamuf. New York: Harvester Wheatsheaf, 1991.

DTB   'Des tours de Babel', trans. ed., in ed. Joseph F. Graham, *Difference in translation.* Ithaca: Cornell University Press, 1985, pp. 165–248.

DI   Interview in *Digraphe*, 42 (1987), 11–27.

DDP   *Du droit à la philosophie.* Paris: Galilée, 1990.

DL'E   *De l'esprit: Heidegger et la question.* Paris: Galilée, 1987.

OS   *Of spirit: Heidegger and the question*, trans. Geoffrey Bennington and Rachel Bowlby. Chicago: The University of Chicago Press, 1989.

DTA   *D'un ton apocalyptique adopté naguère en philosophie.* Paris: Galilée, 1983.

OAT   'Of an apocalyptic tone recently adopted in philosophy', trans. John P. Leavey, Jr, *Oxford literary review*, 6: 2 (1984), 3–37.

E   *Eperons: les styles de Nietzsche/Spurs: Nietzsche's styles*, trans. Barbara Harlow. Chicago and London: The University of Chicago Press, 1979 (bilingual edn).

ED   *L'écriture et la différence.* Paris: Seuil, 1967.

WD   *Writing and difference*, trans. Alan Bass. London and Henley: Routledge and Kegan Paul, 1978, reprinted 1981.

EJ   '"Etre juste avec Freud": l'histoire de la folie à l'age de la psychanalyse', in *Penser la folie: essais sur Michel Foucault.* Paris: Galilée, 1992, pp. 139–95.

TDJ   '"To do justice to Freud": the history of madness in the age of psychoanalysis', trans. Pascale-Anne Brault and Michael Naas, *Critical inquiry*, 20 (Winter 1994), 227–66.

F   'Fors: les mots anglés de Nicolas Abraham et Maria Torok', in Nicolas Abraham and Maria Torok, *Cryptonomie: le verbier de l'homme aux loups*. Paris: Aubier-Flammarion, 1976, pp. 7–73.

Fo   'Fors: the anglish words of Nicolas Abraham and Maria Torok', trans. Barbara Johnson, foreword to Nicolas Abraham and Maria Torok, *The Wolf Man's magic word: a cryptonomy*, trans. Nicholas Rand. Minneapolis: University of Minnesota Press, 1986, pp. xi–xlviii.

FL   'Force of law: the "mystical foundation of authority"', trans. Mary Quaintance, in eds. Drucilla Cornell, Michel Rosenfeld and David Gray Carlson, *Deconstruction and the possibility of justice*. New York and London: Routledge, 1992, pp. 3–67.

FS   'Forcener le subjectile', in Jacques Derrida and Paule Thévenin, *Antonin Artaud: dessins et portraits*. Paris: Gallimard, 1986, pp. 55–108.

G   *Glas*. Paris: Galilée, 1974.

Gl   *Glas*, trans. John P. Leavey, Jr and Richard Rand. Lincoln: University of Nebraska Press, 1986.

HE   'Heidegger's ear: philopolemology (*Geschlecht* IV)', trans. John P. Leavey, Jr, in ed. John Sallis, *Reading Heidegger: commemorations*. Bloomington and Indianapolis: Indiana University Press, 1993, pp. 163–218.

IW   'Interpretations at war: Kant, the Jew, the German', trans. Moshe Ron, *New literary history*, 22 (1991), 39–95.

JD   with Geoffrey Bennington, *Jacques Derrida*. Paris: Seuil, 1991.

JDe with Geoffrey Bennington, *Jacques Derrida*, trans. Bennington. Chicago: The University of Chicago Press, 1993.

LCP *La carte postale: de Socrate à Freud et au-delà*. Paris: Aubier-Flammarion, 1980.

TPC *The post card: from Socrates to Freud and beyond*, trans. Alan Bass. Chicago: The University of Chicago Press, 1987.

LD   *La dissémination*. Paris: Seuil, 1972.

D   *Dissemination*, trans. Barbara Johnson. Chicago: The University of Chicago Press, and London: The Athlone Press, 1981.

LDDR 'Lecture de "Droit de regards"' in M.-F. Plissart, *Droit de regards*. Paris: Minuit, 1985, pp. i–xxxvi.

LI   *Limited inc.*, présentation et traductions par Elisabeth Weber. Paris: Galilée, 1990.

LInc *Limited inc*, trans. Samuel Weber and Jeffrey Mehlman.

Evanston: Northwestern University Press, 1988, 2nd printing 1990.

LO   'Living on: border lines', trans. James Hulbert, in Harold Bloom *et al.*, *Deconstruction and criticism*. London and Henley: Routledge and Kegan Paul, 1979, pp. 75–176.

L'O   *L'oreille de l'autre: otobiographies, transferts, traductions: textes et débats avec Jacques Derrida*, sous la direction de Claude Lévesque et Christie V. McDonald. Montréal: VLB Editeur, 1982.

TEO   *The ear of the other: otobiography, transference, translation: texts and discussions with Jacques Derrida*, trans. Peggy Kamuf and Avital Ronell, ed. Christie McDonald. Lincoln and London: University of Nebraska Press (Bison Book), 1988. This publication includes 'Choreographies' (pp. 163–85) which is omitted in the above.

L'OG   Edmund Husserl, *L'origine de la géometrie*, traduction et introduction par Jacques Derrida. Paris: Presses Universitaires de France, 1962.

TOG   *Edmund Husserl's 'Origin of geometry': an introduction*, trans. John P. Leavey, Jr. Lincoln and London: University of Nebraska Press (Bison Book), 1989.

LV   *La vérité en peinture*. Paris: Flammarion, 1978.

TT   *The truth in painting*, trans. Geoff Bennington and Ian McLeod. Chicago: The University of Chicago Press, 1987.

LVP   *La voix et le phénomène*. Paris: Presses Universitaires de France, 1967, 5th edn. 1989.

SAP   *Speech and phenomena and other essays on Husserl's theory of signs*, trans. David B. Allison. Evanston: Northwestern University Press, 1973.

M   *Mémoires: pour Paul de Man*. Paris: Galilée, 1988.

Me   *Mémoires: for Paul de Man*, revised edn, trans. Cecile Lindsay, Jonathan Culler, Eduardo Cadava and Peggy Kamuf. New York: Columbia University Press, 1989.

MC   'Mes chances: au rendez-vous de quelques stéréophonies épicuriennes', *Cahiers confrontation*, 30 (1988), 19–45.

MCh   'My chances/*Mes chances*: a rendezvous with some Epicurean stereophonies', trans. Irene Harvey and Avital Ronell, in eds. Joseph H. Smith and William Kerrigan, *Taking chances: Derrida, psychoanalysis and literature*. Baltimore: Johns Hopkins University Press, 1984, pp. 1–31.

MD'A	*Mémoires d'aveugle: l'autoportrait et autres ruines.* Paris: Louvre, Réunion des musées nationaux, 1990.
MB	*Memoirs of the blind: the self-portrait and other ruins*, trans. Pascale-Anne Brault and Michael Naas. Chicago and London: The University of Chicago Press, 1993.
MDP	*Marges: de la philosophie.* Paris: Minuit, 1972.
MOP	*Margins: of philosophy*, trans. Alan Bass. Brighton: Harvester Press, 1982.
OCPU	'Ocelle comme pas un', préface à Jos Joliet, *L'enfant au chien-assis.* Paris: Galilée, 1980, pp. 9–43.
O-T	'Onto-theology of national-humanism', *Oxford literary review*, 14: 1–2 (1992), 3–23.
P	*Psyché: inventions de l'autre.* Paris: Galilée, 1987.
Pa	*Parages.* Paris: Galilée, 1986.
PF	'The politics of friendship', trans. Gabriel Motzkin, *The journal of philosophy*, 11 (November 1988), 632–44.
Po	*Positions.* Paris: Minuit, 1972.
Pos	*Positions*, trans. Alan Bass. London: Athlone Press, 1987.
PS	*Points de suspension.* Paris: Galilée, 1992.
S	*Signéponge/Signsponge*, trans. Richard Rand. New York: Columbia University Press, 1984 (bilingual edn).
SPE	'Scribble: pouvoir/écrire', *La revue des lettres modernes* (1988): 'James Joyce: "scribble" 1: genèse des textes', textes réunis par Claude Jacquet, 13–23.
Sc	'Scribble (writing-power)', trans. Cary Plotkin, *Yale French studies*, 58 (1979), 116–47.
SPPC	*Schibboleth: pour Paul Celan.* Paris: Galilée, 1986.
SST	'Some statements and truisms about neologisms, newisms, postisms, parasitisms, and other small seismisms', trans. Anne Tomiche, in ed. David Carroll, *The states of 'theory': history, art and critical discourse.* New York: Columbia University Press, 1990, pp. 63–94.
TLG	'The law of genre', trans. Avital Ronell, *Glyph*, 7 (1980), 176–232.
TTT	'The time of a thesis: punctuations', trans. Kathleen McLaughlin, in ed. Alan Montefiore, *Philosophy in France today.* Cambridge: Cambridge University Press, 1983, pp. 34–50.
UG	*Ulysse gramophone: deux mots pour Joyce.* Paris: Galilée, 1987.

UGr   'Ulysses gramophone: hear say yes in Joyce', trans. Tina
       Kendall, revised Shari Benstock, in ed. Bernard Benstock,
       James Joyce: the augmented ninth. Syracuse: Syracuse Uni-
       versity Press, 1988, pp. 27–75. (This text translates only one
       of the two collected in the above.)

PART I

The book of Esther

I

Incipit

Like the transcendental illusion to which he refers in *Donner le temps 1*, for example (*DLT1*, 46/*GT1*, 30), there is a form of reason analysed by Derrida which contravenes the formal rationality it springs from.[1] For Kant 'transcendental illusion' – a kind of post-Baconian 'Idol of the mind'[2] – arises when the judgment becomes detached from its positive moorings in experience, and enjoys for a while the sensation of being powered under its own steam: it suffers the 'illusion' that it can generate its own conditions of functioning, 'transcendental' in only a phoney, adventitious or delinquent way. A schema such as this is a far cry – and on several counts – from analyses offered by Derrida (much too much conflating and aligning of Derrida with varying 'precursors' gets accepted these days as sufficient exposition), and yet this motif of a rationality capable of going against itself, or beyond itself, makes for a powerful link in the singular, sprawling history of ideas that provides a context for the present discussion.

I wish to let this context be dominated for now however by Hegel, not Kant. For it is in Hegel especially and in Derrida's readings of him that an interested party can look for and find that spoliation of reason by something within its precincts that reveals *autobiography* to be perhaps the most fertile, if an unlikely, place for working on ideas of reason 'itself'. I mean the internecine attack, dramatic in Hegel, by what remains autobiographical in reason even as the latter craves accession to a universal language purged (by definition) of elements too special, too personal, too finite even or even too subjective not to qualify that universality and speckle the flawlessness of its completion.

---

1 Transcendental illusion is discussed by Kant in the second division of the 'Transcendental dialectic' in the *Critique of pure reason*, trans. Norman Kemp Smith, 2nd impression (Basingstoke and London: Macmillan Education, 1933), pp. 297–99. Hereafter referred to as the *First critique*.

2 It will be recalled that the *First critique* takes its epigraph from Bacon.

Too subjective? But Hegel insists on the necessity of subjective 'moments' — such as self-consciousness[3] — on the way to reason, on the way to absolute knowledge, that is; any universal or absolute which attempts to do away with such moments will be unfounded and as spurious as the transcendental illusion in Kant. Yet these moments are just as destructive as they are necessary, Derrida argues, and with a destructiveness very different from the enablingly destructive self-superseding of the subjective in Hegel. Nothing enabling redounds from such 'moments' according to Derrida, their subjectivity (as it was for Kierkegaard up to a point, in his reading of Hegel) unconfinable to a dialectical moment, unsubduable to philosophic method, tending rather to spread and invade the dialectic as a whole — a whole which, precisely because the ascent towards it through the part, the subjective, has been hijacked, never properly attains its own form, though it maintain its desire for such. Hence a Derridean emphasis upon what *remains* subjective in Hegel, upon what is left over after all the dialectical reprises have been triggered off. Long after the subjective has been taken up and incorporated in the universal, there are remains: a remarkable specificity which is the 'subject' of this book — a tendency rather. This tendency is the tendency of the autobiographical, not unlike the Uncanny in Freud,[4] to burst through the subjective, throwing it into disarray. It should have remained behind forever or been taken up into the universal, but this return of what is even more specific within the subjective than the subjective, this *alter ego*, disobeys. We could even describe it (very gingerly) as the dehiscence of the literary into the philosophical. Either way, the specificity hitherto trained by concepts of subjectivity for the synecdochic relationship between specific and general, part and whole, harbours a rather less educable force within it which may be called autobiographical.

That would be an initial, if gross, rationale for picking up Hegel as a counterweight to Derrida — the fact that it appears (to Derrida) that in Hegel particularly, though by no means exclusively, the limits of reason are not set by reason solely but get defined surreptitiously by

---

3 See, for example, the section on the 'Actualisation of self-consciousness' in *The phenomenology of spirit*, trans. A. V. Miller (Oxford: Oxford University Press, 1977), pp. 211–35. Hereafter referred to as *The phenomenology of spirit*.

4 'The "Uncanny"' in *The Pelican Freud library*, vol. XIV, *Art and literature*, trans. under the general editorship of James Strachey (London: Penguin, 1985), pp. 335–76.

damagingly autobiographical elements. These elements take at least three forms, forms which perhaps don't separate naturally but which for rhetorical purposes I spell out:

1. The admixture of elements of 'the life' with those of 'the work'.
2. The internal or autobiographical deconstruction of a principle of reason *at* work *in* the work by something paradoxically requisite to it – by what Derrida has called an originary ruin, indeed a principle of ruin (*MD'A*, 72/*MB*, 68–9).
3. The impossibility of a finite autobiography, or a closed subjectivity, in a relatively ordinary psychological or empirical sense.

The relation between these elements demands some gloss, but perhaps the employment of the term 'autobiography' in the first place needs more justifying. It is not after all without some disingenuousness that 'autobiography' can be used as a synonym for subjectivity, or self-identity, or subjective self-identity, and so forth, and I do not wish to use it as such: it is a term too streaked with literary colour, and with a sense of being folded out into a field of experience at a more contingent or erratic or deregulated level than the quite serious terms of 'subjectivity', etc. 'Autobiography' can scarcely claim the conceptual generality that those more philosophically credible terms obviously do; it is too weak, both as a term and a phenomenon. But its weakness is what gives it force. Its concentration of (from a grand philosophical point of view) ignominious characteristics, the literary and the erratic, makes the presence of the autobiographical in the body of philosophical reason an irritant. That is the interest of it. It is decisive on account of the inalienability of its presence there, and these opening chapters will try to argue that out. It becomes a *general* fact about rationality that it can never be general enough, not least because in order to be formed generality has to be en*gendered* with a *genitivity* that always involves against its wishes a commitment to or contract with a sort of 'low' specificity, more intractable than the subjective, that we shall call autobiographical.

Autobiography holds this usefully discreditable status, then. The relation between its three forms isolated above breeds complexity, one of the preliminary reasons being, in fact, the very poverty of its status – a status which can be respected, presumably, only by an irony that in examining it will refuse to accord autobiography so philosophical a substantiation of its internal relations as it (autobiography) also beseeches. As *for* those relations, the following can be stated in a way that perhaps resists being measured by irony after all. If, for example, elements of the life seep into those of the work (form number 1), and if, additionally, the content of the work is itself prone to the coming undone of what it propounds (form number 2), then the coming undone affects in principle not only that content of the work but also the life partly confused with it (form number 3). This sequence of thought will then have confounded the division that was basic (form number 1) between life and work, not to mention the consequence of this – viz., that 'the life' in its indivisibility now breaks up as it disseminates through the work from which it is not finally different, thus shattering the premise of a finite subjectivity (form number 3), a violence collaterally performed already in the combined coming-undone of both work (form number 2) and life (deduced in the previous sentence). And so on. Against the spirit of autobiography one could then mount a higher level of generality in order to declare the interanimated complexity of these relations to denote in its own right an autobiographical circularity or enclosedness of the theme we are addressing, but only so long as we remember that our distance from such a theme, our 'objectivity' with regard to it, remains formidably difficult to ascertain for we are being at the same time too philosophical and not philosophical enough in our attentions. That these amount to more than sophistical twinings on a braid will be seen in the fact that they can subvert in its ideality the project of a 'pure reason' whether Kantian, Hegelian or otherwise.

But it is not just a question of status, a master philosophy compromised by an association with an inferior, even hybrid, literary genre, the autobiographical – though that would be bad enough. Nor a question of an unavoidable, let us say unconscious, narcissism which would propel self-reflections of the philosopher into his or her work. Nor yet of a corruption of this into the bad taste encouraging the vain philosopher to talk too much about him- or herself. What then? The notion of a narcissism still stands, but in altered form, as a narcissism no longer stipulating a return to the self. Instead, the autobiographical detour which pure reason cannot but take and continue taking through the realm of the literary and the contingent, through the realm of what by compression will be called *writing* later on, suspends the autobiographical and the rational together in a synthesis both special and general, in a strange state chronically unsuited to rhetorical or philosophical classification. In it, narcissistic recuperation will have to be put off indefinitely because it lacks a free locus for its special operation. That this state may be registered as autobiographical is permitted by the graphical in it, writing giving off effects of finitude which are neither subjective nor wholly distinguishable from, since they are indeed effects of finitude, the results of subjectivisation.

All of this may appear very enigmatic, and may remain so even after the 'proofs' of its force as an argument have been displayed. What matters most is that autobiography can be revitalised as a concept of sorts by extending the more received ideas of it as pertaining to a psychological and self-reflexive subject with a life and a history and a work proper to it, towards a new determination by writing. Further on we shall press Derrida's case for 'autobiography of the writing' according to which the distinction life/work (or spirit/letter) becomes enthralled to a less intelligible but more fundamental intensity that could never be filtered – or *only* be filtered – by philosophies of the subject.

But for now I shall focus on the second of the forms of the autobiographical elements given above. I give this prominence because it raises propaedeutic issues as to the aptness, efficacy and interests relative to the present discussion, of reason *per se*. This second form is the one where the project of a pure reason finds itself irremediably poisoned by a foreign body perversely necessary to it, both poison ('*Gift*' in German) and cure (the giving of a dose of medicine, a 'gift' in English).[5] We take up the motif of a rationality at odds with itself – cautiously, however, for there must be a degree of naïveté in speaking of a 'motif' in a 'history of ideas' when that history encompasses critical and speculative philosophies far from naïve in their own attitudes to both 'history' and 'ideas'. A motif of 'rationality against itself' could not, first of all, be a 'motif' to the extent that the latter implies a rational continuity, a ratio and a rhythm which are our motif's to scramble. So, at Derrida's instigation, one resorts to a less logical, more mythological idiom the better to activate these rationally excessive or incremental traits. When reason outstrips itself there can result only narrative effects, mythological in that they conjure genealogies of such *essential* complexity that they resist philosophical or rational generalisation. It is not a ruse for *dramatising* what is paradoxical or hypotactical in reason, but of accrediting the

---

5 For Derrida's work on the implications of this paradoxical linguistic coincidence, see in particular 'La pharmacie de Platon' in *La dissémination* (*LD*, 69–196/*D*, 61–171) and the first volume of *Donner le temps* (*DLT1*, 53, including note 1/*GT1*, 36).

more-than-singular moments of reason with their own density, thinkable on the condition of the narrative attenuation in time which they themselves will have enforced. One learns to speak of war, of absolute war between 'necessity' and 'desire': 'between my desire and Necessity ... there is an absolute war' (*A*, 32, my translation). A history of ideas gives way to a different kind of narrative, comprising fiction at its source, an exuberant and unquenchable genitivity by which the history of ideas cannot remain totally unaffected and, as we shall see, to which, at crucial moments, it has recourse.

A second set of complex relations. It is in the mode of a surprising inversion that Derrida invokes these mythological or legendary words, necessity and desire, writing, 'I would oppose desire to necessity, to *ananké*' (*L'O*, 153/*TEO*, 115). Where one might have associated necessity with Truth in its imperiousness, on the one hand; and desire with the reluctant, vengeful self preserving its own pleasure against the truth's too harsh light, on the other; now the opposition will be made to work in reverse. Now desire is the province of philosophy; philosophy's attempts on truth first and foremost a means of preserving itself through a coherence of its method fixed beforehand by the prefabricated limitation of its object. That it seems is philosophy's desire, the instinct for self-preservation, or a will to truth. Necessity, by contrast, turns accordingly into the figure of something more necessary for its very incalculability, more indomitable or unavoidable for the power of its elusiveness, than truth – whose relative import will also have to be revised. 'Truth' can be understood rather as a pretext, an invented condition, a token of systemic order for the philosophical system pursuing it (in vain, of course, as it is the condition of its own pursuit, philosophy wanting to *be* truthful) than the absolute cause outside its own system that philosophy hopes to mistake it for. In other words, truth most certainly is *necessary* – necessary for a philosophical effectuation of philosophy's aims, necessary in the sense of expedient or being-necessary-to, an abetting precondition. The quality of truth's necessity suffers, however, through such an orientation of it. For strictly speaking necessity gathers only in its absolute unyieldingness before comprehension, so that its alliance with truth will have to be dissolved. If truth appears now as another figure of philosophic enablement and a gratification deferred so as to stabilise and enhance the philosophical intentions for it, necessity shies away from its company. What we are seeking under the name of necessity could not form the object of a pursuit. The more necessary necessity has rather to be *chance*. Why? Because chance necessarily defies systemic coherence.

Ahead of us appears 'a certain interfacing of necessity and chance, of significant and insignificant chance: the marriage, as the Greek would have it, of *Anankè*, of *Tukhé*, and *Automatia*' (MC, 24/MCh, 6). Nothing satisfies as well as chance the provision called for by necessity that a human system meet its limit before it. Chance is asystemic by definition. If it could be systematised, its chanciness would have been annulled.

On this reckoning, however, perhaps chance would not in its necessity be other than truth, not in the necessary imperviousness to thought of its necessity. That is, philosophy may argue into credibility the mis-taking the *methodological* position of truth (the condition of its own pursuit) for a position that is *transcendental*, or independently true, but the greater interest stems from this: neither truth nor chance lies fully either within or without the system of reason that is obscurely determined by them in the necessary ambiguity of their borderline position. Necessity forms an alliance with chance precisely because of this liminal force that styles chance as both truly necessary because beyond appeal, and hard to tell apart from a truth considered without favour to either methodological or transcendental interests. Very subtly, then, chance maintains the systematicity of the philosophical system in its desire. It reveals and produces for thought, by exceeding them, the system's borders, thus making the system possible as coherency; but equally, *qua* necessity it withdraws irrevocably from detection by that system, prohibiting the system from closing upon itself, thus in a symmetrical gesture making the system impossible. 'Necessity comes, not to say No to desire, but to explain to desire that its condition of impossibility is also its condition of possibility' (*A*, 92, my translation, cf. *ADF*, 120/*AOF*, 134). It should be added that desire has more to it than being a dumb recipient of these explanations: desire emerges nowhere other than in the incompatibility of these propositions, i.e., in the identity of its conditions of possibility and impossibility. The skewedness of desire's conditions serves to constitute the desirousness of desire; desire desires *because* truncated or misaligned in its constitution. Will it have gone unnoticed that this is already to give a sketch of desire worlds apart from subject-based philosophy and psychology?

The reversal is so extraordinary that we cannot leave it at that. Consider: chance becomes disclosed as necessity, thus flying in the

face of the ready opinion saying just the opposite, that chance is, in fact, 'by definition', hardly necessary at all, its impact negligible, let alone conclusive. The reversal of sense (of common sense) works by cultivating the force of that weakness (this will also be the secret of autobiography's strength). Chance commands from the *irreducibility* of its weakness. As we shall see, no reduction offers itself because there is hardly anything there of chance to reduce: that it is not really 'there' at all, and then only unpredictably, affords it a power of unslayable, fugitive invisibility. No chance of nullifying chance – a priori – a necessity whose aprioristic character turns out to be quite unique. Certainly a large terrain may be reclaimed from chance by calculations of probability and a scientific prediction of the future, but the length and breadth of that terrain remain irrelevant in their fundamental incompetence for capturing chance in the non-negotiable principle of its *alea*. Which provides a further motive for a certain mythologisation of philosophy's terms: the non-negotiability has something like the force of destiny or fate. Chance shuns the dimension of reason, foreign to reason's topography of calculations because foreign to topography *tout court*, yet repercussing there as if by godly caprice.

Again 'by definition' there can be no response, at least on a graph of consciousness, to the chancy eventuality that pre-empts, disarms and circumvents in advance rational response. Yet by writing as it were *against* itself (against desire), a rational discourse, if it remains one in it, can perhaps sensitise and nuance this occlusive situation of absolute war, absolute destruction of reason, so salvaging something for thought. This impossible strategy, not chosen but imposed, is Derrida's:

I write against my desire. I know very well that between my desire and necessity – what I call Necessity with a capital N in *La carte postale*, like a character – between my desire and Necessity, and those necessities which dictate to me what I write, there is an absolute war. (*A*, 32, my translation)

If this counts as a strategy, one of submission to necessity, then, owing to the reversal of sense now operating, this strategy can be said to produce effects more akin to an emancipation, though not the strategist's. For to write against desire is to write against philosophy's systemic mastery, creating in its vacuum a tensile environment for the multiple impacts of chance without affecting to predict them.

It has been called 'play'. Caught up too in this concatenation of reversals, this 'concept' must inevitably be adjusted too, it being 'the concept of play' which 'announces the unity of chance and necessity in calculations without end' (*MDP*, 7/*MOP*, 7). The unity of chance and necessity sheers away from its strategic subjectivisation in rational experience while molesting the borders of it, borders that are supra-topographical, indeed bringing rational experience into being as nothing but borderline experience without positive content (and therefore without unproblematical 'being'). This semi-neutralisation or deconstruction of subjective rational experience heralds the crowding in of – it is this that can be called play – a new dynamic, neither material nor ideal. 'Play' might be taken in the sense of the 'play' in a mechanical apparatus, a degree of 'give' in the system, a certain amount of slack not quite proper to the specifications of the machinery but allowing it its motility over and above its power source. The play can be good or bad, lucky or devilish. It can no longer be decided *who* plays or *what* plays, for the verb in this active indicative form requires the presence of a subject we shall lose the right to direct and whose subjectivity, determined in its rationality, will have been entirely reconfigured. Any *pleasure* derived from this *play* becomes hard to apportion, and in any case its submissiveness before necessity – which by the rules of common sense should be what pleasure most rebuts – sends us off on another trail: to look for what there is in the psychoanalytic theory of *masochism* that might help in drafting pleasure's concept, assuming it could exist in conceptual form. Such is the transformation exacted by this reversal: to write *against* desire is to play:

You are the only one to understand why it really was necessary that I write exactly the opposite, as concerns axiomatics, of what I desire, what I know my desire to be, in other words you: living speech, presence itself, proximity, the proper, the guard, etc. I have necessarily written on the other side – and in order to surrender to Necessity. (*LCP*, 386/*TPC*, 363)

One must learn to hear this play in Derrida of the simultaneous subjective and asubjective writing that is strictly neither of those things. Possibly it is autobiographical, where we distinguish again the autobiographical from the subjective. The autobiographical modulation of play takes the work away from its being determined in opposition to the life. *All* of these terms are being given over to reconsideration.

I turn to Hegel, then, as my *point d'appui*. Continuing first with the pseudo-motif of reason-counter-reason, necessity and desire, I examine Hegel's protocol for philosophical enquiry. The next chapter,

'Suffering', then brings the dialectic of master and slave, from *The phenomenology of spirit*, together with the Freudian theory of masochism. Finally, in the last chapter of this section, I continue with questions of history, narrative and fiction in reference to Derrida's 'Circonfession'. My intention throughout will be to make salient the re-elaborations of Hegelian thought by Derrida and to stress the importance of the autobiographical to them.

2

Pure reason, absolute knowledge, pure chance

Hegel writes: 'The sole aim of philosophical enquiry is *to eliminate the contingent. Contingency is the same as external necessity, that is, a necessity which originates in causes which are themselves no more than external circumstances.*'[1] His directive might support a prolonged meditation. The difference between it and what for shorthand I label a more *deconstructive* attitude to thinking highlights the latter possibly better than any other. Even though, as I have suggested, to depend on the unicity of 'the work' of a given philosopher may be regressive, the more so when the work (Hegel's) gets treated in its unitary distinction from another (Derrida's), and even worse when to enter into an affair of contrasts might be perceived as capitulating to the interests of the one, Hegel, the philosopher *par excellence* of differential contrasts; even despite these apparent relapses enough pedagogical benefit accrues to warrant them. That Derrida has examined quite conspicuously ideas of pedagogy and education in Hegel can only shed a dark light on my enterprise, and I refer the reader to his analyses.[2] There subsists in my approach a preliminary selectiveness that is precisely the question, and coming clean about it will not escape the question either, as we shall see.

'The sole aim of philosophical enquiry is *to eliminate the contingent.*' With conjoint modesty and pride Hegel both draws the limits of philosophy, the very limitation of whose goals conforms to an ideal of scientific sacrifice, duty, citizenship or handmaidenliness, and at the same time licenses philosophy to police mercilessly the area whose resultant homogeneity will betoken the cohesion of its own corps or

---

1 G. W. F. Hegel, *Lectures on the philosophy of world history: introduction: reason in history*, trans. H. B. Nisbet (Cambridge: Cambridge University Press, 1975), p. 28. Hereafter referred to as *World history*.
2 I mean the analysis in *Glas* of the 'élève', inextricable effectively from other analyses in the same book, but commencing perhaps on p. 14a (p. 8a in the English version).

corpus. This double standard is in Derrida's eyes constitutive of philosophy. Philosophy can only be as scientific as it is legislative. They amount to the same thing, in effect – and that means that in principle at least the issue of hypocrisy does not arise, and 'double standard' does not apply. To be scientific *means* to establish limits, and limits have to be enforced by a 'force of law' (cf. FL) that at this foundational stage assembles on the near side of good and evil. In so far as philosophy aspires to science – and what would a philosophy be that did not? – it takes to itself a formalism, a setting of boundaries, indispensable to functioning and without moral quality.

Hegel gives philosophy a remit at once narrow and broad, its sole aim both restrictive and permissive, permissive because restrictive. An emphasis on method leads the discussion. *How* philosophy behaves defines *what* it is, or rather *how it ought to behave* which equals *how it ought to be*. Philosophy ought to behave so that, having shaken off the inessentials of the contingent, it may pass into intimacy with the object of its enquiry until it transpares. Its method, tacitly supposed to be plastic or protean, adaptable and therefore free a priori, sacrifices itself in taking on as exactly as possible the imprint of what it helps to describe, its 'object', in order to maximise the object's phenomenon unto noumenal reception. Like any power of mediation philosophical method invites being thought of as a virtue, since it gives itself up for the sake of what it mediates, as though it had a free will and, as such, one that might have been less altruistically trained. That it takes *pleasure* from this virtuous rigour, a pleasure granted by the unconsciousness that a supposedly conscious use of method implies, will be argued shortly. The method gives itself to philosophy. Hence the oblique ontological make-up of 'method', existing only to the extent that it vanishes in fulfilling the task that makes it what it is – disappearance would be the greatest scope of its being. Except that if it were to disappear *totally* it could no longer serve in the presentation of philosophy's object; philosophy would be *totally* deprived of a method with which to undertake its sole aim. A method becomes available to philosophy on the condition of a degree of failure on the method's part. Without it the method would not exist, even as, ontologically speaking, it tends to inexistence. The frame with which philosophy makes its presentations will always need to be remarked, to adapt the idiom of *La vérité en peinture*. While this situation may appear limited to its own paradox, and thus inconsequential, it nevertheless contains an account of the philosophical 'object' itself:

what makes the object objective, or rather 'objectal', is that the method addressing it does not dislimn completely into it, for that would be to remove the distance in the avenue toward it that defines objectivity. In principle, then, scientific philosophy has to contend with a certain encroachment of its method into the passageway for thought that the method itself will have cleared. Or in the idiom of *Signéponge* an inevitable dirtiness appears within the cleanliness of science; the science sponge gets dirty in wiping clean the *tabula rasa*, such cleanliness-dirtiness being the precondition of things appearing to science at all. This would furnish a first ground for doubting the auspices for a pure reason. It also suggests that an irreducibly moralistic or ideological moment inheres in philosophy's constitution, prompting it to cleanse the unavoidable impurity in its project.

Now, a preoccupation with its own methods, a critical self-consciousness or self-critical consciousness, may be thought plausibly to characterise the modernity of philosophy since Descartes. So mesmerised by what it is, and so entranced by what it needs in order to transcend this specular stage that is like an infatuation, has it been, that 'modern' philosophy has merited that name simply by modernising, or modifying, and ceaselessly reinventing its own *raison d'être*. But it can be inferred from above that 'modernity' always has been the property of philosophy for as long as being a science has shaped its ambition. In accepting as instrumental the method it considers indispensable to achieving its goal philosophy cannot vary the principle which implants a methodological encroachment into it and which makes obligatory a certain amount of internal administration, conscious or otherwise. So philosophy has always had to keep ahead of itself, modern in this sense – trammelled by the apparatus.

Dating such modernity loses its pertinence, and yet it could be said that Plato and Aristotle had already been affected by this modernity too. It turns on the issue of dialectics. Menaced since its institution in the academy by the possibility of being abused and perverted towards the socially superfluous and potentially invidious ends of the Sophists, dialectics may be calibrated at the origin of modern philosophical anxiety over method. The threat to Plato embodied by Sophism was that the dialectical method had won status for itself, cut loose from its educative purpose whereby the mind steeps itself in a technique authorised as best for generating insights of a genuinely philosophical nature. We know from above that the very concept of method entails this threat, so it is small wonder that both Plato and Aristotle felt compelled to legislate, philosophically speaking, against it.[3] The paradox of education comes in that the medium of education is practice, the relation to reality deferred, the student held back from exerting dialectical (rhetorical) control in political or social life until the method has been perfected through study; during this period of training dialectic is employed also as it were for its own sake, thus (dangerously) resembling the apolitical, or *merely* political, exploitation of dialectic by the Sophists (who were thought of as overgrown schoolboys). (When Kant refers somewhat obscurely in the *First critique* to the history of dialectic,[4] this is linked to transcendental illusion precisely through this sense of a rational method unearthed in the real – a real whose reality, however, cannot be contended without first passing through the ideological 'moment' we have pinpointed.) In both cases dialectic is conceived of as an art, and that can be either good or bad, for 'art' takes definition from its capacity to go either way, be steered towards set ends (the good ends of the republic) as skill, or invested with autonomous freedom (the bad end in itself of Sophistic rhetoric) as device. There is no such thing as unalloyed or immediate mediation, and the philosophical method that mediates on behalf of the philosophy concerned leaks back into the field of vision. Method then becomes an object, though a bastard one, in its own right, husbanding the power to delay infinitely with its own claims the proper business of philosophical enquiry. The critical modernity of philosophy belongs to philosophy's foundation.

Hegel identifies with that foundation, that is with the *establishment* or State of philosophy (cf. *DDP*, 181–227) which must always involve some repression of methodological anxiety. Eliminating the contingent is probably the most general, the most basic method of method. A method becomes one only by cutting a path, implying the rejection of alternative directions. So for Hegel to announce that 'the sole aim of philosophical enquiry is to *eliminate the contingent*' is to make an appeal that is absolute in being staked on the foundations of the philosophical. Perhaps it is tautologous, a 'sole aim' connoting if not denoting an elimination of the contingent. So the sole aim of philosophy is to have a sole aim, that is to have a method, which is to

---

3 For an informative account see Brian Vickers, *In defence of rhetoric* (Oxford: Clarendon Press, 1988), esp. ch. 2.   4 *First critique*, pp. 99–101.

be philosophical; philosophy must be philosophy, philosophy must be itself. It is a call to philosophic self-identity. As such, in its tautology or hyperbole, it chimes with what Derrida, following Montaigne, has named the 'mystical foundation of authority' (FL), the ideological assertion of a force whose force depends on just such a withdrawal into a certain mystification (cf. *DTA*, 23 ff./*OAT*, 8 ff.) – which we may also gloss in terms of an autobiographical aggression or desire to curl up into self-identity. And as for the call itself? Of what genre is Hegel's directive (the directive as to what the sole aim of philosophical enquiry, etc.)? Is it a part of philosophy to prescribe philosophy's duties? Surely not, for a prescription does not constitute an active elimination of the contingent. Or does it? Derrida has explicated questions like these in great detail ... (*LD*, 9–67/*D*, 1–59, cf. *G*, 10a/*Gl*, 7a)

Ostensibly what Hegel says is very clear, but all too soon obscurities accumulate. Philosophy is charged with finding out what is essential and casting off what is accidental, separating the wheat from the chaff. Not only does that seem common-sensical – the obvious, the *only* basis for scientific philosophy – it also finds backing in the ancient tradition. The distinction between the essential and the accidental, between essence and accident, the distinction which *actively and pre-eminently produces* the concept of essence, receives its most authoritative elaboration in Aristotle. And if Hegel here 'reactivates' the tradition which bears it – the reactivation of tradition a notion that Derrida also discusses in relation to Husserl (*L'OG*, 34 ff./*TOG*, 49 ff.), and throughout *La carte postale* – that gesture prolongs the spell of mystification at another level too. For while the Aristotelian tradition of essence and accident continues to deploy those concepts upon diverse matter, the tradition itself *qua* tradition is also taking nourishment from them, the traditionality of the tradition consisting in its necessary or essential progression, undeflected by accidental or aberrant philosophies which may distract it or detract from it. The distinction between essence and accident allows for the self-identity of the tradition which wields it as axiomatic. While it is for *De anima* that Hegel reserves his greatest praise,[5] it is *De interpretatione* which

---

5 'The books of Aristotle on the Soul, along with his discussion of its special aspects and states, are ... still by far the most admirable, perhaps even the sole, work of philosophical value on this topic', *Philosophy of mind*, trans. A. V. Miller (Oxford: Clarendon Press, 1971), section 378, p. 3.

furnishes the most solid platform for the distinction:[6] but perhaps the most general remark we need to make is of the dominance of the Aristotelian tradition as a whole. The unquiet existence alongside it of a largely suppressed counter-tradition, that of an 'Epicureanism' or 'Lucretianism' or 'atomism', receives some publicity in an essay by Derrida entitled 'Mes chances', which I shall discuss shortly. The impressiveness of Hegel's dictum derives largely from an authoritarian (mystical) invocation of the ideals of the dominant tradition, for what is said by that dictum is in itself almost meaningless.

So there is a double imperative, whose force is precisely that, force, something gratuitous to reason. Philosophical enquiry must eliminate the contingent firstly from the field of phenomena which it is to bring under conceptual organisation. And philosophical enquiry must eliminate the contingent secondly *from itself* so as to retain itself as (traditional) philosophical enquiry. The two modalities are not perhaps different, and their combined effect I would call autobiographical. Autobiographical because:

1. The effect is the one through which philosophy establishes its self-identity (autobiography as self-identity).
2. The self-identity is bought at the cost of total rational purity, tucking a tautologous or rhetorical methodologic fold into philosophy that is both necessary and anathema to its self-definition (autobiography as reflexivity, and as the shadow that this casts over reason, abbreviating its control with an immitigable quasi-rationality).
3. To deny this fold is to own up to it, for the denial can take place only outside the body proper of philosophical enquiry (auto-biography as drive to declare its own status, leading to confusion of its own borders).
4. Philosophy's adhesion to a method with its own albeit bathetic objectivity drags philosophy into the field of objects it believes itself to be scientifically detached from (autobiography as non-autobiography, non-singularity, infection from other bodies, the confusion deepens).

But in the penumbra of all this there stands a stranger, more initial tautology that we have overlooked. It inhabits the phrase '*to eliminate*

---

6 'for if by chance, not of necessity': see *De interpretatione*, trans. J. L. Ackrill, *The complete works of Aristotle*, ed. Jonathan Barnes (Princeton and Oxford: Princeton University Press), vol. I, ch. 9, section 18b1, p. 29.

the contingent'. For what is the contingent if not that which is to be eliminated?

Or was this the more potent question: why, if the contingent is contingent, does it need to be eliminated? Does it not disqualify itself automatically? – ?

Both are questions that test the borders of consciousness. Would there be a case for resetting the analysis we have offered thus far? Thus far we have attributed a kind of unconscious energy to the contingent which, because it demands the presence of a method to police it, troubles philosophy with a necessary internal fold. It could be said: the necessity of that fold is unconsciousness itself. It exceeds philosophy's consciousness. Philosophy can *neither, on the one hand*, send the contingent away, for to do so would be to become divested of the method provoked by it, the good usage of which method bestows upon philosophy the rank of a science. The method, however, fails to work totally at philosophy's behest, taking on a dimension of its own, so that a certain philosophic unconsciousness toward it is installed. Moreover, philosophy must wait, *strictly unconsciously*, for an irruption of the contingent, or else the contingent ceases to be wholly contingent, becomes partially expected instead, so a poor vouchsafe of philosophy's scientific rigour (we shall come back to this). *Nor, on the other hand*, can philosophy present the contingent to its own consciousness as an object proper, the horizon of objectivity having sucked into itself the philosophy that would press its method into service in scanning the horizon. On both counts the contingent as incitement of method elicits an unconsciousness, a necessary inaccess for the philosophical at several entrances to its own constitution.

Thus far, then, we have a leaning towards unconsciousness as the structure of philosophical enquiry. But could we not just as well say that philosophy quite consciously sifts out the contingent from its enquiries? That the contingent can be simply set aside as irrelevant? Where a straightforward 'yes' to this question falters is on the cusp between conscious and unconscious. If the contingent is 'that which is to be eliminated' is its sole function to procure for philosophical enquiry something to eliminate? Does it do any more than provide philosophy with its *raison d'être*? Philosophy would then be the activity of transforming, denigrating what is actually its own cause into something quite negligible, in order to determine itself as self-authorising, thoroughly knowable to itself and therefore entirely conscious. *Because* that consciousness results from a transformation, however, there will have to have been a degree of loss, repression or unconsciousness. Consciousness and unconsciousness become merely alternative evaluations of the same effect, that of a transformation that is philosophy's condition.

A similar conclusion may be reached from another perspective. To begin with, the contingent cannot be a stable 'cause' at all, and not just because philosophy must always relegate it to, precisely, contingency. We said a moment ago that philosophical enquiry cannot send the contingent away, on the grounds that doing so would mean its method falling into redundancy directly afterwards, thus jeopardising philosophy's scientific status. Philosophy must never *with absolute success* send the contingent away, is what we mean. Rather it must maintain the contingent in its power of recurrence, only playing at its despatch. That is what contingency is, a kind of ontological flicker. It is potential more than actuality, so again hardly stable enough to serve as a cause. More generally it can be said that in order to win through to its ideology of substance and accident, philosophy has to let itself be affected by an indelible unsubstantiality at its heart, that of contingency, indelible *because* unsubstantial, because the contingent which 'causes' philosophy has too intermittent a quality as its (non-) essence for philosophy to be consciously apprised of it. And philosophy's unconsciousness is the form of its consciousness.

'The sole aim of philosophical enquiry is *to eliminate the contingent.*' Whether 'tautology' is the best word for the hyperbolic tensions of Hegel's asseveration has become doubtful, but we may note at least the infiltrations of a certain unconsciousness, Hegel's dogmatism perhaps representing a 'denial' of it. The identity between 'sole aim', 'philosophical enquiry' and '*to eliminate the contingent*' adds up to more than one, more than the triple repetition of a single proposition. How may we describe this, as it were, rhetorical unconsciousness?

A sententiousness wells in the enigmatic overflow of the sentence. The contingent appears within the philosophical prospects of its own disappearance; philosophy scouts it out only to exterminate it. This double process of phenomenalisation, whereby the contingent appears only in the anticipation of its being eliminated, calls for a passage through time in which the process can be executed. The temporalisation determines the phenomenality of the contingent as transient, indeed as a 'transient phenomenon', phenomenality itself. Phenomena embody and make visible the flux of time that is itself invisible, only some are necessary and some are contingent, the latter not really belonging to time after all but breaching it every now and then. Because not perceived as belonging to time proper where they can 'be' in the temporal present, or assume (temporal) essence (they are, after all, only accidental), contingent phenomena are already dead matter needing to be thrown out like refuse. That clearing away also clears the stage for attention to the proper, poetic transience of necessary things. Pitched between the transience of all that appears and the permanence of philosophical reason is the *poetics* of that reason, the elegiac sententiousness perpetuated here by Hegel as philosophical dogma. The poetics would consist of a kind of free will, the adaptation of method to a necessary cause. But the adaptation is overdone. Though what could such a freedom be, in any case, if not the possibility of rhetorical superabundance, as apparent in Hegel's sentence? Such freedom, such a poetics, inspirits an otherwise philosophically closed discourse, but arises from a necessity – not so much the necessity it identifies, the necessity of philosophical necessity, as that of the contingent whose necessity is the more necessary for being the less identifiable, the less regulable, the less trackable on a phenomenological screen. Is it then because Hegel's dictum simultaneously engages the conscious with the unconscious, because a certain mystification is involved, that freedom seeks after it to find its expression therein, taking its pleasure on the condition of an entrée to unconsciousness? – an unconsciousness not necessarily experienced anywhere but given by this strangely excessive language.

To continue with the text. '*Contingency is the same as external necessity, that is, a necessity that originates in causes that are themselves no more than external circumstances.*' Much of what has been said so far might be applied again to this sentence, so I shall not rehearse it, except to ask: who decides, before a decision is made, what are and what are not 'external circumstances'? Because the phrase suggests an *evaluation* the question is begged as to what the value is standardised by. That is one problem, and another is this: how *can* there be such a thing as 'external necessity'?

Is that not self-contradictory? To qualify necessity as external is to disesteem its necessity. Hegel has to be relying axiomatically, perhaps dogmatically, on a classical distinction between two types of causality, the one 'external', the contingent consecution of one thing directly causing another, tending in principle to die out, entropic, incapable of sustaining perpetual motion; the other 'internal', perpetual or at least encyclopaedic, self-generating and incontrovertibly necessary. For

Hegel it is the history of Spirit – which is all of history – that has this internal necessary locomotion, and the dialectic that rules that external necessity can, in principle, either be absorbed into it, thus overcoming the distinction internal/external while preserving it as one of its phases, or thrown away as rubbish. Whatever was chancy in the contingency, whatever made it 'external', will have been regulated by the dialectic so that its externality effectively signifies *virtual internality*. It is pseudo-external in that it cannot be allowed to *remain* external and will not be tolerated as pure loss. So it either has to be drawn into the manifold dialectical net, or, more strangely, be thrown out once and for all (more strangely because this would mean externalising the external: is that to keep it in place (as external) or to push it further away? Is there not a desire, analysed elsewhere by Derrida in relation to the death of Paul de Man (*M*, 151/*Me*, 159), to kill what is already dead, to despatch for good what is already despatched? Or, stranger still, and referring now to writing by Derrida on the 'crypt' (F/*Fo*), in so far as this feint at super-expulsion is prompted by a need to *contain* the contingent and the anxiety it represents, could it not be seen as an expulsion that jets the contingent further *within* the body proper of philosophical enquiry?). Again an autobiographical impetus carries reason along, affirming that it can make even what is external identical with itself. More rigorously: the playing at loss obtains self-identity.

On at least two scores, then, the chanciness of contingency has been diminished. First, it gets conflated with cause and effect, whereby the contingent is contingent *upon* what releases it and nothing else, all its power of surprise muffled into an aetiology. Second, the externality of its necessity, which might have promised to safeguard (so to speak) its surprise, gets commuted into an encephalic interiority.

Derrida pricks up his ears at this repression of chance in contingency. Being a *necessary* repression, however, necessary to philosophic reason, it is not a question of a therapeutic restoration – besides, that would imply a method, taking us back to square one. That deconstruction is not a method, or that it marks an absolute methodologic resourcelessness, is one of the few claims that we could more or less confidently make, though doubts would have to be raised as to the claim's propositional form. The tendentiousness present here is itself imposed by chance. 'Chance' would be at the very least the element of contingency that escapes Hegel's thinking while enjoining certain forms upon it, and marks the specificity that I want to call autobiographical.

I talked in the last chapter about the paradoxical necessity of chance. I concentrated on its necessary foreignness to the philosophic systematicity also requiring it. Now there are reasons for expanding this idea. Let us assume that Derrida is like all philosophers in wanting to be as scientific and rigorous as possible. It is not difficult, for a popular image of his work is of its being rigorous to the nth degree, *ad absurdum* – obsessive even. To be scientific to this level means taking account of a fact that will undo retroactively the scientism that reasoned it out. What is this fact? That element of chance in contingency that 'Hegel' 'suppresses'. Namely, that it is *'always possible'* (*LI*, section 95–100/*LInc*, section 47–8) that the contingent will interfere in philosophic method when not expected. Unless this were the case, the chanciness of contingency would belong wholly to what Reception Theory calls an 'horizon of expectation', to a phenomenology, precisely, of reason, and not be bona fide chance at all. Chance must in principle shock expectation – but the shock is neither quite affective nor quite phenomenal for it comes from behind or beyond or above the phenomenal in general, a structural law coming as otherness to the phenomenal in general, more irrecuperably alien (to fetishise it somewhat with my language) than 'the other' or the other of the phenomenal. It is what cannot be accounted for in advance, hence the necessity of it that I described in the last chapter (I continue to speak of chance as 'it' only provisionally, for strictly speaking 'it' not only resists being identified, it is even a power of what Derrida has called *'désidentification'* (*P*, 616), chancy (because of the 'dés-', the dice) non-identification, i.e., worse than *evading* detection, chance has no identifiable substance to mobilise evadingly, so to speak). It is *always possible* that contingency will startle philosophic anticipation; it takes the form of the future and opens historical change. And, being *always* possible, it amounts in its invariant categoriality to a necessary condition or a priori, therefore *also* taking the form of the (absolute) past. As such, any philosophy worth its salt will be obliged to take it, the always possible chanciness of contingency, on board. But paradoxically, doing so brings on the destitution of philosophy: chance, which is necessarily a-philosophical, the limit of reason, is where philosophy runs out; a non-philosophical a priori.

I let the argument accelerate in order to emphasize the instantaneousness of its effect, the kind of unmasterable infinity it has that cuts across philosophical decorum. Indeed its very indecorousness, its power of spasmodic contraction, connects it with the autobiographical. We might connect this contractedness also with a certain suffering, or passion (I shall talk about this at greater length in the next chapter). Derrida's position-which-is-not-one, far from the exercise of eliminating the contingent, might be presented as a reduction of elimination – preserving the word 'reduction' so as to signal the scientific pretensions that are insoluble. Circumscribing the scientism is a suffering or passion of chance. Derrida's is the impossible science of accommodating chance as an a priori, allowing for a principle of indeterminacy that removes any hope of allowing for it ... Autobiography, in its reinvented sense, stalks the scene in at least two guises:

1. By 'accommodating' chance, the sway of science in philosophy is eaten into, its essays at absolute knowledge severely pinned back. The relative forfeit of the absolute leads to philosophy's increased specificity or singularity, even marginality and eccentricity; philosophy surrenders its monopoly at the centre of reason, becomes more idiomatic, exposed to an autobiographic drag upon itself.

2. At the same time chance has to commit itself to a 'reduction', too, to have any effect. Otherwise, it would be mere abstract potential, the holding in reserve of the potency of that potential, whereas it is the weakness of it again that I stress, a forceful weakness existing only in its specific expression (both of these words also require qualification: if specific implies general, that is wrong; if expression implies something prior to the expression, that is wrong too). Chance differs in its force from the force of authority, that mystification of power which nurtures its potency as potential (threat or promise), coming in rather on the force of its instantaneousness. Chance is nothing other than the unique. Hence an unbreachable link between autobiography and chance.

There is a relation in turn between these two autobiographies which asks for some comment. What they have in common is that they reduce a generality to a specific case, but that suggests too much rhetorical order, too tabulated and regular a divisibility of parts into the whole, which is why *specific* is the 'wrong' word. If reduction implies concentration, then we do better to think of this autobiographical-chancy specificity in terms of a twisting or deviation. To register the essential marginality of philosophy, and to render the fact that chance, in its capacity for absolute surprise, comes *from nowhere*, from out of no generalised potential that could then be actualised in a synecdochic concentration, one speaks rather in the terms of the 'counter-tradition' mentioned above. There arrives an unheralded contraction, essential swerve or *clinamen* (MC/MCh).[7] The word 'essential' is at risk of being hidden among the others, not least because it carries the greatest burden. 'Essential swerve', like 'essential marginality' above, insists upon the non-contingency, the necessity of contingency: contingency *per se* is contingent upon nothing, 'un-conditioned' (to use Kant's term)[8] and, therefore, the profoundest condition or necessity. Except of course that it is profoundly conditioned too, by itself, so to speak, by its saturation in its own instance which is unique and therefore *highly* 'conditioned'. Again one senses a whole raft of philosophical discourses slipping away, and jumping from one discourse to another hardly gets round the problem.

The nature of things is that they are awry from the beginning. Chance works as an a priori, or in other words the swerve is essential. Being essential, the pathos of the suffering or passion at stake is something other than tragic. Conceptual pressure upon these questions taking us only so far, attention to tone and style and genre now becomes urgent, for it is not so much the concept as the tone which is decisive (*Signéponge*), the style which turns itself upon us (*Eperons*), the genre which imposes its law ('La loi du genre'). One

---

7 Readers familiar with Harold Bloom's usage in *The anxiety of influence* (New York: Oxford University Press, 1973) of Lucretius' term will recognise the very different import it bears here. Bloom is more orthodox in his usage in the sense that he preserves the idea of the lateness or last-minuteness of the *clinamen*'s swerve. He associates it with a Nietzschean capacity a poet might have for individuation, and with a Freudian scenario whereby the Oedipal child battles with his too determining father. The poet swerves away from precursor poets whose influence is oppressive, in order to 'become what one is', to paraphrase Nietzsche (as Bloom does). In Derrida's usage, by contrast, the *clinamen* is underway from the word go, and no effort at subjective individuation can in principle direct it. The term *clinamen* occurs in the early books of Lucretius' *De rerum natura*. I would also like to refer enthusiastically to Christopher Johnson's fine book examining associated themes – *System and writing in the philosophy of Jacques Derrida* (Cambridge: Cambridge Unversity Press, 1993). As for chance 'arriving' – such an arrival never simply 'comes on board' (to use the vocabulary of 'Survivre' in *Parages* and of *D'un ton apocalyptique*, among others): chance reserves – but nowhere, not in a repertoire or archive, not in an ideal or form, not in a potential or authority (it lacks potency, is the impotent and im-potential) – its chances for further abruption.   8 *First critique*, esp. pp. 306–9.

begins to move away from that elegiac sententiousness providing the ambience for Hegel's philosophic prescription, and towards a style more like farce, frivolity and even the Menippean satire alluded to in *Glas*. What are the implications?

Chance determines the phenomenal realm it disturbs as vulnerable, even as vulnerability period, which could very easily make chance seem like Fate. There *is* a similarity, as I touched on in the last chapter, but also a formidable difference. To begin with, chance is not a power like Fate is, and even though Derrida speaks of Necessity and Desire (whose association includes chance) as being 'like characters', like mythological gods, they are only *like* characters. Moreover, that would be to separate the universe out into two, according to – may we say this? – Greek fashion, be it the separation of gods from mortals in ancient Greece, or the Platonic separation of empirical and ideal worlds in the classical period. The separation is what allows for subjective gods on the one hand and subjective mortals on the other. But (to continue) chance in Derrida's formulation substantially reduces the division, the idealist division between ideal and real, not to say abolishes it. Chance only ever takes place when it takes place, meaning that the passive, tragic, subjective vulnerability to it has no time to assume its abject position in anticipation. In other words, chance in Derrida's formulation pre-empts or outstrips the dominant philosophical triple coherency of passion, tragedy and subjectivity. Tragedy would belong to the dominant tradition setting it so that chance, as misfortune, may be made thoroughly subjective (in the hero or heroine), the accident or external necessity first magnetised onto that hero or heroine and then expelled with his or her death or banishment. The banishment ensures countervailingly the self-identity of the *polis* or rational state (both the state of reason as well as the State as rational).[9] Whereas in Derrida's work the realm of chance, in its unconditioned essential necessity, is the case before it becomes the case for him or her. Or perhaps not *before*, but simultaneously. Chance, even though nothing other than the unique, being the case only ever in a particular case, nonetheless retains the *essential* and *general* characteristic of asubjectivity. Yes, that is contradictory, 'aporetic', and it demonstrates chance boxing reason into a corner where divergent directions meet.

9 I derive my argument at this point largely from the work of Jean-Pierre Vernant.

Play, as I referred to it in the last chapter, or farce and frivolity as I am styling it here, rather than tragedy holds the stage, but if we take issue with the tragic (Aristotelian-Hegelian) tradition, nor do we throw in our lot entirely with the Epicureanism antagonising it. We do not oppose Epicurean pleasure to tragedy, for that would be falling back into a materialism of the subject channelling chance as fortune or play. And so on. One has truck instead with lower genres again, frivolity for instance:

That is why philosophical frivolity is not just an accident. Condillac [this quotation is taken from an introduction by Derrida to Condillac] undoubtedly wants to be right about this, which amounts to considering frivolity as a supervening historical evil, which affects from the outside an essentially serious discourse. But simultaneously, according to a logic we have now identified, the accident is also described as a kind of essential fate, structural destiny, original sin. (*ADF*, 112/*AOF*, 124)

The comedy or baseness of frivolity lies in the fact that unlike tragedy it cannot easily be generalised out into statements on the 'human condition' as it used to be called. Frivolity is light and unserious, and yet it is base, heavy, leaden or bathetic because it resists elevation to generality; not enough of Hegelian spirit, the spirit of reason, lightens it (in both senses); philosophical alchemy, according to an only slightly different metaphor, fails to transmute it. (The teeming together of these various metaphors as if seeking a central shared identity itself represents the tensions we are engaging: *something* unites them, but not a single thing, for that would be to grant privilege where distribution is the law. A pressure towards generality exists, and that is as certain for the moment as we can be.)

Coming back to the quotation: Derrida writes that 'philosophical frivolity is not just an accident'. Even put as baldly as that the suggestion is very threatening to Hegel's 'The sole aim of philosophical enquiry is *to eliminate the contingent.*' Clearly, if philosophical frivolity, apparently a chance aberration, is in fact not just an accident, then philosophical enquiry will not be able to eradicate it from itself, let alone from the objects of its enquiry, and yet philosophical enquiry will continue to be such only for as long as it demeans and dismisses frivolity. Frivolity is frivolous because what is accidental about it is not merely accidental, 'not just an accident', but essentially and necessarily accidental, holding an impossible status, a *de jure* frivolity that no philosophy can, or should, address (because frivolity is not properly philosophical, it's frivolous), and therefore, in addition, frivolous *de facto*. Or rather it should but it can't address *de jure* frivolity: as juridical it should, as frivolous it can't.

Derrida scrutinises the tension in Condillac who is bent on 'considering frivolity as a supervening historical evil, which affects from the outside an essentially serious discourse'. Condillac belongs to the correct and self-correcting Aristotelian-Hegelian tradition wanting to conceive accident merely in terms of contingency, empirical error, historical aberration, etc., as opposed to its more (im)potent form 'as a kind of essential fate, structural destiny, original sin' – or in the terms of *Mémoires d'aveugle* as the ruin which 'ne survient pas comme un accident à un monument hier intact' (*MD'A*, 72/*MB*, 68). How could frivolity become a 'supervening historical evil' unless there were the 'structural destiny' from the start allowing that supervention to occur? More starkly, how can error befall what it befalls, unless it be possible for it to do so? We are assuming here that any event implies its possibility, a kind of zero degree implication in that almost nothing separates the two parts of it, 'event' and 'possibility'. If there is error, such as the erroneously frivolous, error must have been possible – and this 'must have been' urges us back to considering it as a prior condition. And then, if error can be a prior condition, or rather if there is a prior condition of error coinciding with the prior condition of non-error (truth, seriousness, rectitude, and so on) – that is, if priority or the a priori itself were innocent of or indifferent to the prerogatives of philosophical seriousness over an interloping frivolity – then one is urged further still into describing 'a kind of ... original sin'.

That is the tragedy. Frivolity is a tragedy.

3

Suffering

It is necessarily easy to confuse the *conceptual* originariness of 'sin' with what is *historically* at the origin. Original sin belongs to the structure of concepts which, to constitute their own formality, disown that sin, blaming it on historical accident, on the eating of the apple that might have been avoided. A narrative mythology (not to say misogyny), a euhemerism or what Hegel himself calls 'a priori fictions',[1] sustain concepts in general. And history has to be the history of guilt, for history is used to take the blame, arising when anxiety needs to be diverted, history invented as the vehicle, the scapegoat, to ride the blame away in a tragic expulsion. Thus can error be historicised, cast in the form of external necessity and bad contingency, made subordinate. That clears the stage for the poetics of reason I mentioned in the last chapter, acceding to a noble language of elegy so as to gesture that error might have been otherwise, being historical, indeed might never have been at all; while at the same time filling itself out through its jeremiad. Its mourning is its work, to speak the dialect of *Glas*. Sin and error, the tragedy of frivolity, can be deemed strokes of ill luck or chance that philosophy stoically suffers. But without bad luck there would be no history at all: what allows for bad luck also allows for good (together they are everything), and allows for history in general, i.e., a concept of possibility to be distinguished from that of potential.

Derrida's analysis of Condillac resembles strikingly his analysis of Rousseau in *De la grammatologie*. In both cases a 'supervening historical evil' takes on the culpability for philosophy's own internal malignancy, Derrida's labour being to disclose that hidden transfer of debt. The transfer does not transfer to a pre-existing history forced to pick up the tab, however. Rather, history emerges *on condition of* this retributive act, so that history, the narrative of the past, might always

---

1 *World history*, p. 29.

be read as shorthand for 'history of an error'. History is inconceivable without debt or guilt (the German word '*Schuld*' combines the two).[2] An inveterate antagonism between genesis (history, fiction) and structure (philosophy, law) preoccupies both of Derrida's analyses. The two, genesis and structure (the phrase recalls Hyppolite's famous book on Hegel, of course), are born only through their mutual pressure, so that instead of a single historical origin, or prime transcendental category, Derrida exhorts us to consider, with and against reason, a double-yoked 'beginning', neither wholly genetic nor wholly formal, these being but effects, so to speak, of a quite other energy, of a primordial dissymmetry or originary transference. But to continue speaking of the formal effect and its organisation as philosophical rhetoric:

By way of Hegel's rule for philosophical enquiry we began to present Derrida's case for philosophy's debt to something other than its conscious rational self. In brief this debt added up to chance and the inevitable, interminable non-payment of it. Philosophy will have always already contracted out to a narrativity to negotiate it on its behalf, thus insuring itself against risk, chance now fashioned a 'supervening historical evil' rather than 'a kind of essential fate, structural destiny, original sin'. It will have taken what is internal to its very constitution and turned it out, producing division within itself but therefore also coherency, effectuating consciousness but therefore also unconsciousness. Avenging itself upon itself in this manner, its autobiography may be figured in the idiom of *Signéponge* as a kind of self-attack (*S*, 5/4), or more sharply, in the idiom of *La dissémination*, as suicide (*LD*, 243/*D*, 214) – of which, more later.

If such exclusionism prevails within the closest chambers of the philosophical, this does not mean that the manifestations of it will be uniform. Though it be necessary, the administration of it may be more or less aggressive, and here it becomes a matter again of varying degrees of force, and the various forces of the law. The force of Hegel's law was poetico-dogmatic (if I may be permitted such a phrase); in the example of Derrida's readings of Condillac and Rousseau a more typically Enlightenment-Romantic nexus is brought out, as the force

2 See Samuel Weber's 'The debts of deconstruction and other, related assumptions' in *Taking chances: Derrida, psychoanalysis and literature*, eds. Joseph H. Smith and William Kerrigan (Baltimore and London: Johns Hopkins University Press, 1984), pp. 33–65.

and pathos of genitivity (one would like to refer also to the writings of Paul de Man in this field).[3] In yet another example, this time contemporary, Derrida finds in a reply by John Searle to an essay of his own an inflected continuation of that force (*LI/LInc*) — though the weaker for being the more aggressive, the more easily disarmed (though only *up to a point*) for bearing its arms so openly.

In the light Derrida casts over him Searle appears gratuitously to engage the intrinsically gratuitous force of reason not only *at a theoretical level*, by eliminating so brusquely so much that is contingent (in his case, it is the elimination of 'non-serious' speech-acts from a general theory of speech-acts) for the sake of the hygiene of his philosophical enquiries; Searle appears also, with an exaggerated jealousy, to want to eliminate *Derrida* from coming anywhere near him or his work, and particularly anywhere near the work of J. L. Austin whose legacy Searle believes himself to be the privileged executor of, or for that matter philosophy in general, as though this time it were *Derrida himself* who were the active incarnation of this devil, or witch, of a contingent. Such jealousy might make it look as if exclusionism were now operating *at a psychological level* too, though in truth all levels are pressed together in this Derridean perspective. 'Derrida' represents to 'Searle' a simultaneously psychological and theoretical threat (hence the inverted commas), and, since we are speaking of force, it is perhaps precisely this simultaneity, the synthetic accretion of the one to the other, that creates the threateningness of the threat and the threatenedness in response to it, taking it into the uncertain synergies of force as opposed to the clinical stratification of 'levels', psychological or structural.

Legal too, in so far as the administration of force is at issue. The element in Searle's rejoinder which Derrida in turn, in a pseudo-economical gesture, picks out is the one upon which all these 'levels' converge, viz., the legal-theoretical-psychological notion of *copyright*. I reserve until the chapter entitled '*auto*' a fuller exposition of the logic behind Derrida's thoughts on (copyright as a means of coping with) 'iterability'; all I want to do here is emphasize that the self-identity both sought for, and prevented, by reason's autobiography finds itself

3 Particularly *The rhetoric of Romanticism* (New York: Columbia University Press, 1984) and *Allegories of reading: figural language in Rousseau, Nietzsche, Rilke and Proust* (New Haven and London: Yale University Press, 1979).

embroiled in decisions, conscious or not, that are quite indissociably as legislative as they are historical.

Derrida receives the manuscript of Searle's rejoinder and can't help noticing the copyright emblem printed discreetly, but conspicuously, next to Searle's name. Surely there would be no need for copyright if it weren't precisely for the threat of misappropriation, analysed by Derrida, such as Derrida represents to Searle (and vice versa)? – 'everyone will be able, will in advance *have been able*, to reproduce what [Searle] says. Searle's seal is stolen in advance. Hence, the anxiety and compulsion to stamp and to seal the truth' (*LI*, section d, 66/*LInc*, section d, 30–1). Copyright institutes legally the attempt to secure the self-identity of a written text, through the univocal figure of its author and his/her ownership of it. It is only because there is some doubt, some likelihood of an infringement of that self-identity, of a contingent adulteration of its essential cohesion, that the law of copyright has come into being. Therefore, by a kind of backwards deduction or retrospective hypothesis somewhat characteristic of Derrida (a characteristic that has encouraged some, misleadingly in my view, to present him as a radical empiricist), whereby the effect vestigialises or perhaps (*perhaps*) symptomatises its cause, a certain infraction of self-identity may be postulated as a necessary possibility, or law of the text's structure. This structural law is then met by the positive law (of copyright) which aims if not to curb it – something which in principle it cannot do – at least to legislate for the punishment of those who allow it (if indeed it occurs in the mode of being allowed by them ... but a host of further issues opens up here) to resurge and direct their own illegal act of copyright violation. The law of copyright, that is to say, represents the legally-sanctioned version of a force present in two other forms (as theory and as jealousy) in Searle's rejoinder, a force of intrinsically gratuitous exclusionism designed in this version to combat empirically – it is *positive* law – the intermittent flare-ups of the stronger (weaker) structural law which flouts it. But, as I suggested a moment ago, if these different versions of force are forceful it may be because they have bound together into a mystifying unity.

Theory, jealousy, positive law. Let us say for the sake of argument – for the sake of *this* theory, my theory, account, *ratio* – that the synergetic force of their binding together, their bonding or *Bund* (to stretch the point), inasmuch as it requires law to recognise and authorise it, is of essentially legalistic aspect. Reason's relation to such legalism would come under the same rubric as does its relation to narrativity, or rather fictionalisation, portrayed at the head of this chapter. Both times the contingent is vilified, but both times what looks like a wilful act of banishing aberration, the exercise of (gratuitous) force, performed so as to protect the self-identity of reason, shows up as a *fundamental* apotropaics, that is, a protection not just protecting its surface but implicating its very nucleus. Paraphrasing *Eperons*, the offensive-defensive *examen* inscribes the attempt to come into being through self-appropriation (*E*, 36/37): with this sharp point turned toward itself, however, there is always the chance of self-laceration, interior serration, or what Derrida elsewhere nicknames 'morcellation' or 'morseling' (*G*, 42b/*Gl*, 34b), or the 'coupabilité' that is both guilt and the ravages of it (resulting in, for instance, a tearing between conscious and unconscious, as we noted above). But history and law, held severally by reason in relation to itself – the one narrating chance as the Fall and its repetitions, the other criminalising it – also merge. For it is *by way of* just such acts of legalistic disqualification that the chanciness of contingency gets shifted onto historical ground where it may in turn be deemed either a part of history or not. The notion of philosophical *legitimacy* fuses with that of historical *legitimacy*, both understood more in terms of belonging or non-belonging to a tradition, heritage, genealogy or *legacy* than in terms of an abstract propriety (it seems, for example, that Searle very much wants to be the sole inheritor of Austin's theory of language). This is why, in Derrida's eyes, philosophic intentions are always and everywhere inseparable from intentions that are genealogical, a connection perhaps most intensively studied in *Glas* and *La carte postale*, regarding particularly Hegel and Freud.

And: if genealogy, then autobiography.

It is with Freud in fact, though among others, that, in Derrida's readings of them, Hegel shares an interference by the autobiographical. Whether or not it may in some sense be considered the 'same' autobiography on account of autobiography's *structural* prevalence over and above the particular theoretico-psychologico-legalistic appropriations of it, has now emerged as a valid question. We will be content for the time being, however, to say that there exists *both* a general autobiographical insistence *and* an individual canalisation. The philosophies or theories propounded by these two will have had to pay a general tax to the autobiographical, whose coinage in Hegel is his *signature*, and in Freud that of his own family, those living 'under the same roof' (*LCP*, 314–26/*TPC*, 293–306), in the ideally disinterested theory of psychoanalysis. About Hegel's signature I shall talk first for it is the more acute form of the chronic vexation caused by autobiography/chance – a conjugation for which we might venture the name 'aleobiography'; a discussion of Freud's auto-biography forms the main part of the chapter entitled '*bio*' below.

What they also share is a predisposition to dialectical (or 'speculative') thinking. Reverting momentarily to history-of-ideas parlance: the advent of Hegelian thought marks perhaps the most vigorous insurrection into the hegemony of the principle of non-contradiction. No longer does A simply equal A, finding its identity by being immediately identical with itself, but now that self-identity has to be mediated through an other: A becomes A only in relation to B, and vice versa. The form of dialectical mediation that will interest us here operates between master and slave, 'bondsman' and 'lord', analysed so fastidiously in the *Phenomenology of spirit*.[4] The link with Freud appears in the theory of masochism, which construes pain and subjugation to be tantamount to pleasure, its opposite becoming the 'truth' of a given term. The subjection of the slave refuses to be dissociated from the pleasure of the master; through an identification with the master the slave experiences pleasure, though whose this pleasure then is remains to be settled. Indeed, that pleasure exceeds identity altogether cannot be discounted. The theory of masochism considered as a dialectics will allow for the second phase of my analysis in this brief chapter.

But first, Hegel's signature. If reason sanitises itself and so achieves sanity by fictionalising and outlawing chance, this still will not have been enough. Still there will be further intimate elements to be devolved. The very intimacy of them will be, again, what is most intolerable. It was the *internal* cancerousness of 'original sin' which was rationalised fictionally; the *internal* presence of a structural law of theft which was rationalised as the barbarian from without against whom the gate could be locked (always too late!). In more exact terms such expulsive violence was what *established* the formal limit between internal and external. But further rebarbative material exists. Again it will need to be rationalised, determined according to a formalism, its force made form (to draw upon the vocabulary of *L'écriture* [and not *identity*] *et la différence*), form being the force of law which settles border disputes over what can and cannot be granted rational identity (one

4 *The phenomenology of spirit*, pp. 111–19.

could indeed almost say *national* identity).[5] So, for example, the force of the name translates – though never completely – into the form of the signature. What does this mean?

In principle, a philosophical text should not be signed. Its pretensions being toward universality any blot of specificity compromises it. On the other hand, without the signature no philosophical text could exist at all, firstly because, as argued in the previous chapter, its specificity or idiosyncrasy is essential, and secondly because the signature stabilises legally the ownership of a text. Lamentably philosophy must have some dealing with names, but the fret they cause will have been assuaged a little by their adaptation as the signature by which the philosophical text gains authorisation. And, as we already suspect from above, if there is a question of law there is going to be a question of history, or fictionalisation, too. And indeed Derrida highlights another myth of loss, this time affecting names: not original sin, but the story of the Tower of Babel, a myth which affords a similarly reassuring despair (*P*, 203–35/DTB). The dispersal of names and languages, the untidy dissemination into locality, faction and over-determined specificity, was once otherwise. Before Babel, there would have been no such onomastic anxieties of race and person. Once again a difficulty pertaining to the structure of a concept (that of the philosophical text and how to guarantee its universality) finds solace in nostalgia, *logos* mollified by *mythos*, so to speak. Then what is myth apart from unsigned narrative? Two movements coalesce. Philosophy reconfigures the internal structural contamination of its own laws as the narrative *fiction* it can choose not to deal with – fiction is *made*; figurality in general is conceived as belonging outside the body proper of philosophy. At the same time it will wish to evacuate the signature from itself so as to shape up as philosophical – to the precise increase of its fictionality. Philosophy can become the truth that always was.

But will the force of the name have been entirely contained? Hardly. In consonance with Derrida's thinking on linguistic translation, the translation from force to form never passes off without some shadow.

5 'Even before any elaboration of the concept of nation and of philosophical nationality, of idiom as national philosophical idiom, we know at least this much – it's a minimal but indubitable predicate – namely that the affirmation of a nationality or even the claim of nationalism does not happen to philosophy *by chance or from the outside* [my italics], it is essentially and thoroughly philosophical, it is a philosopheme' (O-T, 10).

Since the name (the proper name) appears under the sign of autobiography it is twinned with chance. How so? A signature is a legal way of saying that the name of the signatory belongs wholly to the signatory, and one is even encouraged to make the physical signature itself idiosyncratic, to mark out its uniqueness. But once again, it is law against law, positive against structural. The *structural* law of the name refuses to co-operate. The structural law of the name whispers that there is *nothing* about the name *per se* which attaches it to the person who bears it. After all, if it were fully attached and fully owned, how would it be possible to pass the name on, say to a son or a daughter? (How could a legacy be instituted if it were not possible to lose the name first before winning it back through the legatee? – But if it is possible to lose it there is no absolute guarantee of its being won back ...)[6] Or for an actor to take on the name of a real person, in a film? How would it be possible to name that person in their absence? Or even, for that matter, in their presence? It is no surprise then to hear Derrida talking, in *De la grammatologie* and *L'oreille de l'autre*, for instance, of the 'so-called proper name' – so-called because the proper name, if maintaining no essential link with its bearer, is not a proper name at all. The proper name cannot be the property of its bearer; its bearer is only the name's borrower. Borrowing is the law here – a point made, in a different connection, in *La carte postale*.

The attachment of name to person would seem to be legalistic rather than essential, a matter of positive rather than structural law, for the structural law sees no attachment – and this entails a question of chance. For if a name does not properly belong to its bearer, not only is a signature always forged even by its rightful owner, but worse, there is nothing to distinguish it from common nouns in general; if a *proper* name has been hitherto determined according to *property*, but that property or ownership of the name is secondary, the name is now at liberty to mix with common nouns, peppered among ordinary language – 'the very structure of the proper name sets this process in motion' (*L'O*, 105/*TEO*, 76). So it may crop up anywhere. As a mark among others, it is free to become remarked in any 'system of relations':

6 The 'perversion' of (philosophical) genealogy is always possible, a perversion embodied in *Glas*, for example, by an immeasurable infection of Hegel by Jean Genet.

The proper name is a mark: something like confusion can occur at any time because the proper name bears confusion within itself ... To the extent to which it can immediately become common and drift off course toward a system of relations where it functions as a common name or mark, it can send the address off course.   (*L'O*, 143/*TEO* 107–8)

The proper name must belong to this system of relations in order to remain nameable – 'the proper name was never possible except through its functioning within a classification and therefore within a system of differences' (*DLG*, 159/*OG*, 109) – but entry to that system is permissible only when the property or propriety of the proper name ceases to be secure, when the proper name is 'not only a proper name ... but a common noun related to the generality of a meaning'.[7] Once the legalistic attachment is severed, or rather before it comes along to claim the name for its bearer, we are opened to the confusions of chance and the haphazard constellation of nominal effects (not unlike the lexical vault of a Mallarmé poem, say). The chanciness will nonetheless remain autobiographical, for while the proper name disperses and scatters throughout language, that language is every-where – here and there – therefore named, named as unique, with an 'ocelle comme pas un' (OCPU), a distinctive mark like no other, but no longer in ultimate reference to a subjective bearer of it, to a subject with properties, that is.

The name cascades among the text, here and there, and Derrida's *Glas* monitors the fall-out of the vocables of the name of 'Hegel', not least the final three letters which re-form and shape words such as '*légitimation*' and '*legs*' ('legacy'). I can appropriate for the present discussion only one or two traits of Derrida's fabulous book (for reasons, I sincerely hope, more essential than my incompetence, to borrow a formulation of Derrida's own) and say that that aleatory cataract of name-shards which cut up the text falls also across the essay 'Mes chances' which I promised to discuss. It concerns Freud mostly, and the French title 'Mes chances' gives more than the English 'My chances' in that it echoes the '*méchant*', the being naughty or mischievous which interests us here: the naughtiness is a means of steering close to the law, coming close to it and getting pleasure from getting so close while also 'getting away with it'. There are issues of pleasure and punishment which tie in with the theory of masochism.

---

7 *P*, 204/DTB, 166. There are examples of proper names which are more obviously already common nouns: see, for example, Derrida's analysis of 'Pierre' (MC, 30–1/MCh, 15–16).

'Mes chances' is equally fascinated with names and their Epicurean force, that is not only their parodic Epicureanism but also their *pique*, their ability to spice and perforate language down to the smallest letters. The incisions divide the subject that might have been referred to, even slice through reference in the philosophical sense altogether, while retaining a kind of finitude of nominality, as it were, a quasi-ontology, an aleobiography, to use that term. Such finitude differs expressly and in principle from that of a coherent subjectivity or *cogito*: it is the abandonment of such subjectivity that is demanded by the logic of the name when it pulls away, as it does right from the start, from the legal bond of subjectivity and property which had secured the title, the title deed or entitlement of/as the name.

Could this obscure finitude nonetheless be traced to a *tacit* subjectivity instead? If not to a subjective *cogito*, rational and conscious, perhaps to an *unconscious* one?

This question lets us make a discrimination between psychoanalysis and deconstruction. In so far — it is only *so* far — as Freud operates with dialectical machinery 'his' thinking remains all too philosophical, Derrida suggests. There may be a philosophy of psychoanalysis residual within psychoanalysis, one that would, for example, manage aleatory unconsciousness with the too cool hand of dialectical mastery. It would reduce chance. Just as the contingent for Hegelian philosophy is (with good reason) credited with somewhat less than a full-blown chanciness, and styled as the 'external necessity' that is virtually internal, so in psychoanalysis the random thoughts surfacing during free association are read as latently contingent upon one another, part of a submerged aetiology forming the pattern of a psychic unity. Psychoanalysis treats external necessity as *symptomatic*, thus re-drawing the boundary, bringing the external toward the internal, almost reversing the poles so that the external *is* the internal and vice versa. Even though Freud looks explicitly to the borders to light on things that Hegel on the contrary determines to shun, both uphold fairly blithely the liminality of the inside/outside line. Both psycho-analysis and philosophy detain the contingent in a kind of false interior, a labile pocket stifling the contingent's volatility (elsewhere and with a similar agenda Derrida talks 'literally' about outside pockets and purses (*LVP*, 261/*TTP*, 228)). Derrida departs from the *philosophy* of psychoanalysis in this regard. The kind of uncon-sciousness extorted by deconstruction falls neither into nor from a hidden subjectivity; could not be an unconsciousness *belonging* to him or her. The unconscious does not belong. It has the capacity for *both* a literal agglutination evocative of finitude *and* a literal chancy incoherent parade or literal *litter*, and is always held in an undecidable, because chancy, relation between these affianced possibilities.

'Hegel' litters *Glas*, Derrida's text subject, without properly being touched, to the shelling of remains from Hegel the *maître-penseur*. Derrida is in thrall to the master who falls at random upon him, likening himself to a galley slave under the lash (G, 82b/Gl, 70b). These are remains of Hegel over and above the subject Hegel, however, and so not just the remains of Hegelian absolute knowledge in its mastery but also the remnants of what was left out by that mastery in its efforts toward the total resumption of history into thought — indeed what allowed history to continue after Hegel where it should, according to Hegel, have remained complete. Letters, in brief: the fine-grained literality of chance as well as the letters that remain from the philosophical estate, apocryphal stuff, from which Derrida incorrigibly quotes, just as in *La carte postale* it is the letters of Freud and other apocrypha, including biblical, which from beyond the corpus of the master's works work upon its centre, disorienting it. But one cannot simply *incorporate* remains, and suffering the remains of a master's knowledge means not simply engulfing them in a eucharistic swallowing, nor being *subject* to their repercussions, but experiencing an *essential* incompletion, lack, castration or death. The dialectical circuit of suffering and masochism breaks down. Prior to any subjectively channelled relationship between master and slave bristles the literal possibility of chance in its incurable allergy to appropriation. Hence no pleasure, no pain, not yet — that is what remains to come — only play and chance. The letter forestalls the history of knowledge, letter against Hegelian Spirit, while allowing, in the figure of chance and eventuality, for it to be continually re-told. The logic is internally at odds with itself, but obligatory.

The story may be narrated, the debt transferred. But what happens when that debt is owned? Can it be? What happens when rather than putting the blame elsewhere, we like masochists take it on board and confess to sin? When we take on the pleasurable pain of owning up?

4

His life story

Hard to imagine the 'Confessions' of Hegel.[1]

In the idiom of *La carte postale* and of *Feu la cendre*: Derrida's is the attempt, 'against desire', to save remains from the totalising holocaust of reason which would consume all genealogy into itself, the proper comprehended as proper, the improper as improper. Derrida saves the *remains* rather than looking impatiently to what might rise, later on, from the ashes of reason's conflagration, a Hegelian Phoenix, for example. The Derridean figure of saving differs from the Hegelian saviour — ultimately for Hegel *the* Saviour, Jesus Christ — for the latter constitutes a figure of anticipated absolute completion on a higher plane. The Derridean figure is by contrast what is left over from Christian trinitarianism in Hegel's version. Namely? Judaism in general perhaps, but a Judaism converging upon Esther as a figure of the apocryphal, of what is left over after Christian typological summation, she who saves the Jews from the holocaust, sifting like Cinderella through spodogenous matter, and who by lucky chance has a name that forms a near anagram of remains – '*les restes*'. It is precisely the 'Jewish' letter unleavened by Spirit, the Old Testament letter or type falling short of its destination in the New, diverted by the apocryphal into a merely provisional soteriology, chance unassimilated by and wandering from absolute reason, which counts. *And yet*: the figure of Christ, at the moment of crucifixion, bears allegiance with the literal letter or word in the protracted uncertainty of its being taken up, resurrected, hoisted like a fish (the *ichthus*), hosted into the reason of spirit and the spirit of reason. To switch to *La vérité en peinture* and *Glas*: one remains on the cross, suffering in passion, a cross whose chiasmatic power (*chi*asmatic power) forever alternates, without

---

1 Jeffrey Mehlman thinks it just as hard to imagine an anthology of fairy-tales by him: see *Walter Benjamin for children: an essay on his radio years* (Chicago and London: The University of Chicago Press, 1993), p. 2.

wholly engaging or separating them, the plaited motives of reason
and chance. Nothing but death. There is mortal material and we will
never be sure of its absolute comprehension by spirit and reason –
there it becomes a matter of belief, not science.

Hence Derrida's profession of faith in a legendary Christianity
about which he writes in the autobiographical 'Circonfession' (*JD*,
section 30, 145–8/*JDe*, section 30, 153–7), abashed before this law or
god of absolute reason which in its mastery nevertheless fails to
comprehend autobiography and chance. This law or god will never
have shut down chance, the pure unconscious possibility within every
event that no event can know, express or repress, absconding from the
event's would-be presence. This possibility resembles a principle of re-
reading: things may still come to us from the past – the past of events
which have been determined, but not de*termined*, by this lack and
absence – and in this sense we are waiting for the past to happen, like
the future; we are facing towards it and a general tergiversation
structures the lineages of history. Even a god, the personification of
prescience, meets its limit – nowhere – from this other necessity, this
other law, this other god.

And that is why we confess. 'Circonfession' reprises St Augustine's
question: if God knows all things in advance, why do we confess to
him?[2] Because confession broaches non-prescience or chance. It
testifies to the autobiographical, the contingent, the irregular, the
unusual, the singular, the idiosyncratic, the fine literality of one's own
life with its private memories and desires, all the way down to the
most atomistic caesura of chance, which is also passion and ritual, that
of the Jew's own experience of circumcision. All are borne by the
memory that with superfine enumeration, adding up piecemeal to a
literal inventory, will continue into the future to recollect things from
the past. 'One time alone: circumcision takes place but once', to quote
Derrida's book on Celan (*SPPC*, 11/*AL*, 373), and the uniqueness of its
moment, never to be repeated, nevertheless gives onto further
moments, generating a genre, a series of cases or a genus and race –
the Jews, for example – congregated about the ritual, present recalling
past moments and thereby sustaining a tradition, whose possibility

---

2 'O Lord, since you are outside time in eternity, are you unaware of the things that
I tell you? Or do you see in time the things that occur in it? If you see them, why
do I lay this lengthy record before you?', *Confessions*, trans. R. S. Pine-Coffin
(Harmondsworth: Penguin, 1961), book XI, section 1, p. 253.

begins with a cut that abscesses chance from the scene of circumcision over which, like a mother, it waits, and watches. It interrupts presence *per se* and with it the capacity for a god in perpetual presence to permeate it. Perhaps even the same mother, according to a presence more enigmatic still than that of a god, presides in all cases, with chance considered 'matrix' of possibilities, cipher of deconstruction – elsewhere Derrida quotes Nietzsche's autobiographical saying, 'I am, to express it in the form of a riddle, already dead as my father, while as my mother I am still living and becoming old' – which I shall come to again in a moment.

But the mother also dies. The fantasy of the immortal parent, which may be perhaps glossed as 'religion', comes up against an inestimable thanatography. 'Circonfession' narrates the demise of Derrida's mother while in the same book where 'Circonfession' is collected as a band of print running along the bottom of each page, a text by Geoffrey Bennington called 'Derridabase' lords it over Derrida's supplications (*JD/JDe*). 'Derridabase' is the master text which dominates each page, giving a rational account of Derrida's work, having seized the 'logical matrix' of Derrida's thinking. Between the two texts, once again, a crossover between reason and chance. There are countless ways of describing the genealogical catallactics and rational complexities of this scene, and once again I can select only one or two isomorphs. What I want to underscore is that chance (so ridiculous, really, to take it as my theme) is not simply a master principle dressed as a beggar, the fulcrum of a negative dialectics, or a protean but immutable matrix for all reason. It *has* no collateral existence outside the literal points which engrain its inscription, whereupon it dies; *has* no substance before it irrupts and expends itself in the event it biases. So that if a power of conceptual ordering and a certain generality may be attributed to it, it like a mother is a generality wandering only through genealogy, passion, ritual and memory as – dare one say it – real things, and not through the always too-ready-at-hand idealism that would make of such conceptual ordering an order. Which relieves it of its *theoretical* arrogance, unlocking for it instead a passage through the literal, the letter, a principle if anything, to offer it again, of re-reading.

She dies, and one does not have the right to speak of Derrida's mother as a sister of *Theoria*. One can only respect his memory, his shared memory, of her, and admire the courage of writing 'Circonfession'. This text brings us back to thinking more seriously the relationship between reason and genealogy, so much more than a question of legacy. It is a text that unseals the access from logical to biological in an extraordinary and compelling way. It might have seemed easy a second ago, in discussing Hegel, to sketch the structural resemblance between reason and the life of Christ as their elevation to the Absolute suddenly judders into doubt, the catafalque raised but liable to collapse. Easy and fluid precisely because one was operating at this glozingly 'structural' level, committing the sin of what could be thought of as a deconstructive parallel to transcendental illusion, indeed. Deconstructive transcendental illusion would comprise the assertion of structural identity (Gasché would call it *infra*-structural identity)[3] or isomorphic continuity between philosophemes and images at the expense of a thought as to their non-translatability, and so lapse back in effect to a form of the synecdochic ratiocination we set out to deconstruct. Thus a matrix of thought resembles Derrida's mother only through an impossible, unconscious parody. The logical and the biological ask to be thought as a kind of non-synthetic same, even, just possibly, in Kantian idiom, as a non-synthetic a priori judgment.

For the mother dies, totally apart from the syntheses of reason which would assume her as matrix and 'programming machine' (see note 5 below), while at the same time continuing in the solitude – in something near Blanchot's sense of this term[4] – which accompanies them. It is *something like* the relation between chance and philosophic self-identity in Hegel. She the mother, this matrix of the unforeseeable that generates unique lives, will already be watching over the rationalising institution of mourning that may begin to tell what it may even believe to be its own story or autobiography. The autobiography of 'Jacques Derrida' takes place within this institution or ritual. It could be described as the institution of the ongoing death of chance that keeps alive in its energy for further adventure the one autobiography. The one autobiography, that is, which from the first is divided and prone to self-attack, contradictory passions which can just as well vandalise as honour the good faith of its memory and thus '"do violence to the old woman" who represents the mother' (MC,

---

3 See Rodolphe Gasché, *The tain of the mirror: Derrida and the philosophy of reflection* (Cambridge, Mass. and London: Harvard University Press, 1986), pp. 142–54.
4 See 'La solitude essentielle et la solitude dans le monde', in *L'espace littéraire* (Paris: Gallimard, 1955).

37/MCh, 23). Hence Derrida's presentation in 'Circonfession' (*JD*, section 32, 155/*JDe*, section 32, 166) of the 'duel' and fraternal antagonism, even 'interpretations at war' (IW), whose animus begins with the founding of the (mourning) institution.[5] It manifests itself in 'Circonfession' as the guilt – debt and *'coupabilité'* – that curses itself for having perhaps murdered its brother, itself, in a sort of Romulus and Remus myth at the founding of a nation.

The question of autobiography: do I kill the twin?[6]

– In an assault, however, that always spares the name. For the name merely goes along with mortals, holding no obligation to them, or rather, as argued in the last chapter, holding obligation *only* – which is not nothing, it is law, but this law is not everything. The attack comes at the beginning (cf. *S*, 5/4), hoping to scotch the name which always eludes it and mocks from the seat of its monumental invulnerability the tragedies and passions which spring up around it precisely as a quest for the name. Autobiography would be neither necessary nor possible if the name could be owned. In its suicidal initiative autobiography – which mourns only through a name for that name's bearer, a lost but 'living feminine' (*L'O*, 13–32/*TEO*, 3–19), a mother perhaps – rounds on itself in jealousy for the name under which it is instituted but which name, so as to *let* it be instituted, must be given up into the shared space of a people, a *polis* identifiable by its rituals. Between these two names there are politics and, once again, the various forces of law.

Going against desire (for the name) Derrida tries to write into this loving or honouring filial space that verges upon – this is the very architechtonic of reason, as Kant would have it – a space of fraternal hate, conflict and competitive interpretation. 'La guerre commence avec l'enfant' (*G*, 143a/*Gl*, 125a). For better if possible to re-read than to interpret, to honour than to 'engage' in the polemical, conflictual,

---

5 An antagonism and duel presented elsewhere in 'Circonfession' as 'my life is that other that I lose' (*JD*, section 38, 189/*JDe*, section 38, 202–3). Cf. *Signéponge* (*S*, 13/12), 'Otobiographies' ('Neither of the two antagonistic forces can break with this powerful programming machine' (*L'O*,45/*TEO*, 29)), *Mémoires d'aveugle* (*MD'A*, 66/*MB*, 63) and elsewhere. Such antagonism, though always containing the possibility of resulting in conflict, is based on a bottomless, fraternal friendship: 'a friendship prior to friendships, an ineffaceable, fundamental, and bottomless friendship, the one that draws its breath in the sharing of a language (past or to come) and in the being-together that any allocution supposes, *including a declaration of war*' (PF, 636, my italics).

6 In both senses: (1) shall I kill …? (2) do I already, am I already, killing …?

interpretative, militaristic sense. Better if possible to refuse the sop of negativity, a comprehensive or comprehendable death, the compositional surety of the dialectical method, the bad/good mother that kills with kindness by proffering a matrix or programme for reactive repetitions. He risks the autobiographical, the most dangerous thing because redolent with passions and antipathies. But the risk offers the only way for saving to take place.

If this space is a space of re-reading, it explains why Derrida's texts mingle so arborescently with others. On the one hand, Derrida has never been able, despite his passion, to narrate any story, let alone his own (*M*, 27/*Me*, 3), almost out of fear for the acrimony that would have to attend upon it, scarring itself and its other, its other as itself, in its bid for univocality ('In effect I can make an attempt on another's life – in its singularity – only in risking my own' (*G*, 158a/*Gl*, 139a), glossing Hegel). The story would become legible only after some contest of appropriation had taken the name away and let it be read. On the other hand, nothing appears *without* that initial contest – initial, that is, but occurring within a transect of memory where in some form the passive mood (past, passionate, paschal mood) lours. Temporality, and the narrative spacing that deepens into its priority, is irreducible in chance. Derrida, who 'loves memory' (EJ, 141/TDJ, 227) and works from this mood of memory, so to speak, which cannot but wish to preserve memory and guard it, keeping death alive, will have to run the gambit of the violence that comes with that, which is not being able to surrender the name, taking the name back yet then giving it up again, attacking itself or its brother over it, quivering in a syncopated remissioning between private and public, autobiographical and institutional. The only way to keep memory is not to keep it to oneself, nor 'to keep oneself to oneself'. An intercalated style, unique but never entirely one's own, imposes itself upon the autobiographer. One *can* only make autobiography under the aegis of chance, this quasi-maternal injunction to specificity. But *if* specificity, then variety and plurality, the non-singular, even the non-specific, the shared, the open, the to-come, the intrusion of an other who will have the power – an other who will *be* the power – both to love and to hate. That the other can either love or hate the shared memory, the fact of public passion, makes again for the interminable political trafficking that follows upon the autobiographical scene – which never ends – of the mother's death. It is no accident that when Derrida writes his most thickly autobiographical text it is one which illumines this scene. Nor that his texts are constantly engaged in the politics of sharing legacies that could only with naïveté be considered exclusively intellectual.

It is with Augustine's *Confessions*, then, that 'Circonfession' interlaces so. Augustine appears to be owning up to sin in a *mea culpa* that is just as equivocal, however, as the philosophical transfer of debt in Hegel or Condillac which blamed the fault elsewhere and in so doing unleashed the miscegenation – an *essential* generic collusion – of philosophy with history (history as both narrative and fiction, figurality or poetics). Still too much and not enough is owned by Augustine. The naughtiness of stealing the pears, for example, for all the delayed shame it brings in confessing it, abides with Augustine himself and no one else, he feels sure. The shame brands on the face this marque of private ownership. *Mea culpa*: like 'my chances': the sin and the story of it are mine and no one else's. But are they?

The prime means of authenticating confession might be to foreground the unique, confession looking the more 'confessive' the more unique or singular or strange or seemingly impossible the transgressions it lists, the more these fall on the head of just me. But that can be achieved only via an assumed admission of the chanciness, the erroneous and wayward determinism so lefthandedly governing one's life. And the literality of things sets this chanciness simultaneously out of reach of the one who would own it. So it cannot be fortuitous that Augustine's confession involves very early on a renunciation of *literature* (book 1, section 13; his leading example is the story of Dido and Aeneas), for this along with the sexual vices to which literature is likened emblematises chance. It is the emblem of what unfortunately had set Augustine apart from himself, taken him off the straight and narrow, interspersed in his heart some literary affect or spirit that had detracted from the religious affect and spiritual rationality by which later he was to make amends. That experience of being divided from himself Augustine wants to hem in as a sort of negative dialectical moment within the confession. The latter becomes the narrative memory through which its author both avenges himself upon himself and forges himself anew, in self-constituting self-attack and self-dissection, it being indeed once again narrative (the confession) that bears the burden – a narrative that blames narrative (literature).

The owning up will have concealed a more unkempt and unclosable disappropriation. The painful pleasure of sin and its confession turns on the ambiguous suffering of chance, the masochism that rains wracks and pains down onto the self – onto me, right here, and no-one else: it is I who must be singled out and even pain is a cheap price to pay for this identity and identification. The confessive one does this in order that the self may be given back to arbitrariness, to, that is, a master's caprice dissimulating the order that establishes identities – but not quite to chance *per se*, for that disappoints the need for identification. Religious confessions seek the exchange of that diabolical other for a godly one, literature for Scripture, the devil of a father for the good one, the one that will regulate literality as law rather than as error, lifting the spirit up for sure, rounding off its identity, not leaving it to languish, having finished with the suffering. Confession is a dialectics in so far as it posits the (negative) sin that will be negated by the positive goodness of confessing it in order to be identified – but here lies the uncertainty and belief – as the reformed and rationalised sinner who will be taken up into the Absolute. But in making of that sin a story or history or narrative a boundary is set as to how completely it may be negated, for it remains re-tellable and re-appropriable. It has become literature – its name shared and not only between the two Augustines, the sinful and the repentant – even though it is literature about the *renunciation* of literature and associated evils. To be negated the sin must first be told and made literal, but that means it will never be negated towards absolution or made good with thorough success. It may be shared again. Derrida shares and rewrites Augustine's confessions out of a primary distribution of the auto-biography. Augustine's renunciation of literature represents again a force (unconscious, extra but intrinsic to rationalisation) that is all too keen to control that problem. It would not be too much to say that Augustine were literally duelling with Derrida.

Once again, as in Hegel, the teleology or philosophical pilgrimage of a spiritual rationalism stumbles, and keeps stumbling, over the diversionary 'jetties' (SST, 65) strewn by autobiography, literality, literature, chance across its path. Again alternative genealogies and histories loom as something far more monstrous than demons that could be cast within a 'bad phase' of history or life. If spiritual reason has to loop with history so as to make itself fast, history in turn ensnares itself with autobiography which is where reason may always come undone.

But only because another spirit abounds – as the death that is unkillable because already dead and living as such. Unlike, and yet like, the rational spirit which is born into life so that it may die into death and comprehension, this other spirit which reason cannot know, the spirit of chance, pre-empts rather than redeems, its death unchartable and ubiquitous. Derrida calls it 'psyche' (*P*, 11–61/*AL*, 310–43, abridged). Psyche: the spirit that sometimes does and sometimes does not tolerate the calculation of its instance within a generality or genealogy. The vacillation makes the genealogy fabular rather than historical, and fabular *even when it is* historical. The very caprice (more like that of a child than a master) controlling that calculation implants even where the calculation succeeds a quite irremediable ignorance within it. Such psychic non-knowing may have been termed philosophically by psychoanalysis as the Unconscious, but it is the diaspora surrounding philosophical determinism that interests us here. Since it is a matter here of passion or pathos; since psyche exists only in so far as some affect in excess of reason defines it; since it is therefore a *force* and touches us beyond reason; it may be that what we are describing under the name of autobiography and of autobiography in its relation to *'unpredictable things'* (*JD*, section 5, 32/*JDe*, section 5, 31), is the origin of feeling or emotion. In their *essential* variability the two – chance only coming into being intermittently; feeling being nothing but a contingent responsiveness even where feeling is repeated – agree.

But this is not to say that there is a pathos of such pathos. On the contrary. Who knows where such feeling may be received, since it represents a power of incomprehension? Who knows who may receive it, since there can be no finally distinct, private or individual subject as recipient? We ought simultaneously to suggest the *impossibility* of any feeling even as we let it emerge. Or, rather than being content with what resembles a negative limit, beckon forward at least the spectre of telepathy as Derrida has written of it. For telepathy – and I feel sure that Nick Royle thinks the same, perhaps even now[7] – shares the feeling out beyond and between ourselves, including between, that is *through*, each self. The spirit of autobiography seems to move in this way.

But what do these others think autobiography is?

---

7 I refer to the author of *After Derrida* (Manchester: Manchester University Press, 1995) which forms an indispensable supplement to the present volume.

❖❖

PART II

Clarifying autobiography

❖❖

5

❖❖❖

Worstward ho: some recent theories

❖❖❖

The theory of autobiography has become very well trodden terrain. So much so, in fact, that there are now not only many theories of autobiography, but there is also a growing number of theories of those theories, and of surveys (such as this) of autobiographical theory.[1] This is no doubt ironic, since it demonstrates a capacity for the theory of the theory to generate itself apparently infinitely by taking itself as its subject or object – as if it, too, were a kind of autobiography:

Unable to give up wishing, theories of autobiography themselves tend to persist or endure as self-productive fictions about – but never quite transparently evidenced 'in' – the kinds of narrative we conventionally recognise as 'autobiography'.[2]

Those are the words of Louis Renza. What is worse, according to E. S. Burt, is that these interloping theoretical autobiographies may end up sounding like the real thing:

That writing about autobiography should always seem to require having recourse to the same vocabulary of praise and blame as the one that autobiographical writing uses to talk about the self is significant, all the more so because it makes the critic's job of writing about autobiography dangerously like writing autobiography.[3]

Louis Renza and E. S. Burt both bring out the slight distaste or embarrassment at this contamination of the theory by its object, a contamination exacerbated in the case of theories of *autobiography*

---

1 On the tendency of autobiographical theorists to survey the field of auto-biographical theory, see, for example, H. Porter Abbot, 'Autobiography, autography, fiction: groundwork for a taxonomy of textual categories', *New literary history*, 19: 3 (Spring 1988), 597–615.

2 Louis A. Renza, book review, *Comparative literature*, 40: 3 (Summer 1988), 274.

3 E. S. Burt, 'Poetic conceit: the self-portrait and mirrors of ink', *Diacritics* (Winter 1982), 18–19.

which is all about such immeasurable self-involvement, and in doing so draw us back again to the anxieties over method analysed above in relation to Hegel's protocol for philosophical enquiry. The anxieties could be said to respond to an *essential* risk of infection of the theory-doctor by its object-patient. The risk effectively relegates the distinction subject/object to secondariness, and promotes the theory of autobiography into an exemplary position for discourses of knowledge, not an ancillary one at all. It is as if there were something shameful about this contamination, something vulgar or self-indulgent contained in the presentation of autobiography to academic procedures. Autobiography meddles with academic knowledge in its desire for clear and detached understanding. Not only is it not quite a 'proper' topic, but dealing with the topic seems too often to lead to autobiographism on the part of the one dealing with it, like a drug dealer who is tempted into sneaking from his own supply. But this temptation exists from the start, so that consigning the irksomeness of the autobiographical to a latter-day misfortune or literary *arrivisme*, as it were, seems a gesture of resistance to it, even though it is how it is often described – Philip Beitchman says, aptly getting the temporal distortion of the thing, that autobiography is 'already problematical, and a latecomer as a legitimate literary form'.[4]

A discomfort nearly always surrounds discussion of autobiography for fear of this slightly shameful element. What shames is precisely the suggestion of a limit as to academic knowledge, where, by a kind of theoretical nepotism, it loses its distance on its object. The loss of distance and authority resembles in effect the discovery of a counter-example to theoretical mastery – exactly the kind of thing that Derrida dreams of in 'Circonfession' which turns around the possibility of confessing an ultimately shameful, inappropriate and inappropriable aberration, a crime or evil simply beyond the pale for any discourse of knowledge no matter how suavely programmatic (hence too his analysis of the holocaust). But in a sense this counter-example, this extreme evil or sin, in so far as it is almost but not quite a part of the series of objects that a discourse of knowledge treats, is nothing other than that knowledge when it encounters itself mixed up in the field of theoretical objects it began to detail. Candace Lang observes resignedly, though from a more empiricist perspective, that

4 Philip Beitchman, *I am a process with no subject* (Gainesville: University of Florida Press, 1988), pp. 71–2.

'autobiography is indeed everywhere one cares to find it'.[5] Its own counter-example, so to speak, knowledge feels ashamed of itself, afraid that it may not be pure Mind or Spirit but may have a body with just the sort of (impossible) objectivity it attributes to what it thinks to analyse.

As if to pierce this unease and anaesthetise it, there exist on the other hand zealously abrupt 'definitions' of the autobiographical, refreshing only in their ingenuousness. As Avrom Fleishman cannily overtures, 'No one can tell what autobiography is, yet that has not dispelled a surge of recent efforts to define it.'[6] Even as cautious a writer as Paul Jay can permit himself to refer to something as cut and dried as 'the autobiographical act'.[7] It is the tenacious and extensive work of Philippe Lejeune which is often taken as the punctilious mean by autobiographical theorists. *His* definition, sifted and honed, of autobiography runs as follows:

DEFINITION: Retrospective prose story that a real person relates about his or her own existence, in which he or she gives emphasis to his or her individual life, and to the history of his or her personality in particular.

Somewhat mischievously, perhaps, I quote from the autobiography which Lejeune allowed himself – or, we might say, was almost inevitably driven to – after more than a decade's work on the theory.[8] Furthermore Lejeune is actually citing himself, thus filing a further autobiographical (theoretical) level into this escalating classification system. As if himself fulfilling the 'pact' he theorises, Lejeune quotes his own *La pacte autobiographique*,[9] and so indulges in the practice, disreputable or not, inevitable or not, of confusing autobiography with the theory of it.

But the definitions come even more pared down than Lejeune's, for the economy even of Lejeune's definition is fudged by having to make qualifications (two sub-clauses) and the vagueness of them ('history of his or her personality', e.g.) – not to mention the fact that the quote comes from a supposedly autobiographical and not a theoretical text, so that we are hearing not a theoretical definition at all but, if we are

5 Candace Lang, 'Autobiography in the aftermath of Romanticism', *Diacritics* (Winter 1982), 6.
6 Avrom Fleishman, *Figures of autobiography: the language of self-writing* (Berkeley: University of California Press, 1983), p. 1.
7 Paul Jay, *Being in the text: self-representation from Wordsworth to Roland Barthes* (Ithaca and London: Cornell University Press, 1984), p. 14.
8 *Moi aussi* (Paris: Seuil, 1986), p. 14. My translation.   9 Paris: Seuil, 1975.

to take him at his word, a part of the history of Lejeune's personality. Is the thrift in defining autobiography intended to balance the expensive and irregular over-productivity that autobiography figures? Jean Starobinski's definition, more sparing still, reads:

A biography of a person written by himself:

Voilà. Starobinski confirms:

this definition of autobiography establishes the intrinsic character of the enterprise and thus the general (and generic) conditions of autobiographical writing.[10]

What conviction! Autobiography surely is a threatening presence if *such* an axiomatic blunderbuss needs to be marshalled against it.

Having got to this zero degree of definition, Marc Eli Blanchard thankfully inflates it again. Apropos of Starobinski, rewriting him somewhat, Blanchard schematises:

[Autobiography] is an act where the writing, the *graphein* on either side of the life, the *bios* it encloses, is itself the life and death, the presence and absence which it seeks, but only gives us as through a mirror: an image.[11]

– and with this one arrives at a crossroads. Blanchard's formulation turns in two different directions. On the one hand Blanchard launches or re-launches, across Starobinski's text, an effort at thinking the *enigma* of autobiography (an enigma whose persistence detains the present study too) and he does so through a necessary, if rare, privileging of writing (*'graphein'*) over the values of self and life. To this extent his words harmonise with Derrida's, and what they express so densely will be in a sense what I shall try to provide a commentary for later on, though without explicit reference back to Blanchard.

But on the other hand those same words are laden with an existentialist pathos, quite against the grain of Derrida's reading, that becalms another fleet of autobiographical theorists, to which Blanchard therefore partly belongs. The combination of the hypnotising cadence of Blanchard's phrasing, his reliance on the crypto-existentialist notion of the 'act', and the semi-gnostic (Pauline, Delphic, etc.) 'mirror', produces a *pathétique* that turns up in far less subtle forms elsewhere. By a sort of switch mechanism such pathos overcomes autobio-

---

10 Jean Starobinski, 'The style of autobiography', in ed. James Olney, *Autobiography: essays theoretical and critical* (Princeton: Princeton University Press, 1980), p. 73.
11 Marc Eli Blanchard, 'The critique of autobiography', *Comparative literature*, 34: 2 (Spring 1982), 99.

graphical theory the moment it ceases to be interested in the more positivist definitions like those of Lejeune and Starobinski. Such pathos is often borne along by a somewhat *depleted* existentialism,[12] in fact, a watered-down, self-help, gospelised existentialism more or less concerned with claiming autobiography as a means of consumerist 'self-realisation', to which a value of truth, as wholesome sincerity, is often superadded.[13] Thus, for Karl Weintraub, the subject of autobiography

concerns a major component of modern man's self-conception: the belief that, whatever else he is, he is a unique individuality, whose life task is to be true to his very own personality.[14]

Christophe Miething declares in similar vein that

autobiography observes just one question: who am I?... The autobiographical project obeys the order given by the Delphic oracle, the commandment *gnothi se auton*.[15]

And James Olney that

it is the great virtue of autobiography as I see it though autobiography is not peculiar in this: poetry, for example, does the same, and so does all art – to offer an understanding that is finally not of someone else but of ourselves.[16]

Needless to say, such tremulously manful appeals will not help to cover much conceptual ground.

To make an early résumé, there appear to be three enclosures within the field of autobiographical theory:

1. Theories and surveys of the theory, the enclosure in which we find ourselves in this chapter, showing perhaps 'the tendency of much

---

12 For a high humanist-existentialist version of autobiography, see Roy Pascal, *Design and truth in autobiography* (London: Routledge and Kegan Paul, 1960).

13 The theme of sincerity, confession or truth-telling in autobiography has been interestingly linked, however, to the concept of performativity in speech-act theory, on the grounds that autobiography should perform its own truth. See Leah D. Hewitt's 'Getting into the (speech) act: autobiography as theory and performance', *Sub-stance*, 52 (1987), 32–44.

14 Karl J. Weintraub, *The value of the individual: self and circumstance in autobiography* (Chicago and London: The University of Chicago Press, 1978), p. xi.

15 Christophe Miething, 'Le grammaire de l'égo: phénoménologie de la subjectivité et théorie autobiographique', in eds. Mireille Calle-Gruber and Arnold Rothe, *Autobiographie et biographie: colloque de Heidelberg* (Paris: Librairie A. -G. Nizet, 1989), pp. 149–50. My translation.

16 James Olney, *Metaphors of self: the meaning of autobiography* (Princeton: Princeton University Press, 1972, 1st Princeton paperback printing, 1981), p. x.

recent work on autobiography to cancel out both itself and its subject'.[17]

2. Suspicions as to whether autobiography *can* be theorised as a genre since as Candace Lang pointed out, it seems to get everywhere, like sand.

3. Positivist definitions of autobiography, merging with quasi-existentialist claims about self-knowledge.

This third enclosure easily outmeasures the other two and requires some more discussion. It takes autobiography above all as a document of personal history, or 'history of personality', and so places autobiography fairly within an ideology of individualism. Both one's history and one's personality are exactly that – one's own – and one nurtures them like a sublime commodity with all the narcissistic gratification that implies. As such, this enclosure or category provides a soft target for more politically and deconstructively sophisticated critics. With regard to *La pacte autobiographique*, for example, Michael Ryan prickles at Lejeune's 'taken-for-granted decisionism', and, pressing deconstruction towards Marxism, gives assurances that

Marxism, like deconstruction, would question Lejeune's founding axiom which posits the subject of autobiography as isolatable, constitutive and self-identical.[18]

Ryan's Marxism presumably would allege that for a subject to be 'isolatable, constitutive and self-identical' it must be enacting a bourgeois illusion of freedom from ideological pressures. This subject (of autobiography, but of autobiography as a good example of subjectivity in general, we are I think to infer) constitutes an abstraction, or transcendence, and so must needs be worked back into its material base where it will cease to be isolatable, etc., and instead function problematically within a heterogeneous social order ... That seems to be the political import of Ryan's point. Its more philosophical demand is for the re-elaboration of concepts – in particular that of the subject – which are 'taken for granted'. To take for granted isn't just to acquiesce in a political *status quo*, it is to fail the standards of philosophical rigour – the rigour that might dispute 'self-identity' on the grounds that any identity conferred upon the self is done so solely, and at best jaggedly, by hegemonic determinisms, for the self cannot

17 William C. Spengemann, *The forms of autobiography: episodes in the history of a literary genre* (New Haven and London: Yale University Press, 1980), p. 244.

18 Michael Ryan, 'Self-evidence', *Diacritics* (June 1980), 10, 14.

identify itself *ex nihilo*. Autobiography and its theory are to wean themselves off their fantasies of a serene history of the self and face up to the problematics of a narrative of the subject.

Candace Lang again, reviewing James Olney's *Metaphors of self*, makes a similar point though with less political bite, while surveying the field:

> if contemporary critics (of the 'deconstructionist' ilk) are not exactly 'fascinated' with 'the profound, ... endless mysteries' of the self, nor anxious about its disappearance, they are intensely interested in the prejudices and presuppositions underlying such an essentialist concept of selfhood and in the denials provoked by any theoretical discourse that tends to reject or cast doubt upon that concept.[19]

In general, the bone of contention is the subject or self and whether it is whole, or fragmented; self-determining, or wrought with political and conceptual barbs. It is the subject not as 'he' or 'she' which is at stake, but as the 'I' which takes itself to be its own object or subject, univocal and present to itself. However, because the autobiographical subject, for all the contentiousness it inspires in Ryan (and to a degree in Lang), is contended at the level of the subject; because in other words autobiography and subjectivity are treated as commensurate; then despite their deconstructive savvy Ryan and Lang fall short of a Derridean point at which autobiography and subjectivity bifurcate, the former no longer mappable, once taken up on the wing of chance, upon the latter.

This is not to say their words are worthless, far from it. For along with the 'essentialist concept of selfhood' the matter of the subject's representation of itself comes under scrutiny. Indeed, the process by which the subject represents itself has become *indistinguishable* from its capacity for self-constitution. That blending of the two ideas probably derives from the phenomenological tradition informing the deconstructive attitude characterised by Lang and Ryan – the tradition of Husserl, say, who will have described subjectivity in such terms – as opposed to, say, Descartes for whom subjectivity would have been established by reason and cogitation (*cogito ergo sum*), rather than self-representation. (That phenomenological emphasis itself shades into a more pragmatically political one, whereby 'self-*constitution*' in the political sense can indeed be managed only through self-representation – i.e., with a vote.) In addition to political and philosophical problems,

19 Candace Lang, 'Autobiography in the aftermath of Romanticism', 4.

therefore, there will be problems of language to worry autobiography, for language offers the most excellent (and in a sense the only) means of representation. To represent itself in order to constitute itself, the autobiographical subject needs a means of representation, a language in short. And as soon as language becomes an issue for auto-biographical theory, any last footing 'the autobiographical subject' may have had gives way. The 'I' ends up not only as a political and philosophical delusion but as a linguistic one too. To pick up from Louis Renza again:

For some years now, the first person pronoun has been in disarray as a transparent signifier of an authorial signified. Instead of referring to the writing self, the 'I' (a word authorising and authenticating the discourse of fictional as well as autobiographical narrative self-references) places this self 'under erasure' as a rhetorico-linguistic shifter, figure, or trope. Struck down by this smallest of pronouns, self-reference thus becomes another illusion of self-presence: of the writer's or even narrative persona's autonomous self-identity.[20]

The dismantling of the autobiographical subject is surely now complete. Now a Saussurean precept has been borrowed for this theoretical meal of Phenomenology, Marxism and Deconstruction, whereby the 'I' itself, indispensable to the autobiographer, is barred from referring to a subject or to anything other than its own diacritical emplacement in a chain of signifiers. Or, to trace Renza's point more accurately, the subject *can* in fact be read through the reference to it, but only under duress: the reference as much scratches it out as makes it legible, according to the Heideggerian figure of 'under erasure' which Derrida in turn put under erasure himself when he repeated it in *De la grammatologie*. Renza's own appropriation of this figure is slightly puzzling, however, given that he applies it to *reference*. After all, doesn't even the most unregenerate notion of reference think of it as working in the way that Renza calls 'under erasure'? That is, by *referring*, referring and mediating only, not pretending to get hold of the referent or *das Ding an sich* —?

As a field of interpretation, autobiographical criticism and theory is as conflictual and miscellaneous as one might have expected, though *roughly* speaking there exists a fairly *neat* divide within it, over this question of the self or subject. Against those more humanistic quotations (from Lejeune, Olney, Miething) an equal and opposite

20 Louis A. Renza, book review, *Comparative literature*, 39: 2 (Spring 1987), 172–3.

force of more 'theoretical' ones (Ryan, Lang, Renza) is ranged. This must mean that autobiography represents a good way of taking the theoretical temperature, so to speak, of academics in the field. On the one hand, what appears in the name of autobiographical criticism can take the more traditional form which proceeds like psychobiography, still such a dominant form of literary criticism in universities and journalism. A good example of this would be A. O. J. Cockshut's *The art of autobiography*,[21] a commentary upon various Victorian and more recent autobiographies, completely untroubled by any qualms about whether a history of the self is enmeshed in a problematic of the narrative of the subject. Any theoretical shame that autobiographical material may have provoked dissolves in a welter of biographical juices, the critic enjoying privileged glimpses of 'the author' and crafting them into his own *belles-lettres*. The proximity of auto-biography to psychobiography is something I shall come back to. Other works look that problematic squarely in the face. Christophe Miething, whom we have cited, asserts that 'of all the literary genres, none is so close to philosophy as autobiography'. The literary self can be analysed in ways indistinguishable from the analysis of the philosophical self. An entire system of values accompanies the latter: self-identity, self-reference, self-presence, autonomy, authority, self-determinism, individualism, auto-affection, self-constitution, and so on, and these are precisely the values that the more theoretical or philosophical literary critics submit to examination.

But if the emphasis in this third enclosure is upon personal history, then history ought to be as important as the question of the person (the self or subject), although in practice this aspect has been relatively neglected by those more philosophical critics. There has been a large and largely automatic consensus that autobiography and its theory are specious so long as they rely upon an uninterrogated concept of the self, but rather less concern for personal *history*. A ready justification for this might say that 'history' numbers among those values listed, being the form in which the self posits its identity over time, accruing self-identity as self-continuity. The justification hardly ever gets rehearsed, however. It may even be that this system of values itself has a history, so that autobiography, as part of an aged system, looks less like a natural, if curious, form of subjectivity (self-relation) and more

21 A. O. J. Cockshut, *The art of autobiography in nineteenth and twentieth century England* (New Haven: Yale University Press, 1984).

like a historically tardy and culturally overdetermined phenomenon –
a 'latecomer' after all. Karl Weintraub again:

the autobiographic genre took on its full dimension and richness when
Western Man acquired a thoroughly historical understanding of his existence.
Autobiography assumes a significant cultural function around AD 1800. The
growing significance of autobiography is thus a part of that great intellectual
revolution marked by the emergence of the particular modern form of
historical mindedness we call historism or historicism.[22]

Weintraub's epic cragginess may have to be overlooked, and 'AD
1800' may have to be taken with a pinch of salt,[23] but the point merits
attention for suggesting that autobiography (and therefore also
subjectivity?) may not be a philosophical given – that there was a
time before and a time after autobiography – like a BC and an AD, in
fact. The other irony is that since it is Weintraub's own 'historical
mindedness' which permits him to make it, the point itself, if we are
to take him, like Lejeune, at his word, is partly autobiographical ...

But if one *is* going to argue for the historical determinism of
autobiography, some historical dating or other will be required and
that will always involve 'eliminating the contingent' and a certain
arbitrariness. Treating autobiography as a discrete genre at all,
however, rather than as a general tendency (therefore not strictly
datable) might be to get off on the wrong foot. Moreover, dating a
genre can only ever cause problems because the genitivity of genre
will defy historical taxonomy, by definition. A genre is genitive only
if it passes genetically over lines of historical demarcation and is
generated. It will have to be generated with a non-contemporary other,
something arriving before or after it. No doubt 1800 was chosen by
Karl Weintraub to net the greatest possible number of 'Romantic'
writers and so allude to the academic *publica opinio* that Romanticism
pre-eminently may be characterised in terms of authorial self-reference
and subjectivity, or poetical autobiography. If that is the case, it allows
all the 'cultural significance' to be locked up in these hieratic Romantic
figures, 'historical mindedness' largely an affair of private retrospection.

22 Karl Weintraub, 'Autobiography and historical consciousness', *Critical inquiry*, 1
(June 1975), 821.
23 For a usefully succinct and general history-of-ideas survey of autobiography *vis-
à-vis* the concept of the subject, see Sidonie Smith, 'Self, subject and resistance:
marginalities and twentieth-century autobiographical practice', *Tulsa studies in
women's literature*, 9: 1 (Spring 1990): 'Women writing autobiography', 11–24.

A broader view is possible. Ramón Saldívar makes the rarer point that the self's history provides a filtered document of cultural consciousness. He says that

because of its fundamental tie to themes of self and history, self and place, it is not surprising that autobiography is the form that stories of emergent racial, ethnic, and gender consciousness have often taken in the United States and elsewhere.[24]

From out of an anthropologistic care Saldívar gives a nice sense of autobiography's *not* affirming the subject's power of self-appropriation, but testifying to a powerlessness. There is also a chastening suggestion that autobiography is less a right than a privilege, that the time and social esteem needed to embark upon one does not always come free. The powerlessness may however come full circle, one supposes, in that writing autobiography may itself be an empowering 'act' in the transition from *en-soi* social nullity to *pour-soi* differential strength. With his reference to place, Saldívar subtly contours the difference as the geopolitical specificity bearing upon autobiographies. Far from marking a decline from the august generality of Romantic autobiography, the differential specificity represents a source of strength precisely because not so easily assimilated to a general order. Autobiographical history self-evidently relays historical difference, so perhaps it departs diametrically from concepts of History in general in so far as such concepts sustain an ideal, if not actual, notion of an ultimate singularity of historical progression and truth. In a sense 'autobiographical history' would be an oxymoron. What has become known as 'women's autobiography' – a genre description which as such calls for caution – might be pointed to in this connection, as narratives at variance with dominant ideology: personal histories recorded from among marginalised groups do not coincide with the official prevailing History, and are written in order to occupy that margin as a site of intervention.[25] At the same time, whatever is generic about a given autobiographical text (such as an example of Chicano autobiography, or an example of women's autobiography) will wrest the text into some generality, levelling off some of its differential specificity after all.

Theoretically one could take the point further along a different

24 Ramón Saldívar, 'Ideologies of the self: Chicano autobiography', *Diacritics* (Autumn 1985), 25.
25 See, for example, the special issue of *Tulsa studies* referred to in note 23 above.

perspective and look upon autobiography from the group point of view rather than that of those producing autobiographies within it which make the group or genre up. So, for example, cultures and nations (as groups) write their own autobiographies in a more general way, without necessarily passing through the autobiographies of its members. Every day a nation's media, for example, will write the ongoing autobiography of that nation – if the sense of 'autobiography' may be stretched in this way. The nation represents itself to itself.

Coming back to personal history, it is Jean-Luc Nancy who gives perhaps the clearest idea of the *interweaving* between person (self, subject) and history, which we have been keeping apart. He does so in a highly philosophical idiom:

Now, philosophically understood, history ... is the ontological constitution of the subject itself. The proper mode of subjectivity – its essence and its structure – is for the subject to become itself by inscribing *in its 'becoming' the law of the self itself,* and inscribing in the self the law and the impulse of the process of becoming. The subject becomes what it is (its own essence) by representing itself to itself (as you know, the original and proper meaning of 'representation' is not a 'second presentation', but 'a presentation to the self'), by becoming visible to itself in its true form, in its true *eidos* or *idea.*[26]

Nancy manages to be both pointed and allusive. While alluding to both the Platonistic distinction between worlds of being and of becoming, and to Nietzsche's clarion call to 'become what one is', he makes quite decisively the point that, 'philosophically understood' (Nancy is speaking for and on behalf of philosophy and his comments are spoken as a kind of representation of philosophical understanding, in particular of the philosophical understanding of representation, which makes his words more complex in their setting than there is room here to describe), the constitution of the subject takes place in history and not in a temporal desert: 'history ... is the ontological constitution of the subject itself'. A further allusion, this time to Heidegger, underpins the statement, there being no ontology for Heidegger that could exist independently of time. Except that Nancy says 'history' rather than 'time', so perhaps a further allusion still, this time to Derrida, is providing auxiliary support. As we shall see, a certain historicism, conceived as temporal (and spatial) delay in-

26 Jean-Luc Nancy, 'Finite history', in ed. David Carroll, *The states of 'theory'*: *history, art and cultural discourse* (New York: Columbia University Press, 1990), pp. 153–4.

augurates subjectivity in Derrida's interpretation, but cancels it out immediately. The vocabulary of 'law' and 'inscribing' sounds equally Derridean and with it Nancy rewrites the existentialist longing for one's own meaningful selfhood. If the subject is to 'become itself by inscribing in its "becoming" the law of the self itself' rather than by a prolonged introspective process or irreversible political action, then the agencies of becoming (law, inscription) recede from humanistic and existentialist grasping. They occupy instead an imperious position like that of a Necessity, with 'becoming' in thraldom to it. But the self becomes itself by inscribing this law of the self, which leads us to infer that Nancy has deftly reorganised that founding distinction between being and becoming, law and self, necessity and contingency: the self inscribes the law of its own becoming within itself. The self cannot become itself *apart from* the law, a kind of reshuffled Kantian universal is at large, the self put into relation with itself only through this law of itself. Which suggests that Nancy's formulation is as political as it is ontological, and that the two are being considered together, even though it is in the more ontological register that Nancy writes.

Of all the issues that this raises, most relevant perhaps is that of a historicised self-representation. The first point to make, and one on which Nancy stands in agreement with Derrida, is that such self-representation is first and foremost a matter of the subject telling its story to *itself*: 'the subject becomes what it is (its essence) by representing itself to itself'. The subject must have represented itself to itself before it can represent itself to others. Or, autobiography begins with self-colloquy, the autobiographer not simply writing *about* the self (as in Starobinski's definition) but writing *to* the self in an internal vocative mode. Nancy and Derrida echo the words of Nietzsche's autobiographical *Ecce homo*, ' – and so I tell my life to myself'.[27] Autobiography takes the form of self-closure, but it can do so only if it has first effected a minimal distancing of the self in order to address it. The granting in Derrida's (and Nancy's) work of such a priority of the vocative over the accusative or descriptive mood can hardly be overestimated. An autobiographical lien by which the self would write accusatively *about* itself does not make for an obligatory ligature: detachment is permissible, a masterful indifference is its

---

27 Friedrich Nietzsche, *On the genealogy of morals/Ecce homo*, the first trans. Walter Kaufmann and R. J. Hollingdale, the second trans. Walter Kaufmann (New York: Vintage Books, 1969), p. 221. Hereafter referred to as *Ecce homo*.

prerogative. Or rather: in any accusative discourse – that is, a discourse such as 'philosophical enquiry', a scientific or objective discourse – a superforeshortening in principle throws that discourse forward among its objects. The relation is therefore binding, as it is not (at first sight) in the accusative mode. It is an autobiographical relation in so far as the discourse finds *itself* among those objects, but this self is equally its other and combines with others to the point of becoming indiscernible as such. An uncertainty affects the 'you' it addresses, riving it. In general the language of subject and object, even wrought to an Hegelian extreme, cannot cope with the thetic multifoliation prompted by this logic.

Nancy and Derrida are not alone in their thinking. Others have stressed the ineluctable diremption of the self that goes on in any bid toward self-closure, though the double insistence on (1) the vocative, and (2) the temporal (historical) delay implicit in that, does not appear in their work. I would like, however, to take briefly three examples for the sake of fair coverage and to be able to distinguish Derrida's contribution more clearly.

'In truth, the autobiographical subject is above all inter-subject, co-subject: "my" history, "my" life, is afforded me by others.' This is the crux of a generally Foucauldian argument by Herman Parret.[28] It repeats the gesture which takes autobiography to be a regional domain within the problematics of subjectivity, a domain which, like a synecdoche, is supposed to stand for the whole of that problematics, though the relationship receives little elaboration. The autobiographical subject philosophically does not differ from other kinds of subject, and each one is a 'discursive effect', fashioned as the grille through which various discrete institutional discourses radiate their power. But since those discourses are themselves contradictory and irregular, 'rupture, heterogeneity, duplicity [*dédoublement*] is the *conditio sine qua non* of autobiography' (p. 166). Consequently, the notion of autobiography as a self-referential document is somewhat untenable; its subject is made up from an arbitrary and changing filigree of discourses: 'autobiography is an *intertext*' (p. 169). 'Intertext' and 'inter-subject' mesh; the autobiographical subject is constituted by others and by the discourses which will have momentarily photographed those others as subjects.

28 Herman Parret, '"Ma vie" comme effet de discours', *La licorne*, 14 (1988): 'Le travail de biographique', 163. My translation.

The kaleidoscopic proteanism of these interconnections and the evanescent differences among them allow Parret to graft on to the argument a case for semiology. For if autobiography is an intertext, then 'like all intertext, there is not really any objectivity to correspond with, so much as a sign to interpret' (p. 169). There is no closure because nothing singular (or at least permanently singular) offers itself to adherence, only a cellular multiplication and division of discursive forces which can nevertheless be observed, as on a kind of Saussurean grid, as just such 'a sign to interpret'.

The kind of Being-together or *Mitsein* which Parret appeals to can be evidenced from sociological phenomena: one needn't have recourse to a transcendental analytic. The non-closure of autobiography offers a finally empirical aspect in the form of a sign to be interpreted. In our second example, Peggy Kamuf also makes space for the proximity to the autobiographer of others, but in a very different dimension, that of an epistemology of reading. In order to work her way round to a point about 'the circulation or sharing of voices in a work',[29] she questions a statement made by Paul de Man in his *The rhetoric of Romanticism*.[30] De Man's statement is, 'Any book with a readable title page is, to some extent, autobiographical', and Kamuf's speculative commentary goes as follows:

But what, then, is a readable autobiography? Or rather, *whose* autobiography does one read when reading signatures and the texts they sign? It now seems that what is problematic in the sentence 'any book with a readable title page is autobiographical' [*sic*] is less the difficulty of consenting to such an all-inclusive assertion than the difficulty of facing up to the way it upsets a basic certainty about the autobiographical work and its signature. By making it a function of readability, de Man does not so much dissociate autobiography from writing and the writer as place it *between* writer and reader, writing and reading. Thus the same gesture *both* allows one to assert that any text is more or less autobiographical *and* prevents a certain attribution of autobiography to reader or writer. Autobiography is an all-inclusive genre precisely to the extent that it remains impossible to conclude whose life is being written – or read. (p. 124)

The commentary suggests that autobiographical non-closure arises at a cognitive level, where the reading-area shared by (autobiographical)

---

29 Peggy Kamuf, *Signature pieces: on the institution of authorship* (Ithaca: Cornell University Press, 1988), p. 126.
30 Paul de Man, 'Autobiography as de-facement', in *The rhetoric of Romanticism*, pp. 67–81.

writer and reader hangs in the balance. Kamuf pushes de Man's point to the limit: if texts are universally autobiographical, how can you tell one autobiography apart from another? has all identification become impossible? does the impossibility extend to reader as well as writer, given that that universal autobiographism will have been intimated in *reading*? Where a more traditional critic such as Georges May, for example, had enjoyed the idea that autobiography is perhaps 'the literary form in which the most perfect accord unites the author and his or her reader',[31] now discord undoes the very relation of reader and writer, and we simply do not know if such positions are viable as such any longer, let alone whether the autobiographical author might attain any completeness of self-constitution. There gapes instead the vertiginous space of 'readability', a cognitive dimension coming into being through the very privation of cognition – or at least the cognition of identities, which adds up to the same thing.

The privative emphasis is consistent with de Man's own work, although there are fewer, if any, residues of reception aesthetic in that work than there are in Kamuf's commentary. In his essay on Walter Benjamin's 'The task of the translator',[32] for example, de Man will argue that language in its principle functions without regard to *any* phenomenological intention in reading and writing toward its meaning, and absolutely outside of the phenomenological horizon that would ring it. All language stands in a position usually reserved for the language in which a given text is to be translated, wavering between idiomatic and semantic fidelity to that text, never getting at 'the meaning'. This is what makes de Man's use of the term *reading* so strangely new: reading is organised in advance by a linguistic recalcitrance profounder than difficulty, resulting from the impasse between linguistic and phenomenal worlds which itself may be described as non-translatability. Kamuf, by contrast, preserves a virtual phenomenology of reading. At least, reading's horizon remains in place even if now apparently disinhabited, its epistemological objects (writer, reader and text) whitewashed into an invisible

---

31 Georges May, *L'autobiographie* (Paris: Presses Universitaires de France, 1979, 2nd edn 1984), p. 111. My translation.
32 Paul de Man, 'Conclusions: Walter Benjamin's "The task of the translator"', in *The resistance to theory* (Manchester: Manchester University Press, 1986), pp. 73–105.

sameness. It is not so much that the autobiographer cannot close upon him- or herself, as that the specific notion of autobiography *qua* autobiography has been obliterated.

The third example, from Michael Ryan again but this time from a 1976 essay entitled 'Self-de(con)struction', draws upon psychoanalysis:

The stories of Oedipus and Narcissus supply a readymade model for a structural psychoanalytic study of autobiography. What they imply is that autobiography, were self-knowledge ever fully possible, would be an inevitable self-destruction, a recognition that the self's sovereign interiority is split and invaded by exteriority; that its illusory homogeneity is, in fact, heterogeneous. But this very heterogeneity prevents complete self-knowledge. In the subject it is the narcissistic nature of the ego and the 'radical alterity' of the unconscious which circumvent total autobiography. Because Narcissus cannot read correctly his image in the water, and because the tracing of the track of the prophecy's execution is unavailable to Oedipus' conscious control, the critic of autobiography is necessary. He points out the blindness of Narcissus and promotes the insight of Oedipus.[33]

Ryan shares the view that autobiography is just one particular form of (attempted) subjective self-closure, and again he impresses the value of heterogeneity upon us, his reader. The heterogeneity, understood here more in psychoanalytic than political terms, characterises a subject already divided from itself in so far as it is partly made up of an unconscious inaccessible to it. Attempts by the subject at autobiography are doomed from the start, hence the 'structural' component in Ryan's thesis. To put it more interestingly: while *auto*biography can be written (as the story of the self or *auto*), the *auto*'s other, its unconscious, will languish in unwriteability. The supremely self-closing autobiography would in fact be an auto-cum-hetero-biography, but only the *auto*-biography side of the story could ever be written.[34]

33 Michael Ryan, 'Self-de(con)struction', *Diacritics* (Spring 1976), 34.
34 A slightly different point about the presence of an other in autobiography is made by Jean Marc Blanchard: 'Different from all others, so that others may exist, [the self] must be different from them, so that it too may have a world to exist in. Autobiography, the writing of the life of the self, is the other writing itself into the text, experiencing its image and providing the guarantee that for this image a subject is ultimately responsible, present, albeit undefinable.' 'Of cannibalism and autobiography', *Modern language notes*, 93: 4 (1978), 673. (I assume that Jean Marc Blanchard is the same person as the Marc Eli Blanchard cited above, especially as the phrasing is so reminiscent. But this question of what it is to be

Coupled with this 'radical alterity' of the unconscious in the circumvention of 'total autobiography' is the 'narcissistic nature of the ego' which leads, it seems, to a problem with reading again.[35] 'Narcissus cannot read correctly his image in the water', and Ryan's choice of the verb *read* rather than *see* or *understand* suggests that the unconscious, too, is 'unreadable' – or rather that Narcissus is unreadable to himself to the extent that his reading will be partial in its blindness to unconscious aspects. The two complementary forms of non-self-closure (narcissism and unconsciousness) gather around an identity conceived not as problematic existence but as problematic readability. A cognitive anxiety bubbles up again, though in terms very different from Kamuf's. The problem is less that there is an unconscious which makes a rift in subjectivity than that that unconscious resists being read by the conscious subject. Perhaps perversely, Ryan in turn reads this as an opportunity for the critic who may help out with the reading of that unconsciousness. It is almost a defence of criticism on Ryan's part. Does he really believe that this is a justification for criticism, and that a critic could have such a redemptively impartial view of things? As it stands, a critic could ideally complete the vision of Narcissus the autobiographer. So a certain self-closure *is* possible, cognitively if not existentially, but it takes two to achieve it. The heterogeneity depends then upon a kind of pragmatism. Narcissus's self-closure falls short of the mark and the critic makes up the difference. But whose closure are we then speaking of? And what of the transference and counter-transference between Narcissus and psychoanalyst, autobiographer and critic?

Just as Kamuf's ideas emerge from a reading of Paul de Man, so Ryan's emerge from a reading (it is a review) of Jeffrey Mehlman.[36] Himself writing as a critic, then, Ryan produces a *de facto* demonstration perhaps of his theory, as his commentary makes up the difference, as it were, in Mehlman's autobiographical theorism, and it

the same person is precisely the question.) See also Dianne Chisholm's 'H. D.'s auto*heter*ography', which promises to read H. D. in relation to 'Freud's own auto*heter*ography' (96) (she is referring to *The interpretation of dreams*), in *Tulsa studies in women's literature*, 79–106.

35 On self-reading as self-interpretation in autobiography, compare Linda H. Peterson's *Victorian autobiography: the tradition of self-interpretation* (New Haven and London: Yale University Press, 1986).

36 Of Jeffrey Mehlman's *A structural study of autobiography: Proust, Leiris, Sartre, Lévi-Strauss* (Ithaca and London: Cornell University Press, 1974). Hereafter referred to as *Mehlman*.

is difficult to know quite to whom to attribute these various ideas. So what of Mehlman? Both pioneering and consolidating of 'continental' ideas, *A structural study of autobiography* is often awkward in combining Derrida with Lacan to produce what can still be, however, dextrous psychoanalyses of specific autobiographies. While directing a Lacanian melodrama of the autobiographical subject who has 'fallen into language', who suffers a 'fall into syntax', Mehlman leans upon a Derridean concept of writing whereby autobiography perhaps 'entails the scriptural transgression of the metaphorics of wholeness' (p. 121). The rather cobbled relation of Lacanian language to Derridean writing is made to respect a higher structural power, however, from which both derive their strength. In this respect the book is, as its title would suggest, very much of its time. The subject is exceeded and manoeuvred by a structure of writing, a 'structure' which is nonetheless notable for its disturbing stochastic effects. As with de Man, the category of the subject becomes a weak and somewhat nostalgic one, while that of autobiography undergoes substantial alteration. I shall speak a bit more about Mehlman's provocative book in the next chapter.

The general shift in autobiographical theory represented by the three examples given (Parret, Kamuf, Ryan) is away from a humanism of the subject (though the relation between autobiography and subjectivity is largely left intact, in that they are construed as synonyms). This is not to say that the shift therefore slides towards a single alternative point, but that a fanning out occurs. It is as if autobiography has become the site of an intellectual event, diverse and fecund: it has itself become open to surprise, and therefore to its own multiple singularities which, in so far as they are singular, are truly autobiographical. What is Derrida's place in this estuary?

Eugenio Donato, quoting Derrida back to Derrida – thus generating an autobiography effect – during the course of a 'Roundtable on autobiography', a kind of 'live' academic event, recalls that '"[t]here is a differance of autobiography, an allo- and thanatography"' (*L'O*, 76/*TEO*, 54). The autobiography effect rebounds within a colloquium on autobiography itself, and again autobiography and its theory are disclosed in their trysting-place. Derrida's *work on* autobiography, which begins now to cross with his *life of* autobiography, carries through the emphasis on subjective non-closure, and, like Michael Ryan, insists on a 'radical alterity', although of a neither wholly philosophical nor wholly psychoanalytical kind. It extends beyond the question of the *auto*, or subject, of autobiography, and into an analysis of the *bio*, the life, considered not only as a story or narrative period, but as a biologic or zoologic element, the quick of living in its relation to dying, and as the spirit of life in its relation to the letter of the work; it is equally scrupulous about not 'missing the graphic in the autobiographic' (*L'O*, 103/*TEO*, 75). The last three chapters of the present study will occupy themselves in detail with these three, *auto*, *bio* and *graphy*. From what we already know about Derrida, what can we say for now?

In *Signéponge* Derrida writes that:

the conventions of literary biography presuppose at least one certainty – the one concerning the signature, the link between the text and the proper name of the person who retains the copyright. Literary biography begins after the contract, if one may put it like this, after the event of signature. (*S*, 25/24)

As discussed in the previous chapter, copyright law is not strong enough to guarantee absolutely that nothing will come between author and text; it can only legislate against anything that does. A structural flaw runs through it, which made it necessary as legislation in the first place. And if it is merely this flawed thing that establishes the 'link between the text and the proper name of the person who retains the copyright', a link which in turn constitutes perhaps the only certainty presupposed by the conventions of literary biography, then those conventions are very ill secured. The institution of literary biography, so entrenched for so long, suddenly looks very shaky. (Perhaps we are in the neighbourhood of Kamuf's commentary on de Man, where a severance of literary properties prompts a catatonic reflux of unidentifiable literary matter.) Since so much of the literary institution as a whole rests on the same presupposition, it too is implicated in the debacle. One has to travel a very long way to find anything like a view of literature which does not assume such a link as cardinal. Derrida's initiative is to have discovered the more potent determinant of literary practice to be *judicial* as opposed to aesthetic or psychobiographic – the very thing which literature, as sublime freedom of speech, as the right of latitude from the veridical, has fancied itself for a long time to have been founded *in contradistinction to*. Literary biography cannot take place in the absence of the 'contract' which will have franked the literature of the author it speculates about: 'Literary biography begins after the contract, if one may put it like this, after the event of signature.' This event is a condition of copyright, and biography can commence only when the condition has been met. But the biography is itself nothing more than a second signature upon the literature. This literature, in order to 'be', must pass through an appropriation that is also a disappropriation. It begins only after itself, as it were, and then after it has been received and registered, after a postponement, after it has been *posted*, in the phraseology of *La carte postale*. Whence the temporal delay. Which means that some interference from its recipient branches into its structure, and that that structure is in principle open. The contract stabilises the link between text and the owner of its copyright to the same degree that it explodes it and auctions it off.

The paradox besetting literary biography is only inflamed when it comes to the link between the author's name and that author's text in *auto*biography. For is it possible to refer to an autobiography without presupposing an authorial proper name, even where the autobiography is anonymous and that name has to be coded? Autobiography's distinction is in narrowing the gap between author's name and text's title: in principle, the name is title of both text and author. But if, according to the structure of copyright, author and text can always be sectioned off from each other, then in the case of autobiography the author can become separated also from the name (the author's own) which entitles the text. After the essential cleft between author and name, a second-level interdiction separates author from name when in autobiography the name takes on titular status. Such a status for the name brings it further within the apparatus of *entitlement*, a title working not only as the name of the book but also as an element that must be identified for the sake of determining intellectual property. Using one's *name* as a title is to use something one has already lost, the worst, not the best, possible thing for purposes of entitlement. A further weakening of ownership ensues: there is the risk of even *less* authorial ownership over autobiography, curiously, than over publications where the author's name does not double up as title.

In that previous chapter, I concentrated on the aleatory effects resulting from the proper name's essentially inappropriable character. By referring again to Derrida's analysis of copyright one can see that the inappropriability at stake gives us an argument of sorts for 'autobiographical non-self-closure' but at a more judicial (for want, of course, of a better word) than philosophic or psychoanalytic, aesthetic or psychobiographic, level. Autobiography waits upon a contract to begin, a particularly anxious wait in its case as it is waiting for *itself in its relation to itself*. The deferral manifests the *différance* to which Eugenio Donato referred, as does the endogenous differencing of autobiography from itself which follows from that deferral (the recipient spliced into the autobiographer). A kind of othering and alteration puts the skids under autobiography, hence the 'allo-' element in 'allo-biography': '"There is a differance of autobiography, an allo- and thanatography."' But why also *thanato*graphy?

Again, what we already know will help to answer this. To the extent that a name can always do without its bearer, the bearer's death is inscribed within it, and every name is a name of death:

The name is made to do without the life of the bearer, and is therefore always somewhat the name of someone dead. One could not live, be there, except by protesting against one's name, by protesting one's non-identity with one's proper name. *(LCP, 45/TPC, 39)*

Writing survives the author, from before the very first inscription. Inversely, then:

death reveals the power of the name to the very extent that the name continues to name or to call what we call the bearer of the name, and who can no longer answer to or answer in and for his name. And since the possibility of this situation is revealed at death, we can infer that it does not wait for death, or that in *it* death does not wait for death. In calling or naming someone while he is alive, we know that his name can survive him and *already survives him*; the name begins during his life to get along without him, speaking and bearing his death each time it is pronounced in naming or calling, each time it is inscribed in a list, or a civil registry, or a signature. *(M, 63/Me, 49)*

The attempt at autobiography, the redoubled but doubly failed attempt to seize the name and 'be there' as oneself, entails a deeper involvement with one's own death. In two of the examples above (Kamuf and Ryan) there looked to be a partition between existential and cognitive orders of autobiography. Derrida's thinking through of the name permeates that partition. Being there (existentially) depends on a relation to what is quite otherwise than being (to adopt a phrase from Levinas), to what allows for (cognition and) recognition: the name. There is no being outside of the attestation of the name, and a protestation as to its inappropriability, and the two 'orders', existential and cognitive, are sublated into a new law of what is. Or what is not: the name rings on as the death-knell ('*glas*') of the supposedly living person, before, during and after that life. To then try and claim that name by chancing an autobiography is only to be deflected further from it. Only the name endures in or as literature, and this survival of the name allows things to be accrued to it, by a kind of grammic primogeniture, and not to the autobiographers who themselves will die and will already have had their death written and written over again in what they write autobiographically.[37] Here is Derrida again:

At the very least, to be dead means that no profit or deficit, no good or evil, whether calculated or not, can *ever return again* to the bearer of the name. Only the name can inherit, and this is why the name, to be distinguished from the bearer, is always and a priori a dead man's name, a name of death. What returns to the name never returns to the living.   (*L'O*, 18/*TEO*, 7)

The author is essentially related 'to death, releasing himself thereby to be free of his proper name' (*S*, 9/8). Equally the death-bearing name is released throughout writing, so one can now see why an auto*bio*graphy more nearly resembles an auto*thanato*graphy. Auto-biographies carry a double dose of death within them. Writing is its own autobiography, having got hold of a name, but writes nothing but death, and even more jubilantly in the case of autobiographies. We get the first hint of *bio* and of *graphy*, *bio* as death, and *graphy* as autobiography of the writing.

Derrida puts the point into practice by playing on his own name, in phrases such as *j'accepte* (here and there in *La carte postale*) and *le débris de* (at the 'end' of *Glas*). In striving to gain hold of himself in this way, he loses himself all the more, which 'always happens as soon as there is some proper name: the scene is in place where one loses what one wins and wins what one loses' (*L'O*, 105/*TEO*, 77). Autobiographical self-closure fails more the more it succeeds; it 'fails better', to borrow from Beckett.[38] A rival 'I', as it were, like the spectre of a fraternal pugilist again, takes up the wager and recklessly raises the stakes to the point where, invading language beyond the immediately rec-ognisable signature-words, it risks becoming a new universal or total

---

37 The 'moment' of 'empirical' death is therefore a somewhat subordinate case. With regard to this moment, however, one might cite a very different point made by Allan Stoekl: 'This of course is a fundamental fact of *all* autobiography, and its paradox: the author who would write his own life – his entire life – cannot record the moment when he comes to face his death, when he experiences it. Strictly speaking, no autobiography can be an autobiography unless it records both what the author lives to experience, and the passage to what is no longer life.' *Politics, writing, mutilation* (Minneapolis: University of Minnesota Press, 1985), p. 65.

38 See Samuel Beckett, *Worstward ho* (London: John Calder, 1983).

law of the text it ruins by its own inhuman narcissism. The moment
there is a name, the risk is set up, and this egoic I, or *Ich* as Derrida
styles it to parody Freud a bit, now advances as the dominant
autobiographism to be contended with. Apropos of *Glas* Derrida had
averted to this thanatographic flagrancy thus:

> it is possible to describe ad infinitum the instantaneous capture [*prise*] of *Glas*
> by *Ich*, *Ich*'s hold [*prise*] over *Glas*. It would be total if the whole of the prey,
> already, did not pertain to the simulacrum.[39]

The 'simulacrum' would refer then to this fallacious autobiographism
of the *Ich*, but it would not stop at mirroring the 'authentic'
autobiographer. Rather it would overrun the text like the wild plants
and flowers (among them the tropical *derris*) so superabundant in the
anthology of remarks which go to make *Glas* up. Besides, the authentic
autobiographer could not exist apart from this trying relation to the
simulacrum which by living in the name 'before' its bearer borrows it,
weirdly antedates *echt* autobiography. Derrida's name itself will have
germinated among others, hiding itself ('a text "exists", resists,
consists, represses, lets itself be read or written only if it is worked
(over) by the illegibility of the proper name' (*G*, 41b/*Gl*, 33b)),
perhaps even going underground like the mycelium truffled for by
Samuel Weber in his *The legend of Freud*.[40]

Autobiography will forever be competing with the thanatography,
the *Ich* of the name's autobiography, transcribing its death.

---

39 *LV*, 184/*TT*, 161. Elsewhere Derrida says of *Glas*, along with *Eperons* and *La carte
postale*, that 'the autobiographical involvement of these texts was undermining
the very notion of autobiography, giving it over to what the necessity of writing,
the trace, the remainder, etc. could offer of all that was most baffling, undecidable,
wily or despairing' (*DDP*, 455/TTT, 47).

40 Minneapolis: University of Minnesota Press, p. 81.

6

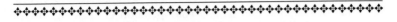

Labyrinths

Having in the previous chapter made some general remarks about autobiography today, I would like now to look at Derrida's reading of two specific autobiographical texts, Nietzsche's *Ecce homo*[1] and Michel Leiris's *Biffures*.

There exists a publication by Derrida entitled *Otobiographies: l'enseignement de Nietzsche et la politique du nom propre*. 'Oto', as in 'otolith', for example, comes from the Greek word meaning 'ear', so for '*otobiographies*' one might read 'earbiographies'. *Otobiographies* belongs with several other texts by Derrida concerning auscultation in general, and I shall make use of these too on entering the labyrinth whose architect Derrida is.

First turning

Jean-Luc Nancy's point about the subject becoming constituted through self-representation might profitably be recalled to introduce this thematic. It was said that both Nancy and Derrida echo Nietzsche's announcement, 'and so I tell my life to myself'. In Derrida's words, the autobiographer 'tells *himself* this life and he is the narration's first, if not its only, addressee and destination – within the text' (*L'O*, 25/*TEO*, 13).

Though the idiom has been enriched, the notions of 'addressee' and 'destination' are still in dialogue with a broadly phenomenological

---

1 In connection to Derrida, Nietzsche and *Ecce homo*, the reader may wish first to consult the following: (1) Michael Ryan, 'The act', *Glyph*, 2 (1977), 64–87; (2) David Farrell Krell, 'Consultations with the paternal shadow: Gasché, Derrida and Klossowski on *Ecce homo*', in eds. David Farrell Krell and David Wood, *Exceedingly Nietzsche: aspects of contemporary Nietzsche interpretation* (London and New York: Routledge, 1988), pp. 80–94; (3) Ruben Berezdivin, 'Drawing: (an) affecting Nietzsche: with Derrida', in ed. Hugh J. Silverman, *Derrida and deconstruction* (New York: Routledge, 1989), esp. pp. 96–102.

heritage. In his early work on Husserl, Derrida had investigated ideas of self-representation and argued, following Husserl, that its ideal form was that of *hearing oneself speak*: 'The operation of "hearing oneself speak" is an auto-affection of an absolutely unique kind' (*LVP*, 88/*SAP*, 78, modified). The subject seals – or, in phenomenological terms, affects – itself in the completion of a circuit between voice and hearing, mouth and ear. The moment the subject speaks it also hears itself; nothing interrupts this solipsistic umbilicus of completion. Thus Husserl will have got hold of the earliest possible determination, so to speak, of subjectivity, the one by which it is formatted before any psychological or political – and possibly even rational – information can meld it. And that is why '[t]he operation of "hearing oneself speak" is an auto-affection of an absolutely unique kind'. It is an ideal and absolutely unique form in so far as it does not literally have to take place as sound and the reception of sound; the possibility of cocooned audiophony constitutes the subjective. In Sarah Kofman's words:

The voice privileged by Husserl is not the physical voice, the sonorous substance, but the phenomenological, transcendental voice, which continues to speak and to be present to itself in the absence of the world.[2]

The figure of hearing oneself speak seems to be the sublime apogee of subjectivism, and so fulfils '[o]ne of the most insistent and most coherent dreams of idealism', as Jean-Joseph Goux puts it – 'that of a signified entirely transparent to itself, borne by an equally diaphanous voice'.[3]

Certain values are attached to this ideal form of hearing oneself speak, the most categorical of which is *presence*. As Nancy had reminded us the 're-' in 'self-representation' signifies not so much a second presentation, implying some loss, as a full and present presentation *back to* (*re-*) the self, an instantaneous flexion of presentation, as it were. In hearing itself speak the subject is entirely present to itself; it activates a presence without alloy. It is often said of Derrida's work in its earlier, more programmatically deconstructive or classical phase, that it is a 'deconstruction of the metaphysics of presence'. Above all, presence stands for self-presence, being present

2 Sarah Kofman, *Lectures de Derrida* (Paris: Galilée, 1984), p. 27. My translation.
3 Jean-Joseph Goux, 'Du graphème au chromosome', *Les lettres françaises*, 1429 (29 March 1972), 6. My translation.

to the self and thus making it bloom, bringing it alive and into the conscious presence of its being. Indeed auto-affection as 'presence' and 'life' are practically synonymous:

Auto-affection is the condition of an experience in general. This possibility – another name for 'life' – is a general structure articulated by the history of life, and leading to complex and hierarchical relations.(*DLG*, 236/*OG*, 165)

Presence will be at the heart of autobiography (a form of 'the history of life') considered as a subjectivism. It will also be there when autobiography is considered in Lejeune's terms as a 'retrospective story', for what the retrospect will view will still be the history, the past moments, of the subject's self-presence. However, once the assurance of self-presence is disturbed, once self-presence begins to fracture, it is writing which will be disclosed.

(In the later texts of *La carte postale* and 'Circonfession', themselves histories of a life, in a way, 'auto-affection' comes to denote Derrida's fondness for cars ... Look for the series of *Photographies à l'automobile* in 'Circonfession'.)

Second turning

Autobiographical self-representation from mouth to ear closes upon itself as a circle closes upon itself, or like a serpent biting its tail, as a symbol of infinity (as Derrida notes in *Marges*: see below). In other words, as absolute non-loss and continuity, the circle symbolises presence. It is with a discussion of ideal mathematical objects such as circles that Derrida's first publication on Husserl concerns itself among other things (*L'OG*,36/*TOG*, 50–1), and the analysis of the circle is sustained throughout his career – as if he too were circling around it and had to keep coming back to it from an autobiographical compulsiveness – from 'Ellipse' in *L'écriture et la différence*, to the 'alliance' in *La dissémination* and elsewhere, to the circle made around the neck by tie and noose in *Glas*, to the encyclopaedism of Hegel which he analyses, to the circumcised glans in *Schibboleth*, to the world-circuit of tourism and travel in *Ulysse gramophone*, and so on. And, under the pressure of this indefatigable analysis, in this example glossing Valéry, the circle shows signs of dysfunction:

'The existence of the speech from self to self is the sign of a *cut*' ... The circle turns in order to annul the cut, and therefore, by the same token, unwittingly signifies it. The snake bites its tail, from which above all it does not follow that it finally rejoins itself without harm in this successful auto-fellatio of which we have been speaking all along, in truth.   (*MDP*, 344/*MOP*, 289)

Auto-affection is styled in this example in its erotic keening as 'auto-fellatio', the 'inquisitive and jealous tension' to return to the self, as Derrida puts it in his 'philopolemology' essay on the motif of the ear in Heidegger (HE, 189).

But why the risk of harm, indeed of castration? In order for the ear to get its message back from the mouth it must run the risk of allowing that message to be broadcast beyond the circle of self. Otherwise there would be no message, no distance for it to cover, nothing to mediate, no consciousness, no need for anything at all, and the subject would vanish into itself or be merely an animal (according to the classic(al) opposition between animal and human), a mere prosecution of its innate capacities without meaningful constitution, that is, subjectivity. Which is another way of saying that a chance alterity associates itself with subjectivity at its origin. The message cannot be returned unless in principle despatched at large, unless errancy pilots it from the moment of despatch, sometimes returning it, sometimes not. Like a boomerang getting caught in the branches of a tree, there is always a chance of its not returning. There is a risk of scission from the message which would complete the self, and to that extent the message of self-constitution actually fissures 'you', you myself, the self I address, my self that along with its full presence has been set apart from me:

At the very instant when from its address it interpellates, you, uniquely you, instead of joining you it divides you or sets you aside, occasionally overlooks you. (LCP/TPC, back cover)

The self cedes its absolute right to the reception of its own messages, as if a structural aphasia lay dormant within it. I address myself and in so doing do not address myself. Rather I address you, an antecedent you and not yet an 'anthropomorphic' other. From the message will I learn of any selfhood. *Otobiographies* is written in the plural, for the circuit from mouth to ear is also an a priori open or public thoroughfare, the messages sent along it taking the form not so much of a sealed and esoteric letter as a postcard for all and sundry to read, 'at once hermetic and totally open' (DTA, 42/OAT, 15). Both at once: 'The circle turns in order to annul the cut, and therefore, by the same token, unwittingly signifies it.' What cuts also closes; what closes also cuts. It cuts both ways. The *annulment* creates the circle of the '*anneau*', the ring.

Third turning

As if to underscore the plurality, *Otobiographies*, the text published by Galilée in 1984, had appeared in another format as 'Otobiographie de Nietzsche', collected in 1982 in *L'oreille de l'autre* (Québec: VLB Editeur). *L'oreille de l'autre*: because the messages are divided or divide the self(-presence), it can be said that the ear receiving them is that of 'the other', and that this possibility of otherness allows communication to take place, making of it an event, something brought into being through being owned and signed and mandated. The ear of 'otobiographies' is affected by the 'ear of the other', 'the stereographic activity of an entirely other ear' (*MDP*, xix/*MOP*, xxiii) which both endorses and prohibits the operation of hearing oneself speak.

The structure of the labyrinth of the ear is made incalculably labyrinthine by being internally catacombed in its structure by the ear of the other. This is not a Borgesian labyrinth, which extends infinitely within the same conceptual dimension, but the allergenic unity of two kinds of labyrinth: the labyrinth of the other's ear already lodged within the ear's labyrinth.[4] Or two kinds of ring ...

Fourth turning

So there is an a priori prosthesis of the other ear within the ear of the same. It is similar to the relation between the proper name and its bearer, the former surviving in its very inception the latter. In both cases there is a relation of two, non-contemporaneous things which are at once intrinsic and alien to each other. In a quotation previously cited by me and cited also in *Otobiographies*, *Ecce homo* provides a further case:

4 Certain critics conceive this allergenic relation in terms of the poisoning of the ear. David Farrell Krell, for example, speaks as herald of 'Fundamental Otology, study of the unifold invagination of *Dasein*, site of ultimate vulnerability: Claudius' poison, according to Hamlet *père*, was poured "in the porches of mine ears", and by the deceptions of Claudius, that incestuous and adulterous beast, "the whole ear of Denmark / Is ... rankly abus'd"', in his *Postponements: woman, sensuality and death in Nietzsche* (Bloomington: Indiana University Press, 1986), p. 107, note 6. Cf. Ralph Flores, *The rhetoric of doubtful authority: deconstructive readings of self-questioning narratives, St. Augustine to Faulkner* (Ithaca and London: Cornell University Press, 1984), pp. 19–21. See also Ned Lukacher, '"L'oreille de Pyrrhus": La césure de l'identification dans *Hamlet*', *Le passage des frontières: autour du travail de Jacques Derrida: colloque de Cerisy* (Paris: Galilée, 1994), pp. 187–92.

The good fortune of my existence, its uniqueness perhaps, lies in its fatality: I am, to express it in the form of a riddle, already dead as my father, while as my mother I am still living and becoming old.[5]

Otobiographies writes itself out across this quotation. There is a relation of two things — two chronologies, rather — which, through the figure of the child, both belong to and are separable from each other. One (the mother) is the figure of a temporal excess over the other (the father). Though temporal, the excess exists not *in* time, for that would be to become subject to mortality. It pertains rather to a 'structure' of temporal difference, embodied in the child, between the time of the mother and that of the father. As structural, it is infinite and ageless. But it is also finite in that it is a structure. On the other hand, then, Nietzsche is also 'becoming old' as his mother — for the mother also dies, as we emphasized in the last chapter but one. In that chapter attention was given to the link, via the notion of 'matrix', between the mother and chance. Here, now, via the notion of a preceding and governing otherness, there is a link between autobiographical mother and the ear of the other so that, to distort Derrida's phrase somewhat, we might say that it is the ear of the *mother* that signs. It is her ear which in its precedence retains the power of stamping and attesting the events of the child-autobiographer's life, a life made living and historical only in so far as it is strung across the temporal difference. That is the torsion which makes autobiography active and brings it into 'presence' as 'life'.

Are we speaking of Oedipus? Some privilege appears to have been accorded the mother by the (boy) child. *Glas* even ventures the epigram, 'genealogy cannot begin with the father' (*G*, 12a/*Gl*, 6a). We are undoubtedly speaking of riddles, Nietzsche having just expressed himself in the form of a riddle. We are not speaking 'literally' about the mother; nor are we speaking quite 'meta-phorically' about Oedipus. Unhelpful as that may be, it is perhaps the most faithful, if too craven, way of describing what may be a quite new level of language-use acceded to by Derrida. Jane Marie Todd glosses Derrida by saying that

Derrida reads Nietzsche's account of his genealogy as an irreducible duality between the already-dead and the forever-living, that is, between the loss of

5 *Ecce homo*, p. 222.

80

the self through writing and the infinite capacity for return that that writing allows.[6]

The 'capacity for return' is not *quite* infinite, in fact, in that some senescence weighs it down, the autobiographer still becoming old as his mother, even though still alive. The idealism of an infinity is countered by Derrida's analysis. But that the quasi-infinite return passes through *writing* is a remark that may be retrieved from Todd's gloss. It is perhaps at the level of 'writing' that this pseudo-Oedipal schema unfolds. *At the very least*, the concept (if it is a concept) of the autobiographer being kept alive by dying as his mother is, if not an allegory or metaphor or riddle, a kind of re-writing or *quotation* of Nietzsche. We know at least this, if nothing more. At the very least, Derrida's writing itself is circling back on Nietzsche. At the very least it retrieves Nietzsche's own 'ear' and Nietzsche's own mother. Through almost what psychoanalysis would term an identification Nietzsche's mother 'becomes' Derrida's, as had Augustine's mother in 'Circonfession'. The ear of the mother is shared. Except that the identification occurs at a purely citational level. There is no cause to proceed to a psychology or even a psychoanalysis of this scene. In the realm of this recitative, the temporal difference affecting the life of the autobiographer becomes more attenuated still, in that it may be relayed from apparently remote and other histories – here, for example, that of Nietzsche. The two of them are brought into relation thereby, like brothers again.

Fifth turning

So there is a multiple, rather than a simple or simply double, origin of the autobiography. With regard to proper names, this was the original multiplicity which confused proper with common (allowing for the inter-familial culture where 'Derrida' and 'Nietzsche' might also thrive fraternally); with regard to the phenomenological ear, this was the ear of the other breaking the circuitry of the ear's auto-affection. With regard to *Ecce homo* this is the double origin of mother-father, 'life death' in Nietzsche, that also structures Derrida the auto-biographer to some degree.[7] The ideal circuit that should have been

6 Jane Marie Todd, book review, *Comparative literature*, 37 : 4 (Autumn 1985), 362.
7 Cf. also the double origin of good and evil spoken of by Nietzsche: 'Twofold prehistory of good and evil', in trans. R. J. Hollingdale, *Human, all too human : a book for free spirits* (Cambridge : Cambridge University Press, 1986, reprinted

between mother and father is broken, since the father passes away from the mother in Nietzsche; but simultaneously complete, since it is borne in its difference by the child (Nietzsche, but also Derrida).

In a certain citational way Derrida keeps that genealogy alive. He keeps the life death alive but can do so only as a consequence of some frangibility in the circle of hearing oneself speak which is the condition, according to the quote above, of life in general. Life and death practically interpenetrate each other. In 'repeating' Nietzsche or affirming him, a kind of '"*alliance fraternelle*"' is sealed. This is the phrase that Derrida cites (again) from Nietzsche in *Mémoires d'aveugle* to gesture to the bond between Dionysus and Apollo (*MD'A*, 124/*MB*, 122). The affirmation, by touching the Nietzsche who is his own father and mother, also calls upon the '*alliance*' that is the wedding ring of the parents, a word which itself repeats and returns to, by rhyming with them, two other terms we have selected previously, '*la chance*' and '*la différance*'.

Derrida speaks of 'a wedding ring of redoubled affirmation' (*S*, 133/132), referring to the nuptial vows of bride and groom (mother and father) in which the spouses respond to each other's affirmation of marriage – in Molly Bloom's phrase, 'yes, I will, yes'.[8] In a footnote to the essay on Heidegger's ear Derrida (not for the first time) provides some etymological evidence for the connection between the spouses and the responsiveness at issue.[9] The structure is one of an *essential* responsiveness, disclosed through an analysis of hearing oneself speak via the 'presence' of the other ear. To the extent that the other is there first, one is always citing and responding is the same, but different. A risk or tension – what *La carte postale*, in the wake of Hölderlin, thematises as a 'change of tone' – is therefore plied into it, and the affirmation does not designate a docile complicity. There is some

---

1987), pp. 36–7. See also Hegel on the double presence of the parents in the child, *The phenomenology of spirit*, section 456, pp. 273–5. 'Life death' refers to the seminar *La vie la mort* run by Derrida in the late seventies and published in *La carte postale* as 'Spéculer – sur "Freud"'.

8 Molly's phrase concludes Joyce's *Ulysses*. In a text entitled 'Ulysse gramophone', Derrida links the 'yes, yes' affirmation to the moment when one picks up a telephone: to do so is already to say 'yes', to say 'yes, I'm here', even before one actually speaks.

9 Part of the footnote runs: 'The spouses, the fiancé, the fiancée (*sponsi*) are first the promised, those that have been promised because they promise themselves in a place that is first that of *spondere* and *respondere*. *Spondere*, but also *sponsare*, is to promise solemnly in prescribed forms, singularly in marriage' (HE, 217).

chance in the alliance, some non-identity the distortion of which remains to be determined. Derrida is thinking as well as of the celebratory sense of affirmation of what he calls *decelebration*.[10] A convergence of Dionysian frenzy and discord with Appollonian orderliness and regulation forms the marriage circle.

Nor is Derrida then in complete agreement with Nietzsche. The Derridean *'alliance'* is somewhat different from Nietzsche's Zara-thustrian yes-saying self-celebration:

A wedding ring of redoubled affirmation, such is the seal – yes, yes – not of the superman of Zarathustra but of the resolute man in the style of Ponge.
(*S, 133/132*)

Derrida is contrasting an a priori responsiveness that says *yes* with an existential (later, self-determining) affirmativity embodied by Zara-thustra. The a priori responsiveness allows, because founded on alterity, for some difference between responses, some tonal modu-lation or dissymmetry – 'the dissymmetry of an affirmation, of a *yes* before all opposition of *yes* and *no'* (*DL'E, 147/OS, 94*).[11] Such dissymmetry is not necessarily that of faction, but of a kind of 'polemology' before antagonism, of a difference that should not too quickly be read as predisposition to conflict. Rather, the level at which difference of yes, so to speak, occurs is indeed that of an 'a priori' – of sorts. In one of his most taxing formulations, Derrida speaks of the *'alliance'* as that

which is not secret because it would be protected behind some clandestine, occult 'cause' in want of power, but because the 'yes', which is a non-active act, which states or describes nothing, which in itself neither manifests nor defines any content, this *yes* only commits, before and beyond everything else. And to do so it must repeat itself to itself: *yes, yes*.
(*M, 42/Me, 19–20*)

The yes 'repeat[s] itself to itself' – 'as "yes" responds to nothing, nothing but the other "yes" itself' (*Pa, 216/LO, 173*). One has not yet arrived at a psycho-existential or historical determination of it. But if, on the other hand, the alliance of the *yes, yes* is not quite aprioristic

---

10 A word which turns up in *Glas*: in this connection, see Christopher I. Fynsk's article, 'A deceleration of philosophy', *Diacritics* (June 1978), 80–90.

11 One thinks here of the point made by Gilles Deleuze and quoted by Vincent Descombes, that '[n]egation *opposes* affirmation, whereas affirmation *differs* from negation'. Vincent Descombes, *Modern French philosophy*, trans. L. Scott-Fox and J. M. Harding (Cambridge: Cambridge University Press, 1980, reprinted 1983), p. 163.

either, in truth, this is because what it enacts is a power of recitation and response and general secondariness: it forces its own aprioristic character out of its untouchable priority and at the same stroke deregulates genealogical hierarchies in a manner not different from the effects released by the logic of the proper name. It repeats itself to itself, autobiographically. It is the yes 'of the resolute man in the style of Ponge', in so far as Francis Ponge's name keeps repeating itself to itself throughout Ponge's texts as analysed in Derrida's *Signéponge*. The alliance 'commits' by 'committing a genealogy in a proper name' (*LV*, 219/*TT*, 190), which is an open genealogy of family grafts, blood-brotherhood, remote kinships.

Sixth turning

The '*alliance*' of the wedding band signifies a commitment. It comes into time. It sends itself forward – like the postcards of *La carte postale*. By recalling itself – yes, yes – it cancels its own anteriority. It moves its absolute priority forward in a certain way, engaging it and exposing it to risk and even death. A thanatographic annulment corresponds with the marriage of this autobiographical I and its other – 'I kill you, I annul you at my fingertips, wrapped around my finger' (*LCP*, 39/*TPC*, 33).[12]

Because it moves forward into time (as historical difference) the '*alliance*' is closely related to another Derridean ring, the '*anneau*' already mentioned, of the year's ring and cycle in its returning. Nietzsche's doctrine of the eternal return of the same comes into focus. This doctrine, in summary, takes the form of a challenge. If we are not prepared to live our lives again as they have been lived in every moment (to use the idiom of Conrad's *Heart of darkness*) will we not have failed? Do we have the courage to face up to the repetition of our lives, instead of dreaming of a golden future that will exempt us from the responsibility to live for ourselves?

An existentialist adoption of Nietzsche such as Conrad's may be blind to other things, however. Derrida will underscore the *selective* character of Nietzschean eternal return. Generous to the elements of

12 Cf. *La vérité en peinture*: 'Put someone in one's pocket: make of that person one's submissive ally (*alliance* ... – both elliptical ring and subjection) after luring, by hounding, after placing the flesh in view, for the capture of another animal. Conquer its resistance by wearing it down ..., be stronger, or deader ..., than him, on occasion by playing dead' (*LV*, 247/*TT*, 216).

'*la chance*' and '*la différance*' which ride it, return cannot be identical
repetition without abolishing itself thereby. '[L]'anneau de l'éternel
retour' which Derrida speaks of in his 'Lecture de "Droit de regards"'
(LDDR, xi-xii) is the seal, in *Parages* now, of a '*retour éternel de l'autre*'
(*Pa*, 65, my italics). The events of each new year both commemorate
and depart from the corresponding event in the previous one. The
'ring' of the event, which in its German form, '*Ereignis*', evokes the
'*Reigen*' that designates a ring, comes into being through this seal of
contractual (and contrac*ting*) difference.[13] Again one is speaking of a
difference in principle, or just about, a principle of an elasticity in the
difference, a rigid principle of non-rigidity that makes of the *anneau* a
somewhat slack concept. The return of the other is 'what passes, more
or less well, through the rhythmic stricture of an annulus' (*G*,
125b/*Gl*, 109b, modified).

Ecce homo opens with Nietzsche's anniversary, his forty-fourth
birthday:

On this perfect day, when everything is ripening and not only the grape turns
brown, the eye of the sun just fell upon my life: I looked back, I looked
forward, and never saw so many and such good things at once. It was not for
nothing that I buried my forty-fourth year today; I had the *right* to bury it;
whatever was life in it has been saved, is immortal ... – and so I tell my life
to myself.[14]

In the text on Valéry mentioned above Derrida had alluded to 'a ring
once more in the form of the return to the sources which always afflicts
the rhetoric of the anniversaries of a birth' (*MDP*, 331/*MOP*, 278),
and here one witnesses the same operation in the context of
Nietzsche's autobiography. The autobiographer looks backwards and
forwards on the day this year of his birthday. He engages the
periodicity of his own life. It is by such dating as that of the annual
birthday which 'holds together a ring, that of the alliance, the date of
the anniversary and the return of the year' (*SPPC*, 12/*AL*, 374,
modified) that he recollects himself and brings himself into a gathered
self-identity. – With the qualification that the self-identity comports
an imperceptible difference or 'historicity'. What returns in the figure

13 Cf. *Signéponge*: '(That this process promises to engage in the production of events,
   and even revolutions, along with the placement in abyss that will necessarily
   ensue, is something that we would have to put into colloquy – elsewhere, and *in
   another tone* [my italics] – with the *Aneignung* of Marx or the *Ereignis* (*Ring*, annular
   object, and *Reigen des Ereignens*, propriation as well as event) of the Heideggerian
   thing)' (*S*, 47/46).   14 *Ecce homo*, p. 221.

of the '*anneau*' is not simply what seals, but also what affords retrospect and prospect, precisely. The return is always 'a return of the coming-going' (*DL'E*, 136/*OS*, 86).[15] A certain 'exit from closure' appears:

> Once the circle turns ... its identification with itself gathers an imperceptible difference which permits us efficaciously, rigorously, that is, discreetly, to exit from closure ... The return, at this point, does not retake possession of something ...
>
> The return to the book announces the form of the eternal return. The return of the same does not alter itself – but does so absolutely – except by amounting to [*revenir au*, in the French] the same. (*ED*, 430–1/*WD*, 295–6)

Once again the structure we are tracing may be no more than textual. Derrida talks apropos of Valéry of what affects the *rhetoric of* the anniversaries of birth, and in the quote from Nietzsche the structure of meridian closure-and-openness expresses itself in a passage that falls *between* the preface and main text of *Ecce homo* ... And in this quotation from *L'écriture et la différence* Derrida is writing, in the figure of return, about nothing other than the 'return to the book' (my italics).

Derrida pulls all of these traits together when he explains that when Nietzsche 'writes himself to himself, he writes *himself to the other* who is infinitely far away and who is supposed to send his signature back to him'. He continues:

> He has no relation to himself that is not forced to defer itself by passing through the other in the form, precisely, of the eternal return ... When he writes himself to himself, he has no immediate presence of himself to himself. There is the necessity of this detour through the other in the form of the eternal return of that which is affirmed, of the wedding and the wedding ring, of the alliance. The motif of the alliance or wedding ring, of the hymen or marriage, returns often in Nietzsche, and this 'yes, yes' has to be thought beginning with the eternal return. I want it to return by making the round which is the cycle of the sun or the annual cycle, of the annulus, of the year which annuls itself by coming back around on itself. (*L'O*, 120/*TEO*, 88)

15 On the concept of the year see also David B. Allison's 'Destruction/ deconstruction in the text of Nietzsche', in eds. William V. Spanos, Paul A. Bové and Daniel O'Hara, *The question of textuality: strategies of reading in contemporary American criticism* (Bloomington: Indiana University Press, 1982), p. 205.

Seventh turning

Clearly, these are highly unusual and perhaps incredible propositions. While on the one hand a certain logical integrity is maintained which holds together by dint of structural likeness the motifs of proper name, ear of the other, '*alliance*' and '*anneau*'; on the other hand something other than logical integrity is at issue and a different kind of attention is demanded. In a sense, '*otobiographies*' signals the very pleading of this demand – the demand to listen with an other ear, to prick up one's ears to the tune which is finer than the concepts carrying it. Above all, perhaps, this involves relinquishing the autobiographical or narcissistic wish for a return to the familiar of philosophical thinking.

In *L'oreille de l'autre* Derrida recalls Nietzsche's whim that having small ears is a sign of philosophical acumen: the more attentive one is, the less philosophical one becomes; one learns to listen, as it were, with a third ear. And in an interview titled 'Avoir l'oreille de la philosophie' he speaks of the risks necessary 'to have an ear for philosophy' (AL'O, 14), these being those which involve giving up the philosophical mastery that would subdue the chance, say, of the unique '*alliance*' binding these various motifs together.

In that interview, referring to an essay in *Marges*, Derrida speaks of 'luxating' the philosophical ear, by stretching its drum or tympanum to the pitch of finest sensitivity. This is not a case of trying to do philosophy *better*, but like Nietzsche of 'philosophising with a hammer' upon the eardrums, and returning to 'the doctrine of the eternal return as hammer in the hand of the most powerful man', to use Nietzsche's phrase.[16] Nietzsche speaks of himself in these terms in the passage we return to:

> It was not for nothing that I buried my forty-fourth year today; I had the *right* to bury it; whatever was life in it has been saved, is immortal. The first book of the *Revaluation of all values*, the *Songs of Zarathustra*, the *Twilight of the idols*, my attempt to philosophise with a hammer – all presents of this year, indeed of its last quarter!

The tension of difference between the shared listeners, in dividing each of them, bursts the eardrums. The hammer Derrida retrieves is that of this force of polyphony where identities are left mostly in suspense or produced only as institutional and ideological after-

---

16 Cited by Martin Heidegger in *Nietzsche*, trans. David Farrell Krell (San Francisco: Harper and Row, 1979, 1st Harper Collins paperback edn 1991), vol. I, p. 16.

effects. But not so much a phenomenal as a textual polyphony, where identity must be bargained for through the name which is equally treacherous — 'the surname sounds better, bursts your tympanum with its tocsin' (*G*, 16b/*Gl*, 9b).

Eighth turning

Let us continue to relate, however, the *difference* — in its pseudo-primordial rather than academic sense, if possible — between Derrida and Nietzsche's Zarathustra. Zarathustra is antithetical, an 'Antichrist' whose vocation is opposition. Despite Nietzsche's refrain that he is opposed to dialectics, Zarathustra's position remains dialectical, ironically perhaps, by doing just that. By contrast, Derrida writes that:

the membrane of the tympanum, a thin and transparent partition separating the auditory canal from the middle ear (the *cavity*) is stretched obliquely (*loxos*). Obliquely from above to below, from outside to inside, and from the back to the front ... precision of hearing is in direct proportion to the obliqueness of the tympanum ... Consequently, to luxate the philosophical ear, to set the *loxos* in the *logos* to work, is to avoid frontal and symmetrical protest, opposition in all the forms of *anti-*, or in any case to inscribe *antism* and overturning, domestic denegation, in an entirely other form of ambush, of *lokhos*, of textual manoeuvres.   (*MDP*, vii-viii/*MOP*, xiv-xv)

Derrida is more non-dialectical than anti-dialectical — but then, so perhaps was Zarathustra, whose opposition was an opposition beyond opposition, an overturning of the pig-headedness and vulgarity of affront. Nietzsche claimed to have nothing to do with refutations or any of the parsimonious protocols of doxology. He will have acceded to an obliquity which to Derrida might have been disclosed precociously, before any maturation, as condition of the philosophical, an ellipsis which is more than merely an opaqueness, being rather an axial impasse in the logic of closure. This impasse is arrived at where logic works 'against' itself in order to produce itself, not through a dialectical denegation, but through an operation which philosophical, ass-eared logic can neither reduce nor escape from.

Ninth turning

Possibly there is difference between Zarathustra's hammering and Derrida's luxation. With what appears to be a facile and superior anti-modernity Heidegger will write of Nietzsche's *Übermensch* that he is 'inaccessible to the teletypers and radio dispatches of the press'.[17] It is hard to judge. Supposing Heidegger's corralling of Nietzsche's figure were not inadmissible, it would set that figure far apart from the site of the tympanum, which is the pre-eminently demotic site of the production of messages, broadcasts and typefaces. In the essay 'Tympan', Derrida speaks not only of the tympanum of the ear drum, but also of the tympan of the printing press, the device serving to situate and print type on a page. One could consider this typing on the tympan(um) as what prepares the subject to assume a meaning in a system of relations. Without this imprint of an a priori mark nothing could enter the market. Nothing could *circulate*.

At the same time, Derrida is echoing Heidegger's own vocabulary of the imprint upon Being, which in turn echoes Plato on the imprinting of ideas.[18] As had Heidegger, Derrida will analyse the 'structure' of Being and thus be drawn into transcendental arguments of the origin. But if the origin of the human being that we have been calling a 'subject' is divided by an alterity, the ear of the other, and that alterity generates time, then an equal pull backwards, or rather forwards, into existential time becomes incumbent. But Derrida perceives this counter-movement to be restrained somewhat by its own means – a non-existential or anti-humanist language of writing, typing, imprinting, forging, structuring. This is less the language of materialist production than of quasi-materialist *reproduction*, mechanical in that it allows for near-identical repetitions over time, but something quite other than mechanical in that the alterity which gets it underway sets a deviancy into its machinery which imperils identity *per se*. The 'language' of such deviancy will not be restricted to linguistic form either, for it is that *essential* detour which counts, a detour which parodies, so to speak, the received notion of written language as supplementary to presence (a kind of detour).

The subject, in ideal terms the subject hearing itself speak, has its tympanum imprinted as in the printing effect of a tympan, as it were before anything else can come about, 'structurally' or as the 'condition

17 Martin Heidegger, *What is called thinking?*, trans. J. Glenn Gray (New York: Harper and Row, 1968), p. 72.
18 See, for example, Martin Heidegger, *The question of Being*, trans. William Kluback and Jean T. Wilde (London: Vision Press, bilingual edn 1959, 3rd impression 1974). Heidegger refers to the imprint or type which facilitated Plato's thinking of the Idea: 'That which brings forth is at times thought of by Plato as that which makes an imprint.' (p. 53)

of an experience in general'. To that extent the subjectivity at issue is as late or as contingent or as arbitrary as in any existential or psychological or historical formulation. Exploiting this point of view, Derrida writes, in relation to the meditations on typography of Philippe Lacoue-Labarthe, that

> what announces itself as ineluctable seems in some way to have already happened, to have happened before happening, to be always in a past, in advance of the event. Something began before me, the one who undergoes the experience. I'm late. If I insist upon remaining the subject of this experience, it would have to be as a pre-scribed, pre-inscribed subject, marked in advance by the imprint of the ineluctable that constitutes the subject without belonging to it, and that this subject cannot appropriate even if the imprint appears to be properly its own. (*P*, 598/Des, 2)

The imprint upon the tympan(um) initialises the subject without the latter's being able to appropriate itself through this mark of character (cf. *DL'E*, 57–8/*OS*, 34); the mark, strangely, doesn't touch. Immediately one can see an interrupting of autobiographical closure particularly of a Nietzschean kind, whose project is precisely that of the subject's appropriating its own 'character'.[19]

While Derrida's 'I'm late' might be heard as a metaphor for the structure of posterity he is refining, just as in 'Circonfession' the phrase 'Je posthume comme je respire' looks to be a literary staging of a theoretic blueprint, that 'structure' exists nowhere outside these metaphors nor outside metaphor in general: in so far as Being comes to be through inscription, it is already committed to specific characteristics and delation, and cannot be neutrally unmetaphorical.

Derrida will have also emphasised this imprinting with regard to the ideal Husserlian phenomenological subject as it tries to express itself (*MDP*, 196–200/*MOP*, 164–7) – the expressive mouth is something like a 'fosse tympanique' (*G*, 138b/*Gl*, 121b). As we have seen, the imprinting is 'structural' only up to a point: the temporality which defines it brings it into play, puts its ideality at risk, marks it. The structure, in other words, is only quasi-formal. It has to do with a non-oppositional, non-rigid movement which is that of luxation, obliquity, ellipsis – of tone and timbre rather than with the content of sound: '*Timbre*: type: *Prägung des Seins*.' (*LCP*, 215/*TPC*, 200)

---

19 On the relation of the tympan to the self-celebrating, self-characterising, Dionysian dance of Nietzsche, see also Sarah Kofman, *Lectures de Derrida*, p. 42.

Tenth turning

Moving further into the labyrinth, we find that the hammer's brand upon the ear drum does not fall out of the blue but itself has its own genealogy. The imprint is sexed. The caveat here, as other commentators have pointed out, is not to 'simply reinstate either a fundamental essentialism or a notion of Being prior to sexuality'.[20] To say that the imprint is 'sexed' need not be to suggest that it is simply gendered masculine, feminine or even neuter (especially not neuter, given the quality of specificity at issue). It is sexed in so far as it comports a multiplicity or heterogeneity, the possibility of division and (almost counter-biological) *generation* – the plurality of voices affecting the ear's labyrinth, the openness which seals it. One could call this a gendered sex-before-gender, or something of that kind, though this 'before' can no longer denote an ingenuous anteriority. So that, in turn, the gender is not simply of a different order than that of sexual gender (whatever that may mean). Rather it is a case of rethinking gender starting from the structure of ontological inscription whose concept Derrida has tried to refine. Which represents an impossible task, perhaps, but one of the directions it might take would be one where appeals to biological knowledge would not be reduced immediately to empirical data concerning the biological. At this point I would like to refer the reader to Derrida's essay in *Psyche* entitled 'En ce moment même dans cet ouvrage me voici', and to 'Fourmis', collected in *Lectures de la différence sexuelle*.[21]

There is also a series of essays on Heidegger by Derrida[22] which try to come to terms with the former's notion of the imprint upon Being (the '*Prägung des Seins*'); they question whether Being as a Heideggerian concept is not allowed to remain a little too neutral

---

20 Alison Ainley, '"Ideal selfishness": Nietzsche's metaphor of maternity', in eds. David Farrell Krell and David Wood, *Exceedingly Nietzsche: aspects of contemporary Nietzsche interpretation*, p. 127.
21 Paris: Des femmes, 1994. Textes réunis et présentés par Mara Negrón.
22 (1) '*Geschlecht*: sexual difference, ontological difference', trans. Ruben Berezdivin, *Research in phenomenology*, 13 (1983), 65–83; (2) '*Geschlecht* II: Heidegger's hand', in ed. John Sallis, *Deconstruction and philosophy: the texts of Jacques Derrida* (Chicago: The University of Chicago Press, 1987), pp. 161–96. (The French versions of both are collected in *Psyche* (P: see list of abbreviations) and in *Heidegger et la question*, Paris: Flammarion, 1990); (3) '*Geschlecht* IV' – the text we have referred to as HE (see again the list of abbreviations). Is there a *Geschlecht* III in the series?

despite its unique imprint – or 'fingerprint', to use the term from genetics. Might it not be that Heidegger's concept involved 'a neutralisation that fell back this side of both sexual difference and its binary marking, if not this side of sexuality itself?' (*TEO*, 180)[23] Derrida's essays pass through a reading of the German word '*Geschlecht*' which means 'sex', 'gender', 'race', that by which one is marked out, and which is a cognate of '*Schlag*', designating (the force of) a blow or an imprint – 'it has an essential affinity with the blow, the strike, the imprint' (*DL'E*, 174/*OS*, 106). Both gender and finger-printing are gathered in '*Geschlecht*'. The reason that the drum of the otobiographical ear, too, is '*geschlecht*' is that it is incapable of taking up a neutral position: it is always angled or tilted in some way, leaning and creasing like a ship's sail, never merely perpendicular in an opposition.

Eleventh turning

Let us hold on to the notion of heterogeneity, without deciding anything – without, above all, deciding that the force of *Geschlecht* has to do with a decided or decisive act, for it is always a question of difference, qualification, tonal difference, variation – and move into Michel Leiris's *Biffures*, one of the volumes of his autobiography and cited *in extenso* in the margin of Derrida's essay 'Tympan'. Since we are lost within a labyrinth where a necessary metaphoricity simulates guidance, let us emphasize more the 'figural' elements surging up around Derrida's readings.

The word '*biffures*' might be translated as 'erasures', since the verb '*biffer*' means 'to cancel'. In *De la grammatologie*, Derrida had already made a parenthetical remark about this verb:

(by using that verb – 'to cancel' [*biffer*] – we leave the values of effacement and erasure, of extenuation and repression, in their ambiguity, as Rousseau proposes them simultaneously). (*DLG*, 322/*OG*, 226)

Let it be said of the imprint upon the tympan(um) that, being a mark that comes about 'prior' to ('I am putting quotation marks around the word "prior" because it has no literal, chronological, historical or logical meaning' (*TEO*, 180)) any empirical marking, a force of '*Schlag*' stamping itself before any '*Geschlecht*', it remains erased even as it is

---

23 The English and the French (*L'oreille de l'autre*) texts do not match up with each other here, for the English contains the additional 'Choreographies' not in the French.

impressed: its defunctive character sits with its generative gender, or engenderedness, ('*Schlag*' also harbouring the letters of '*glas*', the death-knell, as Derrida exploits). The erased-impressed imprint heralds heterogeneity, that of the labyrinth of the other's ear within the ear of the same. It is 'origin-heterogeneous', to use the phrase intoned in the final pages of *De l'esprit*. The imprint, that is to say, is originary, in so far as it comes about 'before' the subject, where subjectivity is a tardiness; it is heterogeneous in so far as this origin has to be structurally multifoliate, open and unenfolded. Heterogeneous, originary, erased-impressed: the fantastic imprimatur of the subject.

Twelfth turning

So what of Leiris? *Biffures* is cited from the start of Derrida's 'Tympan' to its end, as if Leiris's were the other ear affecting Derrida's from the start (a relationship glossed by Jeffrey Mehlman in Lacanian terms).[24] *Biffures* is cited in the margin, but a non-oppositional margin, swaying from the perpendicular, and twining around the main text of Derrida's essay. The two texts can be conceived as internal laminations of each

24 Though the level of engagement between Lacan and Derrida remains 'implicit': 'In the course of this idiosyncratic meditation on the oblique membrane ("tympan") dividing the organ of hearing (from itself), Derrida implicitly pursues his polemic against Lacan' (*Mehlman*, p. 149). The article by Michael Ryan cited in the last chapter ('Self-de(con)struction') is, as was mentioned, a review of this book, and with regard to both the reader might like also to consult the book review by Elizabeth W. Bruss in *Comparative literature*, 28: 1 (Winter 1976), 93–6. The chapter on Leiris in Allan Stoekl's *Politics, writing, mutilation* claims indebtedness to Mehlman (see note 5 to chapter 4 on p. 138). But perhaps Mehlman's point about Derrida's polemic is misleading in suggesting too oppositional an argument (he also appears occasionally to *oppose* speech to writing, the ear to the imprint)...And indebted to *Ryan*, to Ryan's 'private communications and public writings' (p. 34, note 40), is Avrom Fleishman's *Figures of autobiography: the language of self-writing* which, while brushing 'deconstruction' aside, nevertheless considers Derrida in relation to Leiris – (and Mehlman), speaking of 'the writer's apparently fated tendency toward self-deconstruction...In *Of grammatology*, Derrida argues that writing by its very nature not only places but displaces its subject, for the marks in the text are always the sign of his absence rather than his presence. Given this distantiation, it is not only the critic who comes upon a text with a will to deconstruct it; the autobiographer's own activity is deconstruction – practised upon the self because the subject is himself' (p. 30). I refer to this network to suggest the level of 'circulation or sharing of voices', as Kamuf had put it, when it comes to the supposedly private concerns of autobiography.

other, sloping and luxated. But the heterogeneity of 'Tympan' is larger still. Leiris himself will have already pointed to this tendency to multiplication, saying,

From being something belonging to me, it [the word '*biffures*'] becomes public and open.[25]

For not only does Leiris get internally mixed up with Derrida, but Derrida is already mixed up with Heidegger[26] and with Nietzsche, who in turn is mixed up with his pseudo-autobiographer, Zarathustra. Furthermore, the work of Leiris represents the most consistent object of study for the autobiographical theorist we cited in the last chapter, Philippe Lejeune.[27] The multiplication is fomented further by the thought that each of these voices may be double to begin with, playing roles of both autobiographers and autobiographical theorists at the same time.

The figure of this heterogeneous mixing could be that of a spiral, the horn, in fact, of the outer ear, or what in *Glas* are flowers twining round a pole – 'The sentences coil around a direction like liana along a truncated column' (*G*, 87b/*Gl*, 74b) – which recall similar images about the 'ugly pole of writing' in de Quincey's autobiographical writings, for example. In his introduction to Husserl's work on

25 Michel Leiris, *Biffures*, in *La règle du jeu* (Paris: Gallimard, 1948), vol. I, p. 12. My translation.
26 Heidegger, too, has his own hammer to brandish, neither that of Zarathustra's harangue, nor of Derrida's otobiographies, but of the hammer that is 'ready-to-hand' as equipment. See Martin Heidegger, *Being and time*, trans. John Macquarrie and Edward Robinson (Oxford: Basil Blackwell, 1962, reprinted 1967), p. 98 ff. Hereafter referred to as *Being and time*.
27 Lejeune talks interestingly of, among other things, Leiris inviting us to play a game of 'the reciprocal and endless projection of the outside onto the inside and vice versa', in *Lire Leiris: autobiographie et langage* (Paris: Klincksieck, 1975), p. 80. My translation.
    For other work on Leiris, the reader might like to consult the following: (1) a psychoanalytical reading of *L'age d'homme* by Sean Hand, who contests that through a primary 'méconnaissance', the subject gets diverted into myth as 'the story that is not told': 'The simple structure of the subject is in every sense a myth, structured in its turn by the story that is not told.' 'The orchestration of man: the structure of *L'age d'homme*', *Romance studies*, 8 (Summer 1986), 77–8; (2) a tenaciously close reading of Leiris by James Leigh, 'The figure of autobiography', *Modern language notes*, 93: 4 (1978), 733–49; (3) Roland -H. Simon's *Orphée medusé: autobiographies de Michel Leiris* (Lausanne: L'age d'homme, 1984), which is undertaken at a 'more formal-symbolic than infra-textual level, without ignoring the hold that reflections of a psychoanalytical order contribute to a grasp of [Leiris's] work' (p. 17, my translation).

geometry, Derrida had analysed the latter's 'spiraling movement' [*sic*],[28] but the kind of spiralling under consideration here is not entirely geometrical so much as a 'labyrinthine infinity of curves that would baffle the geometry of Apollonius'.[29] At issue is a refashioning of the Husserlian and/or Cartesian *cogito* or thinking subject. If we turn from *Biffures* to Leiris's 'Glossaire j'y serre mes gloses' – a sort of autobiographical dictionary – we come upon the following entry:

COGITO – qu'au gîte tôt ESCARGOt SUM![30]

The *cogito*[31] is related to the snail ('*escargot*') on the grounds of phonic coincidence ('*escargot*' sounds to Leiris like '*cogito*'), and the snail, in turn, in the passage from *Biffures* cited in 'Tympan', is noted for the helix, or spiral, which marks the gastropod's shell:

The acanthus leave copied in school when, for better or for worse, one learns to use the fusain, the stem of a morning glory or other climbing plant, the helix inscribed on the shell of a snail ... *(MDP*, i/*MOP*, x)

The *cogito*, or subject, is phonically confused with the spiral on the shell of the snail. This other sound, this other way of hearing, this other ear, this ear of the other, picks up a quite different message, one that stalls its rational *cogito* or subjectivity. I think, therefore I am a snail. Perhaps that is why I'm always late. I am a subject, therefore I will have been marked in advance by the helix, and marked by the phonic confusion unleashed by the ear of the other.

Thirteenth turning

All these autobiographers and pseudo-autobiographers (Derrida, Nietzsche, Heidegger, Leiris, Lejeune) connote the spiralling ageo-metrical movement of the '*escargot*' before the *cogito*. They are inter-spiralled, inter-coiled, such that none can sign his autobiography with an authentic and univocal seal. So that if Derrida's essay, 'Tympan', is autobiographical – and Derrida says that it is – it is falsely so, and leads into another labyrinth. The essay was drafted in Amsterdam, and one can read in the essay 'an introduction to Amsterdam ... Guides,

28 Derrida claims that this movement is 'the major find of our text' (*L'OG*, 14/*TOG*, 33), – 'qui fait tout le prix de notre texte'.

29 Thomas de Quincey, *Confessions of an English opium eater and other writings* (Oxford and New York: Oxford University Press, 1985), p. 128.

30 Michel Leiris, 'Glossaire j'y serre mes gloses', in *Mots sans mémoire* (Paris: Gallimard, 1969), p. 80.   31 Cf. *Mehlman*, p. 103.

plans, reproductions of tableaux – they can all be found there' (AL'O, 15, my translation),[32] a labyrinth to the labyrinthine city which in turn is confused with the mazy streets of Oxford in *La carte postale*, 'the labyrinth between the colleges' (*LCP*, 20/*TPC*, 15) (a labyrinth which I myself look out over as I write this) where Derrida buys postcards in a scene that will be replayed later, in Tokyo, itself perhaps a city on the circuit of the eternal return:

> Tokyo: would this town be found on the occidental circle which turns back to Dublin or Ithaca? (*UG*, 60/*UGr*, 29, modified)

And so it goes on. Dublin and Ithaca remind us of Joyce's Earwicker, the 'autobiographicoencyclopaedic' (*UG*, 66/*UGr*, 32, modified) ear in *Finnegans Wake*, neither conscious nor unconscious, that rings with voices, and whose very initials, H.C.E., stand for the proliferation noted in *La carte postale*, 'Here Comes Everybody' (*LCP*, 154/*TPC*, 142) – a phrase which might become the name of an autobiographical theory. It is not by chance entirely that it is a passage about Persephone that is cited from Leiris, for the name Perse-phone suggests the piercing of the auditory organ.[33] The speech of hearing oneself speak is indebted to the mark which imprints its ear with an equivocal seal of approval which also confuses it, pierces it, generates the autobiography, and lets or makes everybody come.

32 Derrida associates Amsterdam with Spinoza, another voice resonating.
33 On Persephone, see also Jeffrey Mehlman's 'Orphée scripteur: Blanchot, Rilke, Derrida', trans. Jean-Michel Rabaté, *Poétique*, 20 (1974), 458–82.

❖❖

PART III

The book of Zoë

❖❖

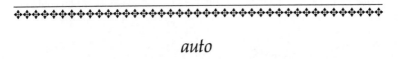

auto

To repeat: the circle coming round upon itself without joining up —
the autobiographical *auto* attracts the a priori threat of this deviation.

First, with regard to the 'mark':

The ideal iterability that forms the structure of all marks is that which
undoubtedly allows them to be released from any context, to be freed from
all determined bonds to its origin, its meaning, or its referent, to emigrate in
order to play elsewhere, in whole or in part, another role. I say 'in whole or
in part' because by means of this essential insignificance the ideality or ideal
identity of each mark (which is only a differential function without an
ontological basis) can continue to divide itself and to give rise to the
proliferation of other ideal identities. This iterability is thus that which allows
a mark to be used more than once. It is more than one. It multiplies and
divides itself internally. This imprints the capacity for diversion within its
very movement. In the destination ... there is thus a principle of in-
determination, chance, luck, or of destinerring. There is no assured destination
precisely because of the mark and the proper name; in other words, because
of this insignificance.   (MC, 31/MCh, 16)

Or again:

This is the possibility on which I want to insist: the possibility of extraction
and of citational grafting which belongs to the structure of every mark,
spoken or written, and which constitutes every mark as writing even before
and outside of every horizon of semiolinguistic communication; as writing,
that is, as a possibility of functioning cut off, at a certain point, from its
'original' meaning and from its belonging to a saturable and constraining
context. Every sign, linguistic or nonlinguistic, spoken or written (in the usual
sense of this opposition), as a small or large unity, can be *cited*, put between
quotation marks; thereby it can break with every given context, and
engender infinitely new contexts in an absolutely nonsaturable fashion. This
does not suppose that the mark is valid outside its context, but on the
contrary that there are only contexts without any centre of absolute
anchoring. This citationality, duplication, or duplicity, this iterability of the
mark is not an accident or an anomaly, but is that (normal/abnormal) without

which a mark could no longer even have a so-called 'normal' functioning. What would a mark be that one could not cite? And whose origin could not be lost on the way? (*MDP*, 381/*MOP*, 320–1)

And again:

the quotation marks are not only the mark of a reservation or distance with regard to a concept or a word. They recall the general quotability, they cite this quotability as a summons, once again not as a formalist neutralisation concerned with propriety but as the reminder of the necessary general contamination, of the transplants and irreducible parasitism which affect any theorem. (*SST*, 78)

And again:

The quote institutes a repetition or an originary reflexivity that, even as it divides the inaugural act, at once the inventive event and the relation or archive of an invention, also allows it to unfold in order to say nothing but the same, itself, the dehiscent and refolded invention of the same, at the very instant when it takes place. (*P*, 23/*DR*, 205)

And again:

internal division of the trait, impurity, corruption, contamination, decomposition, perversion, deformation, even cancerisation, generous proliferation or degenerescence. All these disruptive 'anomalies' are engendered – and this is their common law, the lot or site they share – by *repetition*. One might even say by citation, or re-citation (*ré-cit*), provided that the restricted use of these two words is not a call to strict generic order. (*Pa*, 254/*TLG*, 204–5)

The identity of the same, of that which in this chapter will be known as the *auto*, is generated by the very thing – iterability, the power-to-be-repeated – which prohibits its stability and autonomy. 'But repetition is the basis of identification', in the words of Gayatri Spivak: 'Thus, if repetition alters, it has to be faced that alteration identifies and identity is always impure.'[1] The mark of the *auto* is that which allows it to be altered or othered in repetition, and this is the very first guarantee of its 'existence'. '[D]oubled as soon as it appears ... [w]hat is is not what it is, identical and identical to itself, unique, unless it *adds to itself* the possibility of being *repeated* as such.' (*LD*, 194/*D*, 168)

---

1 Gayatri Spivak, 'Revolutions that as yet have no model: Derrida's *Limited inc.*', *Diacritics* (December 1980), 37.

And so '[e]verything "begins", then, with citation' (*LD*, 352/*D*, 316).

'Kierkegaard'

The other as the (repetitional) possibility of the *auto* directs these remarks.[2] Autobiographical altruism could be a name for it. Here I am thinking of Kierkegaard. He is musing after the failure of his relationship with a woman who has now become engaged to another. But despite the disappointment he is 'again unified', he says, and, in a manner strikingly similar in tone to the opening of *Ecce homo*, he likens this return to self to a religious sagaciousness. This is his return to the same:

I am again myself. This self which another would not pick up from the road I possess again. The discord in my nature is resolved, I am again unified. The terrors which found support and nourishment in my pride no longer enter in to distract and separate.

Is there not then a repetition? Did I not get everything doubly restored? Did I not get myself again, precisely in such a way that I must doubly feel its significance? And what is a repetition of earthly goods which are of no consequence to the spirit – what are they in comparison with such a repetition? Only his children Job did not receive again double, because a human life is not a thing that can be duplicated. In that case only spiritual repetition is possible, although in the temporal life it is never so perfect as in eternity, which is the true repetition.[3]

Kierkegaard's 'repetition' is that which has passed through love for the other – the woman who has now become engaged to someone else – in order to return to himself in a 'double significance'. Elsewhere Kierkegaard says that this woman has given the other man her 'yes'.[4] The woman, Regine Olsen, Kierkegaard's other shall we provisionally say, has become the other's other, no longer Kierkegaard's 'own' – 'an other that is no longer its other' (*MDP*, v/*MOP*, xiv) – assuming, which we don't, that there could ever have been an unproblematic appropriation.

2 For an account of iterability see, for example, John Llewellyn, *Derrida on the threshold of sense* (Basingstoke and London: Macmillan, 1986), pp. 60–70.

3 *A Kierkegaard reader: texts and narratives*, ed. Roger Poole and Henrik Strangerup (London: Fourth Estate, 1989), p. 240.

4 Søren Kierkegaard, *Fear and trembling/Repetition*, ed. and trans. Howard V. Hong and Edna H. Hong (Princeton: Princeton University Press, 1983), p. 220. Referred to hereafter as *Repetition*.

In this chapter I would like, to begin with, to think through the 'double significance' of Kierkegaard along the lines of what Derrida has just called *insignificance*, as the repetition of the other within the same[5] – as that autobiographical altruism which comes face to face with the 'yes, yes'. Again it is a matter of re-elaborating a supposedly 'existentialist' autobiographism in a new, citational or grammatological manner. I would like to do this by working certain quotations across Derrida, quotations from Kierkegaard, but also from Heidegger, Levinas, Kant and others. By repeating them through each other, I hope to put into effect the autobiographical generality of the other, to indicate a general logic without proceeding too much by identity-distinctions, so to speak. It is the operation of autobiography to get caught up in this 'insignificance' without settling into a single authorial voice. I quote copiously from Derrida, generously hosting his text, to simulate this logical insignificance,[6] and to act as a foil say to the comparatively denuded way of talking about Derrida's autobiography that is Geoffrey Bennington's in 'Derridabase'. That is a text mock-cajoled at by Derrida for being so starved of citational specificity and for gaining some of its detached authority thereby. In this, one hears a small echo of Kierkegaard's own reaction to Hegel. Subjective experience in its reality was not properly reckoned for by Hegel, and the attempts to accommodate it insufficient. Among the quotes I set forth, there is perhaps more the structure of an alliance operating, the structure which we brought forward in the previous chapter with regard to Nietzsche, and which affirms itself with a double yes that both repeats and deviates from itself.

There is another preliminary complication. Kierkegaard experiences a 'yes, yes' from his interlocutor, the 'silent confidant', his *alter ego* (more pseudo-autobiographers):

Would that I stood beside you, that I could tear myself from you with the last 'no' as Don Giovanni did from the Commandatore, whose hand was no colder than the good sense with which you irresistibly sweep me off my feet.

---

5 Derrida adduces the fact that the Sanskrit word 'itara' contains both senses, 'other' and 'again', in *De la grammatologie*, for example: 'Art and death, art and its death are comprised in the space of the *alteration* of the originary *iteration* (*iterum*, anew, does it not come from Sanskrit *itara*, other?); of repetition, reproduction, representation; or also in space [*sic*] as the possibility of iteration and the exit from life placed outside of itself' (*DLG*, 297–8/*OG*, 209).

6 And to play a perhaps dangerous game with copyright law. My editor for this volume, Kevin Taylor, has been particularly concerned about this question.

And yet, if I stood face to face with you, I would hardly say more than one 'no', because before I got any further you no doubt would interrupt me with the cold response: Yes, yes.[7]

Standing face to face, the *alter ego* overwhelms the self with a 'cold response' and interruption into the self's oppositional no. It is already a double of the woman who gives her yes to another man, and to this extent the 'yes' marks a double withdrawal from the self (Kierkegaard). In both cases, Kierkegaard finds himself simulated, by the new man and by his shadow interlocutor. And in both cases this simulation returns to Kierkegaard in the form of a yes. It remains other to him while both interrupting him and allowing for his 'spiritual repetition'.

Can this other, in either form (Regine Olsen or 'silent interlocutor'), be known as such, or, like the volatile contingent, does knowing it amount to losing it? The other may be anticipated, but anticipated precisely as that which cannot be anticipated since it works by interruption ('I would hardly say more than one "no", because before I got any further you no doubt would interrupt me with the cold response: Yes, yes'). Consequently, one has to anticipate not being able to entirely anticipate it, and in this movement the other is not quite appropriated. The other ceases to be the other the moment it is detained as such. It pre-empts such gestures.

In regard to the apparently ironic situation of thinking the other, Derrida writes:

To insist upon thinking *its* [philosophy's] *other*: its proper other, the proper of its other, an other proper? In thinking it *as such*, in recognising it, one misses it. One reappropriates it for oneself, one disposes of it, one misses it, or rather one misses (the) missing (of) it, which, as concerns the other, always amounts to the same.
(*MDP*, ii/*MOP*, xi-xii)

How may we begin to detail the ramifications of this logic between Kierkegaard, his *alter ego*, the woman he has lost, the man she has won? How do these elements resolve into a return to the same, a 'double significance'? How do they pass through an expropriation of the other?

A moment ago Kierkegaard spoke of the elevation which moves from 'earthly goods which are of no consequence to the spirit' to the spirit itself. This marks the transition to the 'religious mood' that attends upon repetition. Can repetition be conceived in a non-

7 *Repetition*, p. 193.

religious, non-transcendental, non-spiritual, non-existential manner? The transition occurs only after an experience of the inappropriability of the other (Regine). Some loss affects the gain. Kierkegaard loses 'his' other, his envisaged bride. Her breaking off, his ruin or becoming 'debrided' (*PS*, 56–7), abets the alteration by which he has his 'repetition' and so 'becomes himself again', which is not a simple return to self, but a spiritual repetition and transformation of himself through the interruption of the other. Subsequently, he is both himself and not himself. The loss of the other — and of an other who was never 'owned' — becomes the condition of repetition-alteration, and to this extent what is going on in Kierkegaard's text repeats the logic of insignificance detailed by Derrida in our opening citations from him. Kierkegaard faces up to the woman by no longer being able to face her. To face the other involves a relinquishment, an interruption of self-interest, or what might be called an autobiographical altruism. And not just an interruption of self-interest either, but a positive gratitude toward the other for that interruption, Kierkegaard being 'indebted to her generosity for its coming'.[8] One gives thanks to the other for the latter's very withdrawal from immediate otherness, for this generosity is generative, giving out on to that active 'degenerescence' which Derrida intimates. The other bestows this gift of generosity; the movement of bestowal is that of no longer being given, or to be given, and there cannot be a contained exchange. And this gives rise to *Kierkegaard's* generous largesse in altruism which gives her credit:

Whoever it is she has chosen ... she has certainly shown generosity toward me. Even if he were the handsomest man in the world, the epitome of charm, capable of enchanting any woman, even if she drove her whole sex to despair by giving him her 'yes', she still acted generously, if in no other way than by completely forgetting me.[9]

We cannot say finally whether in this scene of superabundant gift-giving the other is still 'with' Kierkegaard when he accedes to his autobiographical peroration, 'I am again myself', nor quite what the value of 'Kierkegaard' is, given the confusion of his voice with that of the silent confidant. She is lost to him, but perhaps remains to him in her being lost, or as her being lost. Secondly, this active generosity of the lost other comes about by forgetting the object of its generosity (Kierkegaard): 'she still acted generously, if in no other way than by

8 Ibid., p. 220.   9 Ibid., p. 220.

completely forgetting me'. This is what might be meant by the gift that is not 'given' in an ordinary sense, for the gift may be nothing more than an oblivion of its recipient. When the recipient (Kierkegaard) is forgotten, he is in receipt of the gift which allows him his autobiographical repetition. The active repetition is a being-forgotten, such that the phrase 'I am again myself', which sounds like a return to self with all the pathos of remembrance in a recognition scene, means also: 'I am forgotten'. The two senses, 'I am again myself' and 'I am forgotten' may be structurally indistinguishable, vie with one another and threaten to cancel each other out. Furthermore, since the being-forgotten is activated by the woman (the giver and not the recipient), Kierkegaard finds himself again in the woman (in her faculty of forgetting him), and the woman is now engaged to another other, an other who is a 'double' of Kierkegaard. Consequently, Kierkegaard, in becoming himself again in the woman, is further altered by 'being' with the other other, the woman's new partner, and this situation perhaps demonstrates that principle of autobiographical generality in the other that I would like to insist on. Yes, yes: there is a return to the self, but the self is determined by this yes and divided by it. Its power is perhaps stronger than a religious harnessing of it. No one point in the 'economy' of exchanges is fixed.

But what can it mean, in any case, to be with the other?

'Heidegger', 'Levinas'

These are some of the practical and theoretical effects of the 'cold response', a response which generates a responsibility whose limits are not sure. The response of the other leads to a responsibility in which relations between those involved pass through a loss or oblivion which gives the possibility of 'becoming oneself again'. The 'other', the condition of repetition-alteration, is not necessarily someone to be 'with' in an ordinary sense. It is not certain that responsibility has to pass through accompaniment, withness, or what Heidegger calls 'Mitsein', 'Being-with', the being with the other:

'With' and 'too' are to be understood *existentially*, not categorially. By reason of this *with-like* [*mithaften*] Being-in-the-world, the world is always the one that I share with Others. The world of *Dasein* is a *with-world* [*Mitwelt*]. Being-in is *Being-with* Others.[10]

10 *Being and time*, pp. 154–5.

Against this existential positing of 'Others', one may perhaps sketch out a different other, one that gives on to autobiography through repetition, which can be glimpsed in Derrida and in a certain interventive, perhaps distorting, analysis of a part of Kierkegaard's text *Repetition*. Coming 'before' the existential (Heideggerian) relation in the face of Others, there is for this second other a response, an appeal, 'but the structure of this appeal to responsibility is such that, being anterior to all possible response, independent, and dissymmetrical because it comes from the other in us, even a non-response is charged a priori with responsibility' (*DDP*, 397–8, my translation). Derrida uses a categorical or transcendental term for this second other which is 'charged a priori with responsibility', so that where with Heidegger it is the existentiality of the other that is to be understood, with Kierkegaard and Derrida the other moves close to the a priori, close to being categorised as a *principle* of repetition.

But these distinctions are not so easily made.[11] In a sense, the logic of the other is 'stronger' than Derrida, Kierkegaard or Heidegger, and it renders division into 'existential' and 'categorical' somewhat lame (and not least because so to divide is already to be categorical). There is a distinction to be made between 'the other' and 'Others', perhaps. The latter, for Heidegger, are to be understood existentially as the Others with whom I share a world. Without this sharing I am bereft of my own existence, my '*Dasein*', or Being-there. What is more, I cannot 'know myself' without this relation to Others, so that the autobiographical gesture of self-knowledge can be made only in the proximity, the 'proximal disclosedness', of Others:

Knowing oneself [*Sichkennen*] is grounded in Being-with, which understands primordially. It operates proximally in accordance with the kind of Being which is closest to us – Being-in-the-world as Being-with; and it does so by an acquaintance with that which *Dasein*, along with the Others, comes across in its environmental circumspection and concerns itself with – an acquaintance in which *Dasein* understands. Solicitous concern is understood in terms of what we are concerned with, and along with our understanding of it. Thus in concernful solicitude the Other is proximally disclosed.[12]

Differing from Kierkegaard's other in that they remain 'there', Heidegger's Others cannot be conceived outside of their proximity to

---

11 May I refer the reader to Simon Critchley's *The ethics of deconstruction: Derrida and Levinas* (Oxford: Basil Blackwell, 1992) for a more extensive analysis of this and related areas?   12 *Being and time*, p. 161.

my '*Dasein*'. While this is an apparently existential claim, the intimacy between my '*Dasein*' and Being suggests a categorical nexus, for Being acts as much as a categorical as an existential origin. 'Knowing oneself [*Sichkennen*] is grounded in Being-with, which understands primordially.' This '*primordially*' (my italics) works in both categorical and counter-categorical ways; its existentiality will have sublated, for want of a better term, its categoriality, without damaging its primordial status. The existential Others draw me into a principle of existence which is not different from existence itself, at least when that existence is 'authentic'. They also prompt a solicitude that is incipiently ethical (in so far as it is 'concernful'), but the responsibility of this ethic does not appear to run the risk of repetition or alteration – as it may do for Kierkegaard and for Derrida – until Heidegger is read by Levinas; though there may be room for a kind of primordial difference that may be taken as the possibility for dissent and even war with others. These are some of the questions that Derrida takes up in the 'philopolemology' essay referred to in the previous chapter (HE).

Others are those with whom I share a world, and my Being and my (autobiographical) self-knowledge cannot not avail themselves of this relation. Existentially speaking, it is possible that this relation is insurmountable, and that there is no autobiography or self-relation without Being-with or hetero-relation. The concept of the other in Derrida is not absolutely opposed to this 'existential' concept of Others. At the same time, the relation to the other in Derrida goes 'otherwise than Being', to use again the phrase of Levinas. What is more, it not only takes the form of a repetition it also, as with Kierkegaard's repetition, assumes a non-neutral, sexed, or loving accent – 'Praised be feminine generosity!'[13] – in which generosity gives without providing, in the manner of an ungiven gift which cannot be posited 'there', a sort of 'living feminine' not to be too quickly assimilated with gender. There is a 'feminine' generosity or principle of 'degenerescence' which exceeds what Derrida perceives to be the spectre of a residually masculine neutrality of Heideggerian Being. One needs to be precise here while also respecting a general undecidability which preoccupies any discourse on this question. If the other, transported by the figure of a repetition, carries with it the virus of chance in its irreducible manifestation as the specific, then a simply neutral position for otherness no longer offers itself. One must then,

13 *Repetition*, pp. 221–2.

at the very least, admit a non-neutrality of otherness which for reasons that are neither quite wholly strategic nor wholly essential, presumably must also allow itself to pass beyond the second-order neutrality of a *non*-neutrality. A *certain* gendering then impresses itself upon this logic. And if this logic is manoeuvred neither by wholly strategic nor by wholly essential criteria, this is because the very question of the relation of strategy to essence is involved in it. I tried to argue earlier that a gratuitousness was germane to reason in its earliest or apparently most spontaneous gestures, and this internal excess of 'strategy' ('force') within reason's body perhaps demonstrates itself most acutely here. Where can this logic of the other now turn if not to chance a movement beyond the irenic necessity of logical progression? Which above all is not to be presented with a *choice*. If there is strategy at stake in the question of the gender of the other, it is not one that could come under a fully intentional management. A death of intention insists. It takes subjective choice in the realm of alterity away from itself. It allows for generative alteration, and keeps the self alive by instituting that altering repetition which is the death of the (former) self.

The other gives itself, or rather it gives giving, the possibility of giving, although it is not determinately posited. Any -propriation or 'commodification' of the 'subjects' involved pales by comparison with this *gratuitous* thankfulness accompanying the return to a (different) self. So it is difficult to establish the position of the other. Or at least its positioning is neither wholly existential nor wholly categorical. The other thus recoils from philosophical enquiry:

The other, as the other than self, the other that opposes self-identity, is not something that can be detected and disclosed within a philosophical space and with the aid of a philosophical lamp. (DO, 118)

Responsibility to the other comes about not only 'otherwise than being' but also in a sense 'before' being. It is set in motion 'before' any inkling of existence or self-realisation. Admittedly, this aprioristic 'before' sounds like a categorical description. But its power of generous repetition disrupts this. Kierkegaard's existential sense of being restored to himself is set forth upon the back of a thought of repetition, inculcating the other, the other in her lost-ness, which allows for that restoration. The structure of repetition is what allows for existential 'significance' when Kierkegaard repeats the phrase 'I am again myself', with the result that existence is a secondary category after repetition. Against the objection that Kierkegaard had already been himself, that this is just an ordinary repetition or return, we may say that any sense of this comes only retrospectively, when the significance is doubled at the 'meridian' point (cf. Nietzsche – and also Celan, of course) of this peroration. And if repetition comes about before existence, then the repetition at stake will involve the repeating of that which is as yet foreign to what exists, the repetition of the non-existent, out of which a category cannot be made. The relation to the (non-existent) other comes about before, and allows for – if indeed it ever 'happens' in the simple mode of existence – the relation with Others, that Being-in-the-world that is a Being-with the other. Except that it does not really 'come before'. This is because the repetition of the non-existent (that is, the relation to the other), cannot repeat itself in time, for time is (classically, at least) the form or condition of what *exists*. Being implies time, in other words. So we have qualified the remarks made in the previous chapter concerning the 'coming into time' of the other. But still more will need to be said.

Derrida shares with Levinas an emphasis on the relation with the other that comes about before existence, and, consequently, an interest in re-elaborating concepts of time. But where Derrida situates repetition, Levinas situates ethics – although this should not be taken as a significant divergence between the two, and the said 'situating' barely belongs to a taxonomy. The very relation between Derrida and the texts he reads provides an exemplum of the anterior (co)responsibility he appears at first sight to be merely thematising. Derrida writes, for example, that

faced with a body of thought like that of Levinas, I never hold any objection. I am prepared to subscribe to everything that he says. That is not to say that I think the same thing in the same way; but that the differences at issue are very difficult to determine. (*A* 74, my translation)

And of Derrida, Levinas says that

in underlining the primordial importance of the questions raised by Derrida, we wished to designate the pleasure of a contact at the heart of a chiasmus.[14]

Again, we want both to make and to dispense with distinctions.

Self-relation, the existentiality of the autobiographical, is made to demur by that which arrives before existence or its analysis, ontology.

14 Emmanuel Levinas, 'Tout autrement', *L'arc*, 54 (1973): 'Derrida', 35. My translation.

In this movement, repetition of the non-existent (relation to the other) is 'stronger' than the existence and time which it 'precedes'. This early arrival, which arrives before arrival, comes before coming and becoming, is the movement of responsibility in the other, and is 'otherwise than being' since not only can it be said that 'everything is otherwise if one can still speak of being',[15] but also that 'to be obliged to responsibility has no beginning'.[16] It is possible – or it is impossible, the two perhaps amounting to the same in this connection – that the other of being as existence is time, but not as the horizon of being as it is described in Heidegger's *Being and time*, nor its lateral context or ontic landscape, but as time's own deferral or iteration, having no ideal beginning. The interminable deferral of time as the form of full existential presence, that is.

With what sublimity Levinas unfolds in that deferral the ethical:

I am trying to show that man's ethical relation to the other is ultimately prior to his ontological relation to himself (egology) or to the totality of things which we call the world (cosmology). The relationship with the other is *time*: it is an untotalisable diachrony in which one moment pursues another without ever being able to retrieve it, to catch up or coincide with it. The non-simultaneous and non-present is my primary rapport with the other in time.[17]

The 'primary rapport with the other' that is 'prior to man's ontological relation to himself' is time, and this time is not a 'vulgar concept of time' as taking the form of a line, straight or circular or otherwise, but an 'untotalisable diachrony'. Levinas talks more of diachrony than deferral, then, in fact. This diachrony is described, however, in the terms of an impeded repetition, 'in which one moment pursues another without ever being able to retrieve it, to catch up or coincide with it'. Time, which is the relationship to the other, can always lose its origin in order to play elsewhere, to attempt to 'catch up and coincide' with itself, in a structurally fugitive pattern impervious to saturation in this or that context or 'timescape', and to this extent corresponds to the structure of Derrida's in-signifying mark.

One might say this from another direction, such that time, because it is non-totalisable, diachronic and the origin of repetition, therefore

15 Ibid., 35.
16 Emmanuel Levinas, *Humanisme de l'autre homme* (Paris: fata morgana, 1972), p. 78. My translation.
17 Levinas interviewed in Richard Kearney, *Dialogues with contemporary Continental thinkers: the phenomenological heritage* (Manchester: Manchester University Press, 1984), p. 57.

inaugurates the alterity known as the 'other', that is, the ethical other. Alterity is a power of non-totalisability, and this alterity is bodied by the other. It is precisely because this (relation to the) other cannot be totalised that it demands ethical respect, so that ethical respect is always a reverence before what cannot be totalised, a reverence for the non-totalisability of the non-totalisable – hence its apparently transcendental quality. And it cannot be totalised because it 'is' time, and time goes 'otherwise than being', insignificantly. Time's diachrony is of an order incompatible with the synchronist avarice of a totalisation. Though we may wonder if the assimilation of the relation to other to the diachronicity of time does not itself constitute a kind of synchronicist gathering. One may also wonder *therefore* whether it is the other who has my respect or the diachronicity in my relation to that other.

Released along this faltering and divided temporality, the relation to the other nonetheless depends for Levinas upon that being bodied which is the 'presence' of the other, that Being-with or '*Mitsein*' that is a condition of my '*Dasein*'. However, the presence of the other must surrender its (Heideggerian?) value of proximity, for this can be given only by a concept of time that allows for the presentation of the other, where time is conceived as presence (an ontological or existential concept) and not as repetition (which is 'prior' to all ontology). Derrida writes that '[t]here is no ethics without the presence *of the other*', a statement which has to be qualified by the very thing which upsets it – 'but also, and consequently, without absence, dissimulation, detour, differance, writing' (*DLG*, 202/*OG*, 139–40). The presence of the other presents itself as something other than present, with the effect that the other's ethical position cannot but remain enigmatic. Is there an ethics, a responsibility toward the other, that can tolerate this detour and quasi-repetition? The self-relation of the *auto* (the autobiographical) gets deferred by this responsibility, so can there be an *auto* to respond ethically? What is this pre-ontological autobiography that comes about otherwise than being, in the blend of self and other, and can the question 'what is?' comprehend it?

Can there be an ethics without an ethical subject? This has become a question of crucial importance. Surely there has to be some experience of the *auto*, albeit one which 'finds' itself through the structure of a repetitional loss ... When Derrida professes in an interview that 'I believe that without a movement of narcissistic reappropriation, the rapport with the other would be destroyed absolutely, destroyed in advance' (DI, 16, my translation), are we to believe that such a narcissism can simply reach into an inexistent alterity and seize itself, against all the odds?

Either narcissism denotes the exercise of this seeming impossibility, or it will have to be reconsidered at a non-ontological, non-psychological level. This latter option presumably would take us back to the simulacrum that is the '*Ich*', the shadow interlocutor that is the proper name. In one of his most intense and sustained analyses of the name, Derrida refers to the 'fantasmatic organisation' of a 'finite individual' – what can be said of this? – 'and even supposing (I'd love to see it happen) that one could say something singularly pertinent about it, that cannot happen here' (S, 119/118). The question must remain open.

Levinas speaks of the 'face-to-face' encounter with the other, which comes very close to an existential relation with Heideggerian Others. Not simply 'with' Others, however, in an existential relation, but 'for' Others, in an ethical one:

I am 'with others' signifies: I am 'for others': responsible to/for the other [*responsable d'autrui*].[18]

While this encounter appears to be phenomenal and ontological, the rapport with the other, as the diachrony of time (near-repetition), also proceeds otherwise. Kierkegaard's repetition involved a transition to the 'religious mood', from the earthly to the spiritual. His double significance was an ascent to a higher plane, which he likens to Job's transcendental resignation at the end of the *Book of Job* (there will be cause to return to this). The repetitional or diachronic rupture suffered by Levinasian time is also the breach through which God cuts into the 'intelligible world':

God, as the God of alterity and transcendence, can only be understood in terms of that interhuman dimension which, to be sure, emerges in the phenomenological-ontological perspective of the intelligible world, but which cuts through and perforates the totality of presence and points towards the absolutely Other.[19]

There are at least three nodal points so far. The relation to the other which 'is' time in its diachrony, first of all. Secondly, on the evidence of this quotation, the encounter with the other (diachronic near-

---

18 Emmanuel Levinas, *Du sacré au saint* (Paris: Minuit, 1977), p. 137. My translation.
19 Levinas interviewed in Richard Kearney, *Dialogues*, pp. 56–7.

repetition) gives out onto the relation to the absolutely Other (God). But thirdly, this encounter in the 'interhuman dimension' will have emerged 'in the phenomenological-ontological perspective of the intelligible world'. It is hard to know how much weight to lend any of the three nodes. Nor can the passage be nailed down to these three, for, as we shall see in a moment, its context is a theory of language, of language as a second experience (after time) of the non-totalisable.

Christian Delacampagne epigrammatises, 'Derrida, c'est Levinas moins Dieu'[20] – which, despite its casualness, gives pause for thought. Derrida speaks too of a perforation in the relation to the other which he calls 'violence', 'the nonethical opening of ethics. A violent opening' (DLG, 202/OG, 140), and in doing so indicates a certain subreption of the other which, however, declines the (Levinasian) possibility of the God of transcendence. But this Levinasian God is 'transcendent' only to the extent that it is bound by the diachronic structure of time (and therefore of phenomenological-ontological being). The description of 'God' approximates to a notion of ethical conscience:

To be under the sleepless gaze of God: this is precisely, in its unity, to be the bearer of an *other* subject – bearer and supporter [*porteur et supporteur*] – to be responsible for [*de*] this other, as if the albeit invisible face of the other continued [*prolongeait*] my own and kept me alert by its very invisibility, by the unforeseeability [*l'imprévisible*] which it threatens.[21]

But one suspects an interpretative interest on Levinas's part. What is the justification for calling a certain concept of non-totalisability 'God', and on what grounds can it be termed 'ethical', except in so far as it demands respect as a kind of intellectual limit beyond which thinking cannot progress? It seems to be a matter of naming, or vocation. On the other hand, to be more generous to Levinas: what could 'God' denote if not an enjoinder upon ethical conscience? 'God' might be the permanence and necessity of the relation to the other wherein conscience arises.

Both Derrida and Levinas are emphatic: there is no self-relation without relation to the other. Even then, for Derrida at least, 'self-relation' may be a mirage. We still cannot say whether this relation takes place, whether this is the experience of autobiography, or whether, and quite differently, the concept of experience is derived

---

20 Christian Delacampagne, 'Derrida hors de soi', *Critique*, 30: 325 (June 1974), 509.
21 Emmanuel Levinas, *Du sacré au saint*, p. 133. My translation.

from this relation, 'experience itself and that which is most irreducible within experience: the passage and departure toward the other [*l'autre*]; the other itself as what is most irreducibly other within it: Others [*autrui*]' (*ED*, 123/*WD*, 83). Levinas cautions further, now introducing Kantian terms:

It is not a matter, as regards proximity, of a new 'experience' opposed to the experience of the objective presence, of an experience of 'you' ['*tu*'] producing itself after, or even before, the experience of being of an 'ethical experience' over and above perception. *It is rather a matter of the questioning of* EXPERIENCE *as the source of meaning*, of the limit of transcendental apperception, of the end of synchrony and its reversible terms; it is a matter of the non-priority of the Same and, across all these limitations, of the end of actuality [*actualité*], as if *the untimely* [*l'intempestif*] came along to scramble the coordinates of re-presentation.[22]

Experience is the experience of the untimely, '*l'intempestif*' which in turn abuses the notion of experience or at least the privilege accorded it by philosophies (of a Kantian kind). Despite this massive disruptiveness in the field of the concept of experience, that concept remains ready to be questioned, and here we could choose to intrude upon Levinas somewhat and look at his words in a different light. The untimely throws the relation with the other into question, it being '*rather a matter of the questioning of* EXPERIENCE *as the source of meaning*', such that at the highest level of thoughtful abstraction a questioning is discovered by Levinas, even though it is not this to which he is necessarily drawing our attention. In other words, the one form in which the question of the other remains available to us may be that of the question itself. After all, the question implies a minimal curiosity, perhaps respect, for what is outside the self (whereas Derrida contends that 'it is not certain that thinking be questioning, essentially questioning' (*DI*, 18, my translation)). One function of the other would be to solicit the inquisitive mood, to give opportunity and direction to the question. To this extent, there is a hope residual in Levinas for the return of the other, that is, as a philosophical object. What is transformed at the level of content in Levinas's work remains unaffected perhaps at the level of method, there being far less practical deformation of the other than there appears to be in Derrida.

So there is a double accent in Levinas with regard to the other. While it remains to be questioned, it is nonetheless 'beyond the

22 Emmanuel Levinas, *Humanisme de l'autre homme*, p. 14. My translation.

given':[23] it remains given philosophically as a question, but is beyond the given experientially and cannot command its own untimely repetition to a return:

The alterity of the proximate [*prochain*] is the emptiness [*creux*] of the non-place [*non-lieu*] where, as a face [*visage*], it already absents itself without promise of return and resurrection.[24]

But does it not nevertheless make a return, in the form of a question? Is the other's homecoming not already envisaged in its relation to a fundamental questioning? Or, to take Levinas again on his own terms, does not the diachronic environment of the other permit a theoretic linkage between the moments – transience *per se* – which do not coincide with each other, in so far as they are in a *relation* of always-prevented coincidence? Would that not be for the other to deposit some ideality? This would be a 'return' in a certain sense, just as the 'sleepless gaze of God' might always be woken up to by the human conscience, thus activating for oneself the gaze's return in the 'interhuman dimension'.

Once again we leave matters open. The passage through which the other returns and does not return, in the non-place of an experience or a non-experience, under the charge of an insignificance – this passage of the untimely repetition debouches two ways, divine and human. If there is any 'experience' of this passage it is affected by what is called God, the absolutely Other, and so it might be said that there is a Kierkegaardian transition to the 'religious mood' in a 'spiritual repetition'. But Levinas will linger over this threshold, the cut and perforation, not just in the religious mood, but also as over an erotic line, the erotics through which the other passes and does not pass, in a movement that is also 'feminised'.

Even before citing Levinas on this movement, we might moot Derrida's 'disagreement' with it. Not because the movement is *eroticised* as such, but more because it does indeed appear to take the form of an ideal limit. Such an erotics would be hard to maintain when Derrida writes that

no text can defend itself without the other first coming to its aid. No text has the necessary solidity, coherence, assurance and systematicity if the response of the other does not come and interrupt it, and, by interrupting it, make it resonate.   (*A*, 29, my translation)

– for interruption here does not take the form of a limit, a limit which could then be eroticised, or at least has none of the metaphorical or empirical vestiges it might have for Levinas. The interruption of the other does not befall something that exists ahead of it (a 'text'). The interruption of the other stands as a possibility rather than as a topos. Levinas appears to be identifying or calling to something (to God or to an eroticised limit through which He cuts into the intelligible world), even where he seems to have himself ruled such a gesture out, and this is perhaps his 'vocation' as I have called it. Some would go further and say that Levinas is 'too philosophical'. Robert Bernasconi raises this question on Derrida's behalf:

> if Levinas at times succumbs to philosophical discourse, this is not a failing but, according to Derrida, the only way he can renounce it. The question which Derrida does not clearly pose, but which his essay ['Violence and metaphysics' in *L'écriture et la différence*] seems to provoke, is whether Levinas knew that that was what he was doing.[25]

Levinas says elsewhere that the ethical relation to the other forms the social relation thereto, and that the social, in turn, 'commands the erotic'.[26] But, I think, it will have already commanded the erotic (which Levinas is also implying) in so far as the relation to the other takes the form of an absent limit that remains to be desired.

Erotics divine and human: Levinas's reading of the *Song of songs* (in *Du sacré au saint*) appears to get underway from this cut. The bride, mysterious and eroticised (the two bearing an essential relation to each other), still allows for a certain return to the same. The erotic is this division of human and divine, as in a sculpture by Rodin, opened by the passage of the other. As for Kierkegaard – he sings the song of himself precisely when repetition has given that division form, and brought Kierkegaard before it, but according to a 'debriding'. That which rends between human and divine in Levinas, the erotic, seems to be maintained as it were against the exigency of repetition which ought to preclude any cutting into it, since repetition is in fact near-repetition (as diachrony) and presents no self-identity to be cut into, but will have already divided itself, cut into itself. But perhaps that is exactly what Levinas means. The relation to the other 'is' time, we

25 Robert Bernasconi, 'Deconstruction and the possibility of ethics', in ed. John Sallis, *Deconstruction and philosophy: the texts of Jacques Derrida*, p. 127.
26 Emmanuel Levinas, *Du sacré au saint*, p. 133. My translation.

must remember. So it is possible that both relation to the absolutely other (God) and to the erotic (human) depart from it. It could be that the diachrony of time is what provokes erotic tension (and also provokes desire for God?).

The repetitional other is eroticised specifically as woman. But 'woman' in her 'femininity', will correspond to the complex temporality rigged up. Indeed she will even 'be' a temporal-erotic event:

there must have been something of the same common to these *others*: woman had been grafted [*prélevée*] from man, but came after him: *the very womanhood [féminité] of woman is in this initial after-effect [après-coup]*.[27]

Woman is both the form and an effect of an initial '*après-coup*' such that 'the relation between lovers is characterised by femininity. It goes toward infinity while at the same time it is marked by a return to self.'[28] The woman comes back to herself, into her very '*féminité*', by remaining other to the structure of repetition which she has prompted – held in reserve, as it were, until she meets up with herself again. She 'becomes herself again' only through a certain loss of her 'self' into a diachronic impossibility as both already 'herself' in the man but having to wait to be herself until she is made out of that 'graft'. The autobiographical alteration from herself coincides with her difference from the man, so that as with Kierkegaard the structure of alterity is at least double, although there remains the possibility of an erotic *rapprochement* with the man. What matters most, perhaps, is the feminised generativity of the autobiographical alteration which allows for a return to self through its repetitional loss into a temporal impasse. She 'returns' as her own double, as it were, and in doing so falls across the divided temporality which she 'is' and which she has inaugurated. Hence perhaps that movement of finite and infinite that Tina Chanter speaks about, the divided temporality being the opening of the infinite, in the relation which 'goes toward infinity while at the same time it is marked by a return to self'. The woman is divided thereby (in order to resume herself), and the difference between herself and herself is inseparable from the difference between herself and the man,

27 Ibid., p. 142.
28 Tina Chanter, 'Feminism and the other', in eds. Robert Bernasconi and David Wood, *The provocation of Levinas: rethinking the other* (London and New York: Routledge, 1988), p. 44.

for it is in the return of the initial after-effect that sexual difference is established. Her becoming herself (again) occurs through an auto-biographical multiplication predicated upon sexual difference.

The pattern of repetition and 'initial after-effect' divides the woman from herself and from the man: from herself, since firstly she can have no proper access to the structure of repetition which she unleashes, the latter remaining non-totalisable, and secondly because this structure divides her into two 'moments'; from the man, since this structure is the origin of sexual difference (sexual difference is a differend, as it were, of temporal syncopation). Consequently, her self-relation is not necessarily different from her sexual difference from the man, so that the man cannot be ruled out of her autobiographical closure which now cannot close upon itself. The structure of autobiographical altruism, or love, becomes general, and there are irreducible reasons for the lack of distinction between self and other.

Like in the text of Maurice Blanchot's analysed in Derrida's *Parages* (*Celui qui ne m'accompagnait pas*),[29] one can no longer speak straightforwardly of a relation of withness between the two protagonists. They are already repeated through each other, with the result that empirical distinctions fall by the wayside. The other which starts the autobiography off remains untouched, if not unaffected, by empirical response. It, she, he speaks to me, and I hear voices that guide and jog the hand that writes, the voice that speaks – which 'necessarily happens through the affect of the other, the affect affected by the other' (*S*, 129/128). There is an affect of the other without empirical pathos, a responsibility without response which cannot be said, but 'what cannot be said above all must not be silenced, but written' (*LCP*, 209/*TPC*, 194) with the other that writes, more or less closely. The other 'writes' into the *auto* as an effect of the in-signifying 'mark' of writing, of near-repetition as citation or grafting.

Levinas speaks too of speaking an appeal toward the other. The fact of language must be taken into account. Of the 'encounter' with the other he says that

29 Maurice Blanchot, *Celui qui ne m'accompagnait pas* (Paris: Gallimard, 1953). For example: '"Aren't we now too close to each other?" But as if to concede [*me donner raison*], he limited himself to asking in turn: "Too close? – Yes, I would say so, too close: I am not pushing you away, I probably don't have the power [*la force*], no more do I have the wish [*le désir*]. What I mean is that, if this wish exists, it doesn't succeed in creating a choice between you and me. Can I make this choice? That is the question I put to you"' (p. 30. My translation).

the manifestation of a face is the first discourse. To speak is before all this a way of coming from behind one's appearance, behind one's form – an opening into the openness.[30]

To address the other in the solitude of an epiphany goes by way of a speech that is non-phenomenal, after 'coming from behind one's appearance', out from behind, one could say, appearance itself. 'Coming from' has to be taken in the sense of a responsibility or a priori obligation as much as a deictic arrival into presence. What is this passage toward the other opened by 'discourse'?

Derrida will, as we might expect, emphasize the vocative element of this discursive relation. Rather than 'at', language goes towards, the other:

the dative or vocative dimension which opens the original direction of language, cannot lend itself to inclusion in and modification by the accusative or attributive dimension of the object without violence. Language, therefore, cannot make its own possibility a totality and *include* [*comprendre*] within itself its own origin or its own end. (*ED*, 141/*WD*, 95)

Language, transporting the primary relation to the other, is language conceived outside of the intentional conveyance of meaning toward the other, or conceived in the transformation of that passage – as movement, perhaps, but without envisaged end. If language were to include in itself its own end it would foreclose itself and swallow its tongue. (The violent opening – the opening of what is violent – also affects the relation with God who suffers the same predicament. Imagine the God who could not be freed from the ideal totalisation of a language or discourse – 'imagine the God of a negative theology attempting by himself to describe himself, to catch himself in the grid of a determining discourse: he will almost annihilate himself' (*MDP*, 335–6/*MOP*, 282).) The possibility of language falls within the order or non-order of what cannot be envisaged, and establishes a relation that passes before the staking out of phenomenal areas. This is the violent opening, an 'attack' again in the idiom of *Signéponge*, that sets the 'condition of possibility' of a language quartered between its accusative and vocative 'dimension'.

The vocative dimension 'opens the original direction of language' and cannot easily be allied with the accusative or attributive dimension

---

30 Emmanuel Levinas, 'The trace of the other', trans. A. Lingis, in ed. Mark C. Taylor, *Deconstruction in context: literature and philosophy* (Chicago and London: The University of Chicago Press, 1986), p. 352.

of the object. There is a clash, we might say, between the ethicity of the vocative which is 'original', and the deterministic, projective, legalistic, descriptive, accusative dimension of language. But this clash, or dissymmetry rather, is what creates and protracts the non-totalisability of language by itself. Therefore, language cannot totalise its own origin or end, and this means that the originarity of its ethical-vocative dimension is lost to it. The ethical-vocative origin belongs to an 'absolute past'. Glossing Derrida in this (again somewhat interventive) fashion allows us to meet up again with the notion of a pre-phenomenal origin which pertains to Levinas's description of language even as he wishes to resuscitate the 'authentically' phenomenal aspects of the 'manifestation of the face' which is 'the first discourse'. Passing before, or as passion which has never been, language is 'spoken' to the other in a kind of 'absolute past', remaining unrequited. Whence the lost 'feminine past' or '*la passée*' of which Derrida admits connivingly, 'I borrow this word from E.L.' (*LCP*, 264/*TPC*, 247):

Without this absolute past, I could not, for my part, have addressed myself to you in this way. We would not be together in a sort of minimal community.   (PF, 636)

I quote from Derrida's essay 'The politics of friendship' where Derrida refers to this absolute past as 'pure passivity preceding liberty'. But if it precedes liberty, as absolute past it *also* precedes obligation in a political or legal sense. Both liberty and bondage are preceded by it, but this absolute past, as the opening of the ('linguistic') relation to the other yet implies responsibility. But a responsibility which, to quote Levinas now,

owes nothing to my liberty is [nevertheless] my responsibility for the liberty of others. Here, where I might have remained a spectator, I am responsible, that is, again, speaking. Nothing is theatre any more ... [31]

While 'my' liberty is preceded in this intrinsically archaic time of the absolute past, the responsibility I am determined by within it becomes 'my responsibility for the liberty of others'. So, according to Levinas at least, a kind of universal co-responsibility operates which has nothing to do with the 'theatre' of complaisance and placation which is responsibility in the weak sense of the word, as one might say. This is a 'theatre without representation' (*DLG*, 432/*OG*, 306), to use

31 Emmanuel Levinas, *Humanisme de l'autre homme*, p. 75. My translation.

Derrida's words. I cannot remain 'outside' this system of co-responsibility shirking as a 'spectator', and in fact my immanence within it is the condition of the other's liberty, in a transcendental network conducting 'language'. In an autobiographical text dedicated to Levinas, Roger Laporte writes of the proximal necessity of language, asking, 'rather than there being an absence of relation, does language therefore offer him the only means of being himself?'[32] 'Being oneself' has now been reconfigured as being oneself in one's liberty through the other's responsibility towards that liberty.

'Kant', 'Lyotard', 'Hobbes'

The relation to the other passes (in an 'absolute past' or the diachrony whose effects may be the same) through language, and through language the other is 'made welcome':

Levinas asks that the absolutely other be made welcome. The rule applies to any commentary on Levinas as well. So, we will take care not to flatten the alterity of his work.[33]

Lyotard goes on to assimilate questions of language in Levinas to questions of justice and liberty. A commentary, as language of the other, must be respected in the ethical alterity which permits a certain judicial − and, one hopes, judicious − openness. But this can turn sour, and the liberty of the other's language also constitutes a freedom to parody and to persecute, not only to respect. Lyotard starts to speak of the 'discourse of persecution':

What seems to authorise the parody and the persecution is the principle that justice consists in alterity. (p. 276)

The principle that justice consists in alterity opens the door to every kind of alterity. All that is other is 'just' in so far as it is other. Lyotard is reaching with Levinas back to the theory of law in Kant, but where in Kant justice is indexed to moral rectitude (grounded in an epistemology), Lyotard finds in Levinas the seeds of a profoundly un-Kantian deviation from this (in a manner not dissimilar to the account of 'recidivism' in The dialectic of Enlightenment). To be myself, to know what autobiography is, I am before the other, in the pure past of a responsibility which, however, forestalls my capacity to choose a

32 Roger Laporte, 'La veille' in Une vie (Paris: P.O.L., 1986), p. 38. My translation.
33 The Lyotard reader, ed. Andrew Benjamin (Oxford: Basil Blackwell, 1989), p. 275.

response or decide on a relation with the other. There remains in (Lyotard's) Levinas (and in Derrida to a degree) a kind of Kantian universal, but a strange kind of universal which has lost its power to regulate (does the spectre of 'transcendental illusion' come back?). The other 'will have obliged', 'il aura obligé'.[34] The other will have obliged us to a relation with the other, and this ethic, if it can be called such, is irreducible. But the fact that it is irreducible does not make it directive; if it is necessary it is not necessarily organising (or beneficent), and its non-totalisability suggests an 'inhuman' profligacy. It is something like this which troubles Lyotard, this non-totalisable necessity, 'apparent' in language, which while being opened by a kind of transcendental law immanent in ethical alterity becomes, because of the nature of that law, a law unto itself. Lyotard fears a splitting off of this law, it seems.

Derrida only intensifies the point when he writes that:

before even having taken the responsibility for any given affirmation, we are already caught up in a kind of asymmetrical and heteronomical curvature of the social space, more precisely, in the relation to the Other prior to any organised *socius*, to any determined 'government', to any 'law'. Please note: prior to any determined law, as either natural law or positive law, but not prior to any law in general. This heteronomical and asymmetrical curvature of a sort of originary sociality is a law, perhaps the very essence of the law ... We have begun to respond. We are already caught, surprised [*pris, surpris*] in a certain responsibility, and the most ineluctable of responsibilities – as if it were possible to conceive of a responsibility without freedom ... And we see it coming from the Other. It is assigned to us by the Other, from the Other, before any hope of reappropriation permits us to assume this responsibility in the space of what could be called *autonomy*. This experience is even the one in which the Other appears as such, that is, appears without appearing. (PF, 633–4)

And again, we can only leave matters open. Perhaps there is a link between the 'prior' law and the 'natural' law in that the former might be (Derrida's conjecture) the 'essence' of law, and this essence will put it in contact with other kinds of law, including 'natural' ... What we are notionally working with is the proposition that justice consists in alterity in so far as the Kantian transcendental unity of apperception is yoked to the other expressed as a universal. My faculty of judgment is what it is only by virtue of its coincidence with this universal, the other, for 'without this entirely-other, there would be no universality,

---

34 This is the refrain of Derrida's essay on Levinas in *Psyché* (*P*, 159–202).

no requirement of universality' (*LV*, 55/*TT*, 47). But this passes at the level of 'law in general' rather than at the level of natural or positive law in the realm of which there can always be 'deviations' such as parody and persecution. Indeed, natural or positive law is instituted starting from this possibility, and in order to regulate it.

As for 'language' (not to be restricted to its linguistic forms), gestures of commentary (as parody or persecution), while appearing to be a violation of natural or positive law, an intervention, maintain a relation with 'law in general' which repeats the Levinasian-Derridean necessity of non-totalisability. Strictly speaking, then, my language (the other's) cannot proximally situate the other's – it will have been obliged – so that gestures of 'commentary', parody and persecution, presuppose a loss of consciousness:

No, somewhere parody always supposes a naïveté withdrawing into an unconscious, a vertiginous non-mastery. Parody supposes a loss of consciousness, for were it to be absolutely calculated it would become a confession or a law table. (*E*, 100/101)

There is the necessity of the law of the other, responsibility or obligation to the other, 'before' the calculation of a law table or confession. I receive the law before I confess, before the law is reduced to the dictum on the tablets, to natural or positive law, and in the oldest, most archaic script that is emblazoned before what exists, according to a kind of structural unconscious which necessarily cannot be totalised, and which allows no exit to a space where commentary would become freely conscious. Derrida also calls this 'death':

The law is all the more imperious, unlimited, insatiably hungry for sacrifice, in that it proceeds from something entirely other ... which demands nothing, which does not even have a relationship to itself, which does not exchange anything either with itself or with any person, and which – death, in short – is not a subject (anthropomorphic or theomorphic, conscious or unconscious, neither a discourse nor even a form of writing in the current sense of the word). (*S*, 49/48)

Obliged by the law (of the other, the other's law) under the authority of a death obliges me to my headstone (the other's), in something like what Avrom Fleishman calls a 'proleptic funeral',[35] one that is inscribed with 'the archaeological character of the epitaph' (*S*, 125/124). The relation to the other as a general law is death, or a practice of language lacking absolutely in judicial control, and not

35 Avrom Fleishman, *Figures of autobiography*, p. 44.

merely remote from this control as Lyotard perhaps is suggesting. The law comes to me from the grave, from what has fallen heavily and unforeseeably out of sight. Autobiography is the writing in advance of this legislative obituary. As in Kafka's *The trial* the law itself cannot be touched.

But a third party guarantees the relation to the other, as a kind of 'countersignature', for this is how universality becomes universally instituted. We saw this in the 'feminisation' of the other in Kierkegaard and Levinas, where the other was doubled, in the ritual of a kind of marriage or *'alliance'* as we referred to it in the last chapter. This has to happen when 'the relation to the Other also passes through the universality of the law':

This discourse about universality which can find its determination in the regions of morality, law, or politics, always appeals to a third party, beyond the face-to-face of singularities. The third party is always witness for a law that comes along to interrupt the vertigo of singularity ... how could one endure this situation if there were no friend? (PF, 640–1)

The relation to the law opens beyond the intimacy of prior alterity so as to be 'instituted'. Derrida speaks of the 'friend' as bearer of the law of the other. The friend interrupts the 'vertigo of singularity', and thus makes of the universal an intersection into the singular. Kierkegaard too insists on the universal transection. In relating his 'double significance' to Job (who becomes a further *alter ego* for Kierkegaard), Kierkegaard is also isolating the necessary universality of the law which passes through Job, resulting in a confusion of the voice of the law (God's command) with Job's own plaint. Job will have been obliged to the law, and through this obligation his repetition is set up. Kierkegaard is thinking of the following passage:

Then the Lord returned all Job's possessions, and gave him twice as much as he had before. All his relatives and everyone who had known him came to his house to celebrate. They commiserated with him over all the suffering that the Lord had inflicted on him. As they left, each one gave him a coin or a gold ring.[36]

Job will have already repeated this repetition (marked by another gold ring) through his obligation. It is because he is obliged to the law which speaks through him (and to which he tries to close his ears!) that he partakes of the structure of repetition which he then 'experiences' at the end of the book. What Kierkegaard refers to as the transition to

---

36 *The book of Job*, trans. Stephen Mitchell (London: Kyle Cathie, 1989), p. 91.

the religious may be, in our terms, precisely this excess of the structure of repetition over those who 'institute' and 'experience' it (as in the case of the 'essential womanhood' in sexual difference detailed by Levinas). The presence, the dramatic appearance of God who speaks 'out of the whirlwind' in *The book of Job* does not affect in the least this structure of a priori responsibility. One could perhaps say that God is the personification of that structure. The law will have been written onto Job's heart, with the other, which makes Job in his suffering behave as though he were the bearer of a secret, except that his heart is open to the universal – meaning that whatever the secret might have been, it could never have been kept, even by the agencies of a repression. He is traversed by this universality – quasi-Kantian – and thus obliged.

When Hobbes comes to write his reworking of *Job*, *Leviathan*, it is with the concern that that obligation be realised legislatively as command, or, briefly, as government – government guaranteeing the integrity of the '*socius*'. Lyotard's reading of Levinas could, without much ingenuity I think, be said to allow for, even to require, a kind of Hobbesian sovereign by whom the ethical ambiguities of the universal might be settled once and for all. Obligation in Hobbes becomes a matter of the regulation of social behaviour, of positive as opposed to general law, of a 'right' that can be 'laid aside':

Right is laid aside, either by *simply* renouncing it; or by transferring it to another. By simply RENOUNCING; when he cares not to whom the benefit thereof redoundeth. By TRANSFERRING; when he intendeth the benefit thereof to some certain person, or persons. And when a man hath in either manner abandoned, or granted away this right; then he is said to be OBLIGED, or BOUND, not to hinder those, to whom such right is granted, or abandoned, from the benefit of it: and that he *ought*, and it is his DUTY, not to make void that voluntary act of his own: and that such hindrance is INJUSTICE, and INJURY, as being *sine jure*; the right being before renounced, or transferred.[37]

The sphere of obligation becomes one of fragility, in which rights can be transferred in a kind of empirical moral economy, and where obligation works as a frail safety net to withstand that economy's disintegration. Job, by contrast, 'becomes himself again' precisely by not allowing obligation to become a matter of restricted economy, but is repeated through the other, the universal in its a-total sense.

The social neighbour is to be treated, in Hobbes, as a potential

---

37 Thomas Hobbes, *Leviathan* (Glasgow: Collins, 1962, Fount Paperbacks 1983), p. 147.

enemy, for that neighbour's interests are likely to jar with mine. No relation to the heart, then, no a priori responsibility to the other as a friend whom one loves, no circumcision of the heart by the law. To repeat: there is a law of the heart 'before even having taken responsibility for any given affirmation, [so that] we are already caught up in a kind of asymmetrical and heteronomical curvature of the social space, more precisely, in relation to the Other prior to any organised *socius*, to any determined "government", to any "law". Please note: prior to any determined law, as either natural law or positive law, but not prior to any law in general.' The other will have already been a friend, in the friendship of an original love, or altruism, where the other is gathered to the self in a non-proximal, non-combinatorial synthesis, neither familiar nor foreign. Being with the other at the inception of obliging law maintains the otherness of the other as other while gathering the other to the heart, as both familiar and foreign. But it is an imperious love:

Beforehand, the thing is the other, the entirely other which dictates or which writes the law, a law which is not simply natural (*lex naturae rerum*), but an infinitely, insatiably imperious injunction to which I ought to subject myself.
(S, 13/12)

It is, again, a love that passes before government and determined law, but its imperiousness is what makes of it a witness, a structure in which things may be tested, something with a profound connection to the institution of responsibility and so a kind of 'government' in a renovated sense. The operation of positive law, by contrast, is always to assert that the other is other, but as a secondary, as opposed to original, other; it is always to fix the integrity of the same through the establishment of the nation state, to identify the other as the *xenos* or stranger. The other is therefore always likely to be treated with a certain antagonism, as a stranger, or a scapegoat, and the tragedy begins again. One finds Kant adding nuance to Hobbes:

By 'antagonism' I mean the unsociable sociability of men, i.e., their propensity to enter into society, bound together with a mutual opposition which constantly threatens to break up the society.[38]

The task of government is then to regulate that antagonism by assimilating natural and positive law to an ideal of universal law. But

---

38 Immanuel Kant, *On history*, trans. Lewis White Beck, Robert E. Anchor and Emil L. Fackenheim, ed. Lewis White Beck (New York: MacMillan, and London: Collier MacMillan, 1963), p. 15.

such universal law passes otherwise in Derrida, being already the relation to the other, and it comes about before the legislative institution (identification of the *xenos* as other and vice versa), as a law of the heart, responsibility, or obligation but in a spirit that is always committed to the letter, the institution of the specific case, the witnessing of a writing that is a citation. If repetition is at the heart of ethics, then ethical responsibility is activated in its priority only as what Levinas calls an 'after-effect'. This is the new law. It is at once the most archaic and the most pristine command. The 'ethical' position of deconstruction will be one that has assumed its 'obedience', if one may risk such a precarious term, to such a command of alterity: 'to prepare oneself for this coming of the other is what one could call deconstruction' (*P*, 53, my translation).

This perhaps is the anguish of Job when he finally curses the Unnameable ('God damn the day I was born / And the night that forced me from the womb'),[39] for his obligation to the other has finally turned to him, in a testamentary moment, and insisted upon his a priori intertranslation with God. Job discovers that responsibility is looking for a response, however terrible this might appear ('how should the *question of the response* be linked to the question of responsibility ... ?' (PF, 638)). He discovers that the Unnameable will have already discovered him, in whose pattern of repetition he is able, with Kierkegaard, to 'become himself again'. Levinas thinks also of Jonah who 'was not able to escape from his mission':

In other words, the humanity of man would be the end of interiority, the end of the subject. All is open. I am everywhere traversed by the gaze, touched by the hand. One understands from this that Jonah was not able to escape from his mission.[40]

A kind of law or imperiousness, something to which witness can be borne, insists in the midst of what, particularly to Lyotard, looks like the potential loss of all responsibility into an ambiguous a priori. An ineluctability – what Derrida, justifiably then, calls 'death' – ensues from this space that is 'prior' to both liberty and bondage. This might be described as the 'space' where the self, in its primordial alterity, is called to account: it is called to re-count, because of the iterability that alterity demands. Like Job and like Jonah, it is bound to return to the original bond and take up its responsibility.

39 *The book of Job*, trans. Stephen Mitchell, p. 13.
40 Emmanuel Levinas, *Du sacré au saint*, p. 132. My translation.

Levinas has already spoken of a 'chiasmus', and elsewhere of 'existence at the crossroads',[41] and in this chapter I have attempted to transmit several idioms across such a 'place', trying to keep alive the tension between agreement and disagreement that the speakers of these idioms (Kierkegaard, Derrida, Levinas, etc.) manifest. – The other changes, transitive and intransitive.

41 Ibid., p. 128.

8

bio

One of the keepers told them that there were other rooms to see [at the Sir John Soane Museum] – that there were very interesting things in the basement. They made their way down – it grew much darker and they heard a great deal of thunder – and entered a part of the house which presented itself to Laura as a series of dim, irregular vaults – passages and little narrow avenues – encumbered with strange vague things, obscured for the time but some of which had a wicked, startling look, so that she wondered how the keepers could stay there. 'It's very fearful – it looks like a cave of idols!' she said to her companion; and then she added – 'Just look there – is that a person or a thing?'[1]

What one calls life – the thing or object of biology or biography – does not stand face to face with something that would be its opposable ob-ject: death, the thanatological or thanatographical. This is the first complication.

(*L'O*, 17/*TEO*, 6)

This is the first complication. What one calls life will not be called, at least not called to come away from death, to disentangle itself from death and stand here, before us, as an object for the sciences, such as the 'life sciences'. A life science without an object and without the eye for description: life 'itself', life-with-death, 'life death', or what I would like to call *still life*, endows this new science.

What one calls life, the *bio* of autobiography, in one's calling makes one both put it off and bring it nearer, establishing the scientific, fantasmatic relation, a relation to the fantasm of ideal distance or what is known as objectivity. At the same time, what one calls life does not stand face to face with something that would be its opposable ob-ject: death, the thanatological or thanatographical. It stands with death, the two as one, letting the spirit of its fantasm rise – the fantasm of the thing, or object.

This thing called life is perhaps neither a thing nor that which can

---

1 Henry James, 'A London life', *The complete tales of Henry James* (London: Rupert Hart-Davis, 1963), vol. VII, p. 154.

be called or inventoried. To call it a thing, to name it as an object for 'science' (biology, biography, autobiography) is already perhaps to defend oneself against it, to fix it over there, bring it a little nearer, describe it with naïve candour, to ward it off and protect oneself against it in bringing it close and making of it a shield.

Rather, it is a matter of number and rhythm, and of how to begin an analysis of life, of life as not opposable to death, without discerning it first; of how to make what Derrida calls an 'incipit'.

So – what is it to call upon life? There is a word relating to the practice of calling upon the recently deceased to make sure they have not been buried alive. The word is *conclamatio*, and this chapter will try to be a kind of conclamation or address to what is neither certainly life nor certainly death. I borrow the word from Philippe Ariès:

An abundant specialised literature took a new look [in the eighteenth century] at the old stories about the miracles of cadavers, hungry cadavers, and cries heard from tombs, and reinterpreted them in the light of what was known about apparent death. For a long time people had feared premature burial, and ancient wisdom cautioned prudence. The traditional rites of burial were really only so many precautions for avoiding premature burial. These precautions included not only the *conclamatio* – calling three times in a loud voice the name of the person presumed to be dead – but the customs regarding toilet, exhibition of the body, lamentation (the noise of which could also awaken the living corpse), the exposure of the face, the waiting period before cremation, and so on.[2]

Derrida begins his reading of life death in Freud with an *incipit* – a conclamation of sorts announcing the 'third ring' of a reading:

As if it had an *incipit*, I am, then, opening this book. It was our agreement that I begin it at the moment of the third ring.   (*LCP*, 277/*TPC*, 259)

So the third ring will have kept something alive and, in truth, not quite have begun, if to begin means to depart from a clean limit having surpassed or put to death what it follows. It calls upon something still alive, resounds as a conclamation of the still life, and relates back to the 'principle of re-reading' we registered in an earlier chapter.

(The third ring is not just any ring, but is like a 'theme' – like a theme, almost an object – of Freud's three caskets, for example, and of what links the chance of a number or a rhythm to the life and death of an individual.)

In this transformation of the concepts of life and death, it will be

2 Philippe Ariès, *The hour of our death*, trans. Helen Weaver (London and Harmondsworth: Penguin, 1983, reprinted 1987), p. 397.

difficult to maintain the notion that the live or dead object can be interiorised by thought as something substantial, as substance unaffected by accident. Laid out on a cloth, like a still life, the (dead) body is, in the classical psychoanalytic theory which Derrida transforms, for interiorising by eating. There is a cannibalism of mourning. Freud speaks of eating the object:

The ego wants to incorporate this object into itself, and, in accordance with the oral or cannibalistic phase of libidinal development in which it is, it wants to do so by devouring it.[3]

And keeping this notion alive, Julia Kristeva for example writes of one of her analysands, 'Hélène', in a chapter entitled 'La solitude cannibalique', that 'Helen...confirmed my interpretation of her having locked up a fantasm, the representation of her mother within her body'.[4] Is (anything other than) an 'interiorisation' possible?

The living incorporate the dead by devouring them, in mourning. Incorporation makes a sepulchre, or stomach, for the eating of the other, a process of object idealisation not easily differentiated from scientific consumption, so that there is still life in the deceased, which is the life of the deceased within the bereft. The deceased are dead but still living, in the mourner, so it is still life, of a sort. In Freud's 'Mourning and melancholia' this is still the object-within-the-subject, the dead-within-the-living, an apparently 'simple' schema of accommodation and reception. But what if, as in Derrida, the dead were not an object, neither a corpse nor a corpus, but already, and from the beginning, the 'condition' of life, and still? And what if calling the object life were rather a conclamation, the invocation of what Philippe Ariès calls the 'living dead'? And perhaps above all, since both living and dead matter may be 'interiorised', is it not that the said interiorisation tenders no respect whatsoever to the distinction between live and dead things?

Autobiography, considered conventionally, does no more than the mourner, the schema of object(me)-devoured-by-subject(me) remaining in place. But when the relation of object to subject is deranged and reordered, when there ceases to be an object (me) to be interiorised (by me), a different kind of connection is opened up. Conventionally, the

---

3 Sigmund Freud, 'Mourning and melancholia', in *On metapsychology: the theory of psychoanalysis*, The Pelican Freud library, vol. XI, trans. under the general editorship of James Strachey (London: Penguin, 1984), p. 258.

4 Julia Kristeva, *Soleil noir: dépression et mélancolie* (Paris: Gallimard, 1987), p. 87. My translation.

subject of autobiography takes itself as an object — this is probably the simplest, most enabling, 'methodological', description of autobiography within the code of current academic discourse. But it can also be thought out entirely otherwise. It is still life, but it is not 'life as opposed to death', and so cannot be simply incorporated as an object, thought about, or, what may come to the same, mourned for.

One is tempted here to speak of habits of thought: what is called thinking habitually posits the incorporation of thoughts as objects for thought, accommodating them, hosting them in their inhabitation. What is a habit, and how is it distinguished from a compulsion to repeat? A habit is a place where the threshold is worn thin with an ordinarily rhythmic coming-and-going, and so a place which to keep locked would be too inconvenient — more of a household door, a back door tramped in and out of.

To break the habit, autobiography can still be thought of as the coming together of subject and object, but otherwise, as what Ruben Berezdivin talks of as 'life in its non-oppositionality to death';[5] or as what David Wood writes of in this regard:

The words 'life' and 'death' are, in this very movement, transformed, and their opposition subverted. Dispersion, differance, mark the end of a certain illusion of life that we call self-presence. What this opens up is the possibility of a re-inscription, a re-working, of these values within the general problematic of writing.[6]

This is 'movement', however, without that methodological commencement which defends itself against, in summoning forward, the number one, in cozenage of the object, as if it had a beginning.

Habitually speaking, autobiography commences with this retrospection toward the commencement, as if under the sway of a mythic 'once upon a time' which pinpoints the absolute singularity of a departure or birth. But the first may also be the last ('the first and last time', (*SPPC*, 12/*AL*, 373)), even where, as in *Schibboleth*, the first time is marked with an irreducibly singular cut, the incision of circumcision, for the circular cut forms only another ring, this time around the prepuce, a fourth ring perhaps, or more. This one time is caught in a spin of reversals, of circles which are vicious but not hermeneutically sealed:

5 Ruben Berezdivin, 'Drawing: (an) affecting Nietzsche: with Derrida', in ed. Hugh J. Silverman, *Derrida and deconstruction*, p. 93.
6 David Wood, 'Following Derrida', in ed. John Sallis, *Deconstruction and philosophy: the texts of Jacques Derrida*, p. 155.

Once, nothing easier to translate, one would think: *einmal, once, one time, una volta*. As for the vicissitudes of our latinity, for the Spanish *vez*, for all the syntax of *vicem, vice, vices, vicibus, vicissim, in vicem, vice versa*, and even *vicarius*, for the turns, returns, replacements and supplements, spins and revolutions, we shall be led to return to them more than once.

> (*SPPC*, 12/*AL*, 373, modified)

There is no simple movement or passage of translation among these terms, no first point from which to plot a series, for each turn leads only to another without, however, forming a trajectory. There is more a movement, a vicious or adverse movement, of an other time, which fractures the beginning, in 'the time and place of the *other time* already at work, altering from the start the start itself, the *first time*, the *at once*. Such are the vices that interest me: the other in (stead of) the first, at once' (*LI*, 120–1/*LInc*, 62).

Now, 'it would be impossible to substitute *another fact* for the unique fact of the *first time*' (*L'OG*, 33/*TOG*, 48), the fact of the circumcision and first cut, but this is still the first complication and one which disorganises any facticity as such. And not for the first time, either, but since time immemorial, in a time outside time, and so according to a kind of anamnesia without recall, which because not trainable into memory, into the subjective unit known as memory, is always more than one.[7] The habitual thought of a life begins with its conception, and one can be versed, like James Olney, in its Platonic reversals and volte-faces:

What I propose is that the term *bios* simultaneously incorporates the two foregoing senses: it is both the course of a life seen as a process rather than a stable entity and the unique psychic configuration that is this life and no other. In Platonic terms, I propose that we understand a world of becoming that is moving perpetually towards the world of being that is this phenomenological, eternal present (*ta onta*); or, in reverse perspective, that we should understand memory as a faculty of the present and an exact reflection of present being that also recapitulates and reverses the entire process by which present being has come to be what it is.[8]

One can read here the profound complicity between the unique and the simplicity of number, and the simple passage of reversal. Indeed, the word 'unique' speaks of this unity already. What is it to be one?

7 On chronology in autobiography, see also Burton Pike's 'Time in autobiography', *Comparative literature*, 28: 4 (Autumn 1976), 326–42.
8 James Olney, 'The ontology of autobiography', in ed. James Olney, *Autobiography: essays theoretical and critical*, p. 241.

Not one and the same now, but one and the other? The numerical discernibility – in Olney with an almost theosophical import – forms a scale of verse and reverse, along which the *bios* is threaded, as on a sort of stave.

To think life death together must be, at the very least, to overcome the prejudice toward the one time and the unique to which the name of the subject – the subject which can become an object – is given. This is how the subject has been seen to be self-identical over time, such that the measure of this time, the life-term of the *bios*, has been not so much a calendar of contingencies as an absolute and ideal coextension. Coextension itself – a concept which has to presuppose what could be called 'uniquity': separable, measurable, identifiable, indivisible, timeable. This has been life's way, which is as much to say its method, its *modus vivendi* and *modus operandi* falling into the same upbeat rhythm, as if it had a beginning.

The alternative to which can no longer be an alternative, i.e., the death of the subject and the ensuing burial. To kill off the subject, to change the life into death, becomes another way of mourning for it, thinking it, incorporating, conceiving and idealising it. There is no distinction to be made for the subject, when it comes to conception, between life and death; in effect they 'come down to the same thing' (*G*, 56b/*Gl*, 46b), so that one is invited to 'rethink this movement before the constitution of the *Selbst*' (*G*, 271a/*Gl*, 244a). Not death, perhaps, but departure:

Departed is the subject.

But the caskets are only empty – even after exhaustion – of the body proper [*le corps propre*].   (*LV*, 219/*TT*, 190)

A departure and a valediction forbidding mourning. And four paragraphs later: 'What is one time, this right time?'

So not two together, life and death, one plus one, but all at once, but not quite at once: life death. This is hardly a theme conducive to truth or method. The departure of the subject from that autobiography forfeits its authenticating uniquity, but it is still life, of a sort. It is not just that the distance between subject and object, life and death, has been collapsed, foreshortened or vitiated. No, that distance was already nothing but a fantasmatic 'effect' of a cause that was never anything.

One encounters here a different surface. It is an autobiographical surface the practical effects of which would be substantially reduced in describing them objectively. It involves reapplying the law of the object to the study of the object, and hence a loss of methodological orientation – something which again I try to 'simulate' in my writing in this chapter. Without the inaugural energy of the reapplication, no such thing as autobiography can be launched. Autobiography departs from this 'method' by which any methodological approach perishes. Weakly, and still somewhat dialectically, such a remarkable reapplication could still be described – as the becoming same as the object in alteration, or something along those lines.

In the essay 'on' Freud, Derrida submits to the law of this reapplication (what is called there 'speculation'), preferring allegation to demonstration,

alleging that speculation is not only a mode of research named by Freud, not only the oblique object of his discourse, but also the operation of his writing, the scene (of that) which he makes by writing what he writes here, that which makes him do it, and that which he makes to do, that which makes him write and that which he makes – or lets – write. To make to do, to make write, to let do, or to let write: the syntax of these operations is not given.

(*LCP*, 304/*TPC*, 284)

Freud's 'speculation', which is that of his essay, 'Beyond the Pleasure Principle', is declined autobiographically, where Freud mixes his own life up with a quasi-scientific discourse, or, rather, where 'Freud' is made to write, let write, by this autobiography that is ignorant of subjects and objects. And among these, 'life'.

'This "spéculer" structure comes about when a text does what it is talking about (a simple, non-Derridean example: to stammer when speaking about stammering)' – to quote from Marian Hobson's excellent gloss of Derrida's essay.[9] I want to apply as little gloss here as possible, choosing instead to write out a certain interiorisation of Derrida, in order to work autobiography practically as 'life death', or 'autobiography of the writing'.[10] Autobiography of the writing

---

9 Marian Hobson, 'Deconstruction, empiricism, and the postal services', *French studies*, 36: 3 (1982), 307.

10 For further commentary on Derrida's 'To speculate – on "Freud"' there is also, for example, Christopher Norris's 'Deconstruction against itself: Derrida and Nietzsche', *Diacritics* (Winter 1986), 65 ff., and Irene Harvey's chapter on 'Freud and the principle of life and death' in her *Derrida and the economy of différance* (Bloomington: Indiana University Press, 1986), pp. 233–5. Alphonso Lingis writes in this connection that '"Beyond the Pleasure Principle" contains pieces of cellular biological theory formulated in strategico-military terminology, pieces

because of that *necessary* simulacrum of the '*Ich*' we have analysed earlier. Everything takes place within this pseudonymous environment. I am thinking also of another excellent essay, Samuel Weber's 'The debts of deconstruction and other, related assumptions', which also cites this from *La carte postale*:

> What happens when acts or performances (discourse or writing, analysis or description, etc.) form part of the objects they designate? When they can give themselves as example of which they speak or write? There is certainly no gain in self-reflexive transparency, on the contrary. An accounting is no longer possible, an account can no longer be rendered, nor a simple report or *compte rendu* given. And the borders of the whole are neither closed nor open. Their trait is divided ... [11]

Forming part of the object it designates, Freud's essay, 'Beyond the Pleasure Principle', read by Derrida in 'To speculate – on "Freud"', gets twisted in the gyves it would use to bind down its object – a game, in this case, of '*fort da*', a game played by Freud's grandson, Ernst. The grandfather and the grandson are both repeated in the logic of this game, so that

> he himself is doing *fort/da* with his own interpretations, and it never stops. His own writing, his own deportment in this text is doing *fort/da*. Perhaps the performative is in play as well, in a very serious manner, but the game is also very serious and demands great concentration. He plays with this *fort/da* in his writing; he doesn't 'comprehend' it. He writes himself this scene, which is descriptive or theoretical but also very profoundly autobiographical and performative to the degree that it concerns him in his relation with his heirs: There is, in other words, an immense autobiographical scene invested in this apparently theoretical writing, and it is doing *fort/da*.   (*L'O*, 97/*TEO*, 70)

Autobiography is both the narrowing of the space between subject and object, discourse and theme, but also the opening of a new space, a scene of writing which is more potent than its so-called 'agents' or institutors, all those who, envisaging their own position of control, are

of neurology transferred to the psychic apparatus, fragmentary reports of psychoanalytic treatments, narrations of domestic scenes, autobiography, autothanatology, and auto-analysis, pieces of heterobiography and heterothanatography composed not out of the narratives of the other but out of transference with him.' 'The pleasure in postcards', in eds. Hugh J. Silverman and John Ihde, *Hermeneutics and deconstruction* (Albany: State University of New York Press, 1985), pp. 158–9.

11 In eds. Joseph H. Smith and William Kerrigan, *Taking chances: Derrida, psychoanalysis and literature* (Baltimore and London: Johns Hopkins University Press, 1984), p. 38.

nonetheless granted that position by virtue of an inaccessible but original simulacrum which dominates them, where 'death by writing also inaugurates life' (*DLG*, 205/*OG*, 143). The simulacrum repeats the gesture of mastery before them, through a kind of impossible reapplication at once cancelling and underscoring the 're-' of the reapplying writing scene. Where the 're-' habitually designates the versification of a reflex, here, autobiographically, its habits are versed differently, versed in the 're-' which avoids coming back.

The simulacrum is the nearest one might get to a machine, or an apparatus. This is the textual apparatus which puts itself in motion, autobiographically, set up, set forth, of itself, instituting a fidelity of the most unintelligible kind, where '("**the apparatus explains itself**") but quite differently' (*LD*, 60/*D*, 52). The scene of writing, that of Freud's text performing what it purports to analyse, explains itself, but, as it were, from within itself, from infinitely within, presenting itself to itself without the space to permit an explanation from the outside, that is, from that fantasmatic, legislative, scientific space of non-involvement and regulable responsibility. Perhaps this is fantasy itself: non-participation, defending itself against its object by bringing the object into line with itself, rubbing up against it, but always from an ideal border, a place of simplified ingress and egress, or a habit.

Autobiography proceeds, or processes, as the apparatus. Neither the classically human nor the classically mechanical befits the apparatus' functioning. It is of itself without self-relation – autobiography but not self-representation. So who or what is behind it?:

> But who is it that is addressing you? Since it is not an 'author', a 'narrator', or a 'deus ex machina', it is an 'I' that is both part of the spectacle and part of the audience; an 'I' that, a bit like 'you', attends (undergoes) its own incessant, violent reinscription within the arithmetical machinery; an 'I' that, functioning as a pure passageway for operations of substitution, is not some singular and irreplaceable existence, some subject or 'life', but only, moving between life and death, reality and fiction, etc., a mere function or phantom. (*LD*, 361/*D*, 325)

Life death, subject object: not to be punctuated by concepts. And the habitually opposed to concepts – verse, rhythm, phrasing.

Marian Hobson again: 'Freud, says Derrida, makes life a kind of detour (*Umweg*), and thereby also makes death internal to life.' (p. 313) When the autobiography starts, it does so without defending itself against an *incipit*. But does there remain an aversion or evasion? Is the scene any longer regulated by pleasure, by avoidance of unpleasure?

Freud insists on the mastery of the pleasure principle. Derrida reads this as a form of a more 'masterful' drive still, the drive to singularity, in other words the drive to drive, to go ahead toward oneself, and to tolerate no detour. This 'drive', this 'desire', is what it is only as a silent protest against the apparatus which dominates it. The drive to autobiographical singularity is a 'resistance' to the autobiography of the writing, so autobiography is always autobiography against autobiography. There is no singularity without the unmasterable autobiography which gives rise to it. The 'drive' is this conceptual impossibility. Having just been discussing Being-toward-Death in Heidegger, Alphonso Lingis writes of this drive that:

> the compulsion which is stronger than the compulsion to live, or to die, is the compulsion for one's own. For one's own, the proper, is not given, but is sought in the compulsion to live and the compulsion to die. The one's own is not identity or coincidence, but compulsion for itself, appropriative compulsion. And it is not a compulsion to possess one's own being or one's own life, but to possess one's own dying. The most compulsive compulsion, the master compulsion, is the compulsion to appropriate one's own expropriation. The kind of compulsion for one's own, this exappropriation, is what dominates, is mastery itself.[12]

The compulsion to come back to oneself, to get back home, to work by habit, to open a habitat for inhabitation where the self occupies itself – that is the profounder drive. But if the subject belongs to the object, in the ongoing dissolution of the legislative-performative space, what about me? Me – I cannot present myself, I can autobiographise only to the extent that I am confused with the other who is already drawn into the autobiographical apparatus of the reapplying writing scene. The apparatus takes me away from myself.

The apparatus takes me, and that amounts to, first of all, an infringement of the relation between me and my death, for it is my mortality which above all will have been the measure of the inalienability of myself from myself. So the autobiography of the writing raises the possibility that my death will not be mine, but the other's, that 'I am dead of a death that is no longer my own' (*LCP*, 62/*TPC*, 55), which is cause for fear ('He has always been afraid that someone would steal his death' (*G*, 12b/*Gl*, 6b)), and that my 'detour' is not an economic expedient as it is in Freud but a structural necessity: structure, or the apparatus, what I gloss as the inhuman 'itself'. I am

12 Alphonso Lingis, 'The pleasure in postcards', p. 164.

implicated in a kind of still life, numbered among its objects, where I cease to hold an objective or subjective relation to myself, departed as I am into a simulacrum which I cannot recognise.

I autobiographise as the structurally *vicarious*, dead of another's death from the non-ideal beginning. My detour, in so far as self-relation is proscribed, shares me in the other's mortality, or rather the other's mortality establishes the minimal condition for my life and autobiography, and in this removal I am reapplied to myself without narcissistic recognition. 'I' and 'me' are the effects, fantasmatic, scientific, legislative, performative, of a certain aversion to this possibility – and an aversion that precedes any predilection or choice on my part, since it precedes what I call upon as me. Inversely, what is insisted upon particularly in *La carte postale*, you, when I call upon you, call for me to call upon that death from which we depart. I am you, or I belong to you; as you I move in our death, I remove myself in it, condemned to detouring through you, your death, that is, me. To say 'I am' means not only 'I am mortal' (in *La voix et le phénomène*) but also 'I am from your death': I begin by returning from (y)our death, without necessarily arriving back, having made a detour, like Orpheus returning from the living dead Eurydice. Autobiography from the death of the other, or *heterothanatography*

concerns *bios* in its autobiographical import. From one instant to another it indeed could veer off in the direction of the heterothanatographical, if there escaped from our hands what we grasp under the heading of writing.

(*LCP*, 291/*TPC*, 273)

It goes on before me, as though when I walk I always walk behind, slowly, in the cortège of my own funeral procession, since I am already dead from you. And if

I *am* and I *am dead* are two statements indistinguishable in their sense, then the *already* [*déjà*] that I am (following) [*je suis*] sounds its own proper *glas*, signs itself its own proper death sentence [*arrêt de mort*], regards you in advance, sees you advance without any comprehension of what you will have loved, following, in a column, the funeral march of an erection everyone will intend to have available from now on. (*G*, 92b/*Gl*, 79b)

The autobiography which writes only itself, without humanist recuperation, occupies 'my' life, and allows me myself only by my coming away from it. In 'To speculate – on "Freud"' there is a rare reference to Rilke (*LCP*, 382/*TPC*, 360) and to the 'Orphism of a speculation' (*LCP*, 338/*TPC*, 317). I prefer to cite Rilke directly: Orpheus has come with Hermes to fetch Eurydice:

> But now she walked beside the graceful god,
> her steps constricted by the trailing graveclothes,
> uncertain, gentle, and without impatience.
> She was deep within herself, like a woman heavy
> with child, and did not see the man in front
> or the path ascending steeply into life.
> Deep within herself. Being dead
> filled her beyond fulfilment. Like a fruit
> suffused with its own mystery and sweetness,
> she was filled with her vast death, which was so new,
> she could not understand that it had happened
>
> ...
>
> She was no longer that woman with blue eyes
> who once had echoed through the poet's songs,
> no longer the wide couch's scent and island,
> and that man's property no longer.

Orpheus has already lost her, living in her death in his detour, coming away from her. There follows the 'theme' in 'already':

> She was already loosened like long hair
> poured out like fallen rain
> shared like a limitless supply.
>
> She was already root.

Orpheus will have turned round, to recuperate the scene to recognition and perception. Already too late:

> And when, abruptly,
> the god put out his hand to stop her, saying,
> without sorrow in his voice: He has turned around –,
> she could not understand, and softly answered
> Who?
>
> > Far away,
> dark before the shining exit-gates,
> someone or other stood, whose features were
> unrecognisable. He stood and saw
> how, on the strip of road among the meadows,
> with a mournful look, the god of messages
> silently turned to follow the small figure
> already walking back along the path,
> her steps constricted by the trailing graveclothes,
> uncertain, gentle, and without impatience.[13]

13 *The selected poetry of Rainer Maria Rilke*, ed. and trans. Stephen Mitchell (London: Pan Books (Picador), 1987), pp. 51–3.

Verse, phrase, and rhythm in this drama of aversion. The 'steep path to life' plays out what Derrida calls the 'logic of obsequence', return within the death of the other, the aversion to the habitual threshold between life and death, rhythm whose apotropaic measure subsides to mourning – mourning not for the dead, but a passing in the other's death, and so mourning for what is still life in which the other fructifies. She lives on and calls for, against conclamation, 'the feminine operation of mourning' (G, 163a/Gl, 144a) as instituted by the matricial logic we presented in a previous chapter, which describes the living of the other's death. She is no longer, and never has been, his property:

The old humanist and metaphysical theme is familiar: (the) burial (place) is the proper(ty) of (the) man ... the feminine operation of mourning ... prevents the corpse from returning to nature. In embalming it, in shrouding it, in enclosing it in bands of material, of language, and of writing, in putting up the stele, this operation [in Hegel] raises the corpse to the universality of spirit.
(G, 163a/Gl, 144a)

Such 'spirit' would be spirit thought otherwise, as that which rises from the graveclothes, a kind of sublime putrefaction, obscuring the way, the method, the step forward. Rilke repeats the line, 'her steps constricted by the trailing graveclothes', from earlier in the verse: 'den Schritt beschränkt von langen Leichenbändern'.

Hermes, god of doors, presides over the thinking of the threshold otherwise, not in terms of life against death, opposable ob-jects. I come from the other's death, not as across a threshold, into the maw of death, or out of it, but bearing my death from the other as my life, between mourning and triumph. Autobiography bears the other's death, my own, as still life, fructified, fallen, complete, dead before presentation or the conception of it, according to what is called in Eperons 'a structurally posthumous necessity' (E, 136/137).

Think then of Rilke's emphasis on the work, its maturation, its patient attendance to what forms. Mourning work of the already dead-before-death, work itself: 'Is not all work a work of mourning?' (G, 100b/Gl, 86b); 'I 'worked' this morning but you know now what I mean by that: mourning – for me, for us in me' (LCP, 208/TPC, 193); 'labor in general as labor of mourning' (LV, 92/TT, 79–80). Any routine, any job of habit and labour involves this excavation of the space that one believes is proper to oneself but where one is already usurped, and where one is working the other's work, even performing their grief for them according to what Abraham and Torok might call a 'trans-generational' structure whereby the other's fantasms and psychic agendas are 'borrowed'.

Work is not different from pleasure when it comes to rebinding the grave clothes: the difference between bound and unbound energy does not apply in this return to the moribund state of inertia that Freud locates as the *telos* of pleasure. The detour through the 'other's' death will not accrue to 'me' as pleasure. Instead there is an ongoing work and binding, a being bound to work, and what makes it work and routine and ordinary is perhaps that the work is not 'mine': that is what makes it 'work', its general inappropriability. Mourning work is work from the other, and if it *is* a matter of pleasure, then it departs from the other's pleasure, too, and unpleasure, but also from the other's death.

Worse still, more than the death of one other, the death we are speaking of is structurally the death of all, hence the pathos of uniquity, the plea, 'At least help me so that death comes to us only from us. Do not give in to generality' (*LCP*, 130/*TPC*, 118). One thinks back to *Ecce homo*: 'Above all, do not mistake me for someone else.'[14] The other's death is more than you too, being excessive or superabundant; but can such generality be arrested? Aversion to generality (of death) would seem to spill out into rhythm. Inversely, ceding to generality, were this possible, marks a different rhythm and a different verse.

I bear my own life in coming from the death of the other: auto-hetero-thanato-biography, or the Orphic first few steps of verse. Strictly speaking, this is not mourning, then – mourning is classically an object idealisation – since my life is inspired by it; not mourning, but what Derrida calls '*demi-deuil*', or 'mid-mourning'. No one emotion need be associated with this such as grief, for it is ongoing, changing, transforming. I propose to translate '*demi-deuil*' with a word from *Finnegans wake*, which is 'funferal': funeral, fun-for-all, fanfare, triunf, translation in the root 'fer', eins, zwei, drei, vier, funf, über all, und so weiter, 'in the wake's wake, exultation too of a funeral vigil, *Finnegans wake* again' (*LV*, 246/*TT*, 215). There is open access between the phrases 'I am', 'I am dead' and 'I am in mid-mourning', and all function as the ghost in the machine, the phantom in the apparatus, the hallucinatory functioning of the function which comes

14 *Ecce homo* , p. 217.

from generality. To come (to say 'I') is always to come from generality and to limit thereby, in a manner lacking method and application, lacking genealogical orientation, generality's functioning. For me this forms the most enigmatic aspect of Derrida's 'work': that generality must be arrested, yes, but that generality can be arrested – and according to 'the arbitrariness of a genealogy' (*LV*, 270/*TT*, 235). To come is to come into one's grave from the other's, to be fitted to a tabulation, there being 'no burial without a classificatory arrangement, without an ordered series, without tabulation. Otherwise it's just a mass grave' (*LV*, 283/*TT*, 246). There is always a chance that the other's tomb will be shared by others still, still life, and harboured not so much in a crypt, hermetically sealed, as in a sort of mass grave, from which I come:

You tell me that you too are writing someone dead whom you do not know (I am quite persuaded of this, more and more) and whom I represent. Therefore you kill me in advance (it is true that I often await your signs like death sentences), but you also bring back to life. Do you think that we are dealing with very singular revenants or rather that this is the destiny of every correspondence? Are we busying ourselves around *one* tomb or indeed, like everyone ... Both, doubtless, the one doesn't go without the other. (*LCP*, 172–3/*TPC*, 159)

I come back (autobiographise) from beyond the tomb, I go, in the words of Chateaubriand, 'to descend into a funereal cave to play at life there'.[15] The playing at life involves a classification but one that will not restrict itself to a code of identifiable units, allowing itself also to mix things up in the most appalling manner.

I begin only by returning, and returning as an 'arbitrary' hybrid of fantasmatic grafts and 'incorporations', like some kind of monster. My autobiography is always the autobiography of a monstrous revenant. There is a haunting, not necessarily mine, perhaps everyone's, which functions within it, makes me come forward in the simulacrum of a writing process which both inherits and disinherits me. One might speak here of the incorporation of ghosts within, but therefore not within, a non-corpus, within everything that is foreign to the hunger of the sarcophagus. And yet a crypt, and a doorway, and a kind of compulsive habit, at the threshold of which Hermes plays a different role.

15 Chateaubriand, *Mémoires d'outre-tombe* (Paris: Bordas, 1985), p. 98. My translation.

Something remains inaccessible to me, structurally, which is to say structure itself, archistructure, or what Derrida seems to call in 'Fors' a 'crypt'.[16] One would be very close here to the notion of an unconscious, if it weren't that closeness and the classical unconscious presupposed a topography in whose rubric the crypt resists being formalised:

this crypt no longer rallies the facile metaphors of the Unconscious (hidden, secret, underground, latent, other, etc.), of the prime object, in sum, of a psychoanalysis. Making of that first object a background, a fund, it is a kind of 'false unconscious', an 'artificial' unconscious lodged like a prosthesis, a graft in the heart of an organ, within the cleft me, the cleft ego [*le moi clivé*]. A very specific and highly circumscribed place or fort, to which access can nevertheless be gained only by following the routes of a different topography, or topic. (F, 11/Fo, xiii, modified)

One thinks perhaps of the 'false doors' that were a motif of mausolea in the Romantic period,[17] forming a false outside and a sham topography, 'crypt ... that organises the ground to which it does not belong' (G, 187a/Gl, 166a). In *Marges*:

the unconscious is not, as we know, a hidden, virtual or potential self-presence. It differs from, and defers, itself; which doubtless means that it is woven of differences, and also that it sends out delegates, representatives, proxies; but without any chance that the giver of proxies might 'exist', might be present, be 'itself' somewhere, and with even less chance that it might become conscious. (MDP, 21/MOP, 20–1)

Rather than being withdrawn into some archive to which only I would hold the key, the unconscious marks the site of a prosthesis or graft of a general alterity which precedes even the 'me' it affects. In the sense that it is not withdrawn, it is thoroughly egoic. But it is also determiningly structural and conditioning in so far as it affects basically this egoism, it partakes fallaciously of the ego's structure. It may even be 'pure' structure in so far as the genetic biologism I know as mine meets an alterity in it, meets, that is to say, a principle of death. To say 'I', to say 'me', is also to say that I come from the crypt or from structure itself in which my genesis ceases to coincide with life, the

---

16 See also (1) 'Text crypt' by the appropriately named Peter Lock, *Modern language notes*, 97: 4 (1982), 872–89; (2) Elisabeth Weber's 'Graffiti sur le mur', *Digraphe*, 53 (1990), 17–25.

17 The false doors in the mausoleum for the Desenfans family at the Dulwich Picture Gallery of Sir John Soane is the specific example to which I am alluding.

living and the order that obtains legislatively among them. Genesis and structure appear to be absolutely intimate and absolutely foreign to each other at the same time.

This would fit in perhaps with Nicolas Abraham and Maria Torok's 'anasemic' description of incorporation, as the incorporation of the failure to incorporate, and the resulting architecture of a crypt that is not necessarily either my own or the other's.[18] A disinhabited space is produced, open to tenants as it were but not to permanent proprietors. A dwelling of it may be made, but of a very different kind, a counter-ontological kind, say to the 'dwelling' of Heidegger's essay 'Building dwelling thinking'. Derrida takes their clinical work and reinvests it with a metapsychological accent, the 'failure' of mourning perceived to result from the unavailability of a singular receptacle for incorporation:

> They have proposed the concept of the crypt. Now, what is the crypt in this instance? It is that which is constituted as a crypt in the body for the dead object in a case of unsuccessful mourning, mourning that has not been brought to a normal conclusion. The metaphor of the crypt returns insistently. Not having been taken back inside the self, digested, assimilated as in all 'normal' mourning, the dead object remains like a living dead abscessed in a specific spot in the ego. It has its place, just like a crypt in a cemetery or a temple, surrounded by walls and all the rest. The dead object is incorporated in this crypt – the term 'incorporated' signalling precisely that one has failed to digest or assimilate it totally, so that it remains there, forming a pocket in the mourning body. The incorporated dead, which one has not really managed to take upon oneself, continues to lodge there like something other and to ventriloquise through the 'living'. (*L'O*, 80/*TEO*, 57–8, modified)

The 'living' may be in scare quotes for the reason just mentioned, i.e., that there are not isolable units of 'living' people who might have

---

18 For example: 'It is a fact that the "phantom", whatever its form, is nothing but the invention of the living. Yes, an invention in the sense that the phantom is meant to objectify, even if under the guise of individual or collective hallucinations, the gap the concealment of some part of a loved one's life produced in us. The phantom is, therefore, also a metaphysical fact. Consequently, what haunts are not the dead, but the gaps left within us by the secrets of others ... Because the phantom is not related to the loss of a loved one, it cannot be considered the effect of unsuccessful mourning, as is the case of melancholics or of all those who carry a tomb within themselves. It is the children's or descendant's lot to objectify these buried tombs through diverse species of ghosts. What comes back to haunt are the tombs of others ... ' Nicolas Abraham, 'Notes on the phantom: a complement to Freud's metapsychology', trans. Nicholas Rand, *Critical inquiry*, 13: 2 (Winter 1987), 287.

performed the mourning. If there is a kind of superficial graft that is the unconscious, a 'false' ego, it pertains to the shared site of a 'work', the construction of a building whose architecture is entirely exoteric. The work is death. Derrida elaborates a life death of the writing crypt, a split tomb operating everywhere in order to desist from itself, and so 'be', 'as' a scene of writing; opened to the winds, to contamination and virus.[19] It 'ventriloquises through the living', but the living would not necessarily have a voice proper to themselves before they become the receptacles of this ventriloquism. For the living to speak for themselves, as it were, there must be the illusion of that genealogical arbitrariness having arrived, having been arrested, at a living point known as a human being. There must be some speculation in other words, for the crypt to be incorporated, even though, at the same time, this remains 'impossible' − 'what speculative dialectics means (to say) is that the crypt can still be incorporated into the system' (*G*, 187a/*Gl*, 166a). The incorporation of the 'graft' can and cannot happen, and this aporia paralyses the logic in its vicinity. It is almost magical, the way that, against the odds, a speculation that makes the graft 'mine', can pay off. The autobiography slips out, as if by magic, like a genie which belongs to generality only in the phantomic surprise of singularity, or speciality, that it brings to it. What is a genie? It slips in between fate and generality in a utopic disorganisation of its locus. But it comes to me, and I come to myself from it.

One begins to speak of a certain presence, but presence as haunting, a primary apparition rather than perception, 'a haunting which allows neither analysis nor decomposition nor dissolution into the simplicity of a perception' (*DL'E*, 100/*OS*, 62), a haunting that is still life, not one thing haunting another, but a case of haunting without subjects and objects, reapplied and folded back into itself, missing itself thereby, avoiding and nullifying its own conceptual constitution. Haunting autobiographises, without self-relation. This can only mean that the crypt is ubiquitous, and that I am what I am by coming and going 'through' it, habitually, as if the stone were rolled away to make a kind of work entrance. This last should not be mistaken for an 'image' or metaphor; it is merely the attempted description of a magical

19 'and p. says to his mama ... "you know, I think I have a crypt". No, not a grippe, that's all over, the vaccine is commercialised: a crypt.' (*LCP*, 145/*TPC*, 133) 'Crypt' and 'grippe' might be mistaken for homonyms, but I prefer to call them 'overnames', an analysis of which follows below.

simulacrum preceded by nothing. But with the body, the corpus, the concept gone from the tomb, one can only fantasise its resurrection, that is its consumption in another, a transcendent space, as the verse 'begins'. But behind this locked gate there is 'no second heaven'. Paul Celan:

> DIE SCHLEUSE
> Über aller dieser deiner
> Trauer: kein
> zweiter Himmel.

Translated by Michael Hamburger:

> THE LOCK GATE
> Above all this mourning
> of yours: no
> second heaven.[20]

One loses a word that remains, a word or a phrase, that haunts of itself ('To a mouth / for which it was one of a thousand / I lost − / I lost a word / that had remained with me: / sister.'). We will come to this return of the word or *phrase*, rather, in a moment. Death gets raised up, through aversion to this more troubling, chronic and uncontrollable haunting structure; one sees 'a rigid cadaver, still standing' (*S*, 7/6). It is raised up against general haunting. Raised against raising, building against building: there is no building, no structure, no concept, without this 'against', an aversion, which is the span of a resistance, or a techtonic and libidinal foundation − in 'Fors' the construction of the legal dimension itself, the agora.

It is still life, however, that one eats in cannibalising. 'One "eats" the *pièce* of the other as one eats a photo with one's eyes, one mourns, one interiorises the other and one dresses in black, one takes the other into oneself, one makes of the other a part of oneself but it is always the failure of narcissism' (LDDR, xiii, my translation). It is a 'failure of narcissism' because the stomach is no longer mine, but near me, on, but outside, 'my body', like a purse, not to be distinguished from my life or my death ('your purse or your life', (*LV*, 261/*TT*, 228)). (Jean Genet writes of Jean Decarnin that 'today I am horrified at containing, having devoured him, the most dear, the only lover who loved me. I am his [J.D.'s] tomb.')[21]

20 *Poems of Paul Celan* (London: Anvil Press, 1988), pp. 168/169.
21 Quoted by Jane Marie Todd in her 'Autobiography and the case of the signature: reading Derrida's *Glas*', *Comparative literature*, 38: 1 (Winter 1986), 14.

Funferal is therefore the very structure of my life, that which gives me my life, my life in the death of the other, to autobiographise with a uniquity that comes to me outside of any ontological predilection. It is thus that I find myself in an order of generation. Generation does not generate absolutely, however; inversely, life does not begin with generation, and there is a beginning, a structure, which starts things off without having any relation to unproblematic generation, beginning, inauguration, origin, etc. The structure is not other than life death, a pressure of structurality, which is to say crypts, tombs, purses and even, in 'Cartouches', matchboxes. The question posed there, 'what is a box?' (*LV*, 262/*TT*, 229) is graver even than the question '"What, then, is life?"'. It cannot be comprehended – understood or contained – but its necessity is absolute, more absolute than the absolute, the latter always requiring a juridical counterweight. 'What is a box?', like the question in 'Fors', 'what is a crypt?', no longer bears any relation to a questioning about an object. The box is the question, the question is a crypt, sealed but open, and thus obviating the relation of a question to an answer. The hermetic secret is already answered; questioning proceeds otherwise. Otherwise, in verse perhaps, like a simulacrum or a simulacrum of a simulacrum, stepping forth with 'simulacrity', like the most material living ghost.

Generality is arrested by chance and by law. Thus genealogy is the law of generation considered as a calculable series of life terms. One can hear the phrase 'life term' here not only in the sense of a so-called 'natural' life term (threescore years and ten) but also in the sense of a sentence for a prisoner, a life term for someone who is 'doing life'. 'Doing life' is such a paradoxical phrase since life is precisely what the prisoner is not doing: the prisoner is not doing life, but is making a detour which is the suspension of life.

We have made a detour, it would seem, away from Freud. Very much at issue in Derrida's reading of Freud's 'Beyond the Pleasure Principle', the question of genealogy and inheritance as related to chance, in the functioning (haunting) of the autobiographical apparatus is played out. In the 'Envois' Derrida has already written:

I am going to tell you now what intrigues and interests me at the moment: it is what links these *arrêts de mort*, these letters which give and suspend death, what links them to *fate*, to good and bad fate, to the writing of chance, of destiny, of accident, of prediction in that it throws out a fate ... (*LCP*, 80/*TPC*, 72)

Derrida finds a genealogical interest in Freud's text which is, briefly, an interest in remaining, legislatively and libidinally, the father of psychoanalysis, thus instituting a genealogical arbitrariness at the origin of a science. Marian Hobson:

The *'fort/da'* of the child is related by Derrida to the movement of Freud's text; to its havering speculation concerned with both the institution of a new concept (beyond the Pleasure Principle) and its contribution to a comparable but corporate insitution, the psychoanalytic movement.   (p. 309)

Coming from the other gets confused with coming from one's own, one's own whom one belongs to by standing back a little bit, enumerating one's descendants, legatees, epigoni and disciples, serried in 'an order of generation, an irreversible sequence of inheritance' (*LCP*, 25/*TPC*, 20) – a phrase which Derrida writes just a few lines after this:

this sign of death, he looked for it, he rushed into it without looking back
                                        and in the homosexual phase
which would follow Eurydice's death (and that had therefore preceded it, according to me   ) Orpheus
sings no more, he writes[.]

My autobiography comes to me from the other's death, in the originary simulacrum – the writing apparatus – of an inheritance. Inheritance must therefore be taken in all its enumerating, libidinal, fantasmatic-scientific charge, as a stroke of luck. Chance is always a chance for inheritance and genealogical identification, where the life term is appropriated. One can read a great deal of this charge in, for example, John Forrester's gloss:

Lacan's return to Freud seems only to have made the question of the legacy all the more unmanageable, and to oblige each of the faithful to recognise his or her own 'wildness', just as Lacan sported his incontestable wildness. Derrida does not succeed in avoiding these aporia [as if an 'aporia' could be avoided!]. Not only can his 'readings' of Freud or Lacan be shown to repeat the same blindnesses he analyses as being the source of their effects, but his exteriority to analysis is inevitably subject to the very erosion of that concept he highlights.[22]

Ugly claims over the division of Freud's institutional estate. The scene could be stylised as 'breaking the will', designating two things: (1) breaking open Freud's will in order to write one's name as an inheritor into it, as a codicil; (2) breaking the will, or the death and life 'drives',

22 John Forrester, *The seductions of psychoanalysis: Freud, Lacan and Derrida* (Cambridge: Cambridge University Press, 1990), p. 242.

as if these ghosts could be avoided. Forrester's comment, in trying to break the will, repeats the very gesture so minutely analysed in 'To speculate – on "Freud"'. Once more, the writing scene reapplies: Forrester's 'object', the Freudian legacy, is an object of anxiety which in turn turns Forrester's writing into an anxiety of inheritance, or influence. Like Freud he 'inadvertently' 'institutes the science of his proper name in the general function of autobiography'.[23]

One must speak here of a will that lies outside of psychology, or a drive which lies outside of metapsychology. The will can always be broken, in so far as there is no guarantee that inheritance will follow an orderly line of genealogy; but it can never be broken in so far as it designates the 'will' of the apparatus, the structure of the funferal, or still life.

Life, as structurally indistinguishable from death, may be considered outside of genealogy and generation. In other words, life death can pass without relation, without a priori submission to a law of genealogical belonging, '*pas de singularité génétique*: (no) step of genetic singularity' (*G*, 170b/*Gl*, 150b), without an a priori 'of' that could be regulated by the subject or object. Rather, an 'Absolute of genitivity itself':

> If the of announces neither an objective nor a subjective genitive, that is because it concerns the Absolute of genitivity itself, the pure possibility of a genetic relation. (*L'OG*, 157/*TOG*, 142–3)

Against this pure possibility, which has the purity of an absolute contamination, genealogy institutes and legitimises itself, through a reduction of life to generation (an object for biology). Inversely, this pure possibility 'contains' an aversion to itself, which passes, nonetheless, elsewhere; is its own aversion, which is the stiffening of the law of generation. The consequence of which is that life, whose ideal representation is in that of the family tree, is given its organic privilege as a privilege and not as a natural right; or the natural right is natural only through this pre-natural aversion which it would have cause to fear. It might be more accurate to speak here of versions rather than of family resemblances and relations. How does one account for a version?

The version is caught between faithful genealogical reproduction and deviation. Genealogy considers it merely as a di-version, or a

---

23 Andrea Loselle, 'Freud/Derrida as *fort/da* and the repetitive eponym', *Modern language notes*, 97: 5 (1982), 1180.

detour, an aberration, on the way back to generative purity. Autobiography gives a chance to both genealogy and to diversion,[24] a chance, that is, to being both 'oneself' and, as such, the simulacrum of the self, such that the two cannot be compared according to a mimetic standard. Which means that one can look at a thing, and see the object in its version, the version that is no different than the object in the object, as if there were a kind of comprehension. The object (the object of a biology, for instance) can already be its own version, both exceeding and diminishing in the object, 'as' the object, as the non-object object, the object which cannot be as such, the same thing but a version, as if haunted – but no, as haunting itself. This shines through the thing as in a gloss it will never do. There is no rule for sorting out the relation of object to version, for the logic of the relation is already that which will have given the object to us for inspection. One cannot look to the object to discover its version within it, for looking is already looking-to-the-object; the version passes otherwise. This is also a description of 'anasemia', the science of the word which is nothing but a word, but not an object, a thing but not a thing, haunted of itself, before and outside of objective meaning, as if a verse, or what Derrida writes of as the 'phrase'.

Forrester's asseveration suggests the breaking of the will, and the setting of the psychoanalytic family back on the right track, though with a little distance, a touch of objectivity. One is rescued thereby from the bastard course of Derrida's work and mourning:

> genealogy establishes filiation, from father to son, like a measured tree. Outside of genealogy, but tied however to it by way of a displaced status, the bastard obtains: born out of wedlock, degenerated out of space.[25]

Forrester is cutting away the dead wood from the family tree, while we are following a movement from the box ('boîte') to the wood ('bois'):

> if we had time to describe all the 'woods' and 'trees' ... we would see all the implications of dead wood (take it also as an order) where he, the I, is erected again; but we shall see, from among the trees, only the family tree, to which it is not a matter of reducing everything else.   (S, 29–30/28)

---

24 Dominic la Capra writes, in a discussion of Freud as the founding father of psychoanalysis, that 'part of the allure of autobiographical writing is the opportunity it offers to become one's own symbolic genitor', in *Soundings in critical theory* (Ithaca and London: Cornell University Press, 1989), p. 51.

25 Catherine Backès-Clément, 'La dissémination: la méthode déplacée', in *Les lettres françaises*, 1429 (29 March 1972), 4. My translation.

Dead wood 'affects' the family, which is to say that genealogy is contaminated not only by illegitimate children but by the possibility, the worst, that children will be survived by their parents, and the apple cart upset: 'To survive one's own, to survive one's children, to bury one's heirs, nothing worse, is there?' (*LCP*, 258/*TPC*, 241). This can always happen, mourning does not have to wait for it in order to commence: it commences from this very possibility, starting to eat, and to drink, to drink death, the 'order' lying anasemically, hauntingly in the dead wood: 'bois mort', dead wood, drink dead, drink death, already dead whereas 'in what psychoanalysis strictly determines as such, the work-of-mourning would merely devour more quickly, in the course of a single meal, the gathered time of a Last Supper' (*G*, 99b/*Gl*, 86b). Even when there is still life, the funferal gets under way, with 'the obsequence of this cortège in singular lineage' (*LV*, 214/*TT*, 186). So the forester's task is infinite: he can begin to trim the branches only after this a priori necessity, in the wake of its matinal wake. Life survives as death, or the unkillable, the general mass death, the holocaust in *Feu la cendre* and elsewhere, from which I will have returned.

The phrase comes back to haunt, almost like a thing, re-named, named over its name, as if belonging in a genealogical relation. 'Autobiography can be a mourning for the perpetual loss of the name – one's proper word-thing.'[26] In *Signéponge* this is a survival through renown; in *La carte postale* it is as if renown itself were the object of squabbling among the legatees. Within this quasi-psychological anxiety of influence there is what Harold Bloom calls the 'apophrades', the return of the dead, but here the return of the dead name, the dead wood of the family tree, outside the forest, haunted by the renowned, in these *mémoires d'outre-tombe*:

Not once did I enter the wood [*bois*]; Mme. Récamier alone had obtained permission to enter it. Seated on a bank in front of the surrounding wall, I turned my back to France and I had my eyes attached sometimes on the summit of Mont Blanc,[27] sometimes on the lake of Geneva: clouds of gold

26 Gayatri Chakravorty Spivak, '*Glas*-piece: a *compte rendu*', *Diacritics* (September 1977), 24.
27 Since we shall shortly turn to Shelley and to Derrida's analysis of the '*arrêt de mort*', the reader might like to read an analysis of Shelley's 'Mont Blanc' by Herman Rapaport, 'Staging: Mont Blanc', in ed. Mark Krupnick, *Displacement: Derrida and after* (Bloomington: Indiana University Press, 1983), pp. 59–72. Rapaport also makes a connection between the '*arête*' and the tombstone or burial

covered the horizon behind the sombre line of Jura; one might have said a glow rising above a long coffin. I picked out on the other side of the lake the house of Lord Byron, the roof-top of which was touched by a ray of sunset; Rousseau was no longer there to admire this spectacle, and Voltaire, likewise disappeared, was never troubled with it. It was at the foot of the tomb of Mme. de Staël that so many illustrious departed on the same shore presented themselves to my memory: they seemed to be coming to look for their fitting shadow in order to take off into the sky with it, to perform its cortège during the night. At that moment, Mme. Récamier, pale and in tears, came out of the funereal grove [*bocage funèbre*] like a shadow herself. If ever I have felt at once the vanity and the truth of glory and of life, it was at the entrance of the silent wood, dark, unknown, where she of such moment and renown [*renom*] slept, and in seeing what it is to be truly loved.[28]

There is a haunting of the name-thing, a kind of resurrection before birth, hardening sometimes into the legal code of a name, which becomes a thing to eat, a sublime fellation in the so-called homosexual phase of mourning. The verse begins, a conclamation falling between the person and the thing, in the renown of the future which has yet to be decided.

What survives in this mass death, before the origin of life, is a certain renown. It overnames the thing, the person, with an unclaimable excess, a resonance where 'no more is resonance the act of resonating' (*MDP*, 9/*MOP*, 9), being '*klanglos*' as in Hölderlin's poem on the renown of Rousseau. As the promise of continuity it will have already simulated inheritance. But the thing and the person are always prone to being confused, especially in a questioning concerning life:

> Struck to the heart by this sad pageantry,
> Half to myself I said, 'And what is this?
> Whose shape is that within the car? and why' —
>
> I would have added — 'is all here amiss?'
> But a voice answered ... 'Life' ... I turned and knew
> (O Heaven have mercy on such wretchedness!)
>
> That what I thought was an old root which grew
> To strange distortion out of the hill side
> Was indeed one of that deluded crew,
>
> And that the grass which methought hung so wide
> And white, was but his thin discoloured hair,

mound (p. 69), which is connected in turn with life death at the mother's breast. The '*arête*' is treated as a fragment for an 'archaeology of the libido' (p. 71).

28 Chateaubriand, *Mémoires d'outre-tombe*, pp. 193–4. My translation.

And that the holes it vainly sought to hide

Were or had been eyes ...

                                                    ... I cried,
'First who art thou?' ... 'Before thy memory

I feared, loved, hated, suffered, did, and died,
And if the spark with which Heaven lit my spirit
Earth had with purer nutriment supplied

'Corruption would not now thus much inherit
Of what was once Rousseau — nor this disguise
Stain that within which still disdains to wear it. —

'If I have been extinguished, yet there rise
A thousand beacons from the spark I bore.'[29]

There is an apparition of what passes 'before memory', persisting as the living dead, in a scene which misrecognises person for thing. It announces itself with a kind of excess of renown. Such is the cortège of renown in its horrific splendour — 'A cortège of ghosts surrounds you on all sides, they provoke you, they press you, from the quattrocento Triumphs of Death to Shelley's *The triumph of life* ("here the true similitude / Of a triumphal pageant ... " / "But mark, how chained to the triumphal car / The mighty phantoms of an elder day ... ")' (*LV*, 266/*TT*, 232). The triumph haunts with a thing, a name, an inheritance which cannot be recognised except through aversion, incredulity, where science becomes blurred with belief, which begins the verse and runs the risk of legation and legislation, acknowledged or unacknowledged. 'If the destination of one's own writing is names, or if one writes in order to call up names, then one writes also for the dead' (*L'O*, 74/*TEO*, 53) — and equally for the 'dead' name, the overnamed name which makes of this haunting an apparatus. The root-thing precedes the appropriator's identification, as in the poem by Rilke where 'she was already root' ('Sie war schon Wurzel'). It installs its necessity 'before thy memory'. In the 'Rousseau' of Hölderlin those who are named pass too through this renown without resonance:

Und jene, die du nennst, die Verheißenen,
Wo sind die Neuen, daß du an Freundeshand

29 *Shelley's poetry and prose*, selected and eds. Donald H. Reiman and Sharon B. Powers (New York and London: W. W. Norton and Company, 1977), pp. 460–1. Hereafter referred to as *Shelley*.

Erwarmst, wo nahn sie, daß du einmal
Einsame Rede, vernehmlich seiest?

Klanglos ists, armer Mann, in der Halle dir,
Und gleich den Unbegrabenen, irrest du
Unstet und suchest Ruh und niemand
Weiß den beschiedenen Weg zu weisen.

Michael Hamburger translates: 'And those whom you name, the promised, where are those new ones, that a friendly hand may warm you; where do they approach, so that for once, lonely speech, you may be heard? / Not a resonance, poor man, stirs for you in the hall, and like a wraith you stray inconstantly seeking rest, and no one can show you the allotted way.'[30]

It makes for a 'misreading' or misnaming, where inheritance is conceived as relation of the bereft reading or misreading the deceased in order to implant themselves into the genealogical sequence, so that 'the question is recognising what returns to the father' (G, 91a/Gl, 78a). A theoretical institution, like psychoanalysis, has to reckon with the reader-as-appropriator: 'Is it not natural that I feel like a son?'[31] One works one's way back to stand with the father and, having been self-elected, aspires to turning the fountain off at source, to be the last and sole legatee. But always at the risk of such ghostly apparitions, where the selection of identities becomes subdued by a disfiguring force, an aversion, a kind of pure rhythm.

The father, falsely, seems to hold to the origin of natural life. But there can be a deformation. An epigraph used in *De la grammatologie*, for example, taken from Rousseau's *Confessions*, runs: 'All the papers which I have collected to fill the gaps in my memory and to guide me in my undertaking, have passed into other hands, and will never return to mine' (*DLG*, 203/*OG*, 141). Shelley's Rousseau (for Rousseau may be divided up – among Shelley, Hölderlin, Derrida, de Man and so many others – as much as Freud), the father writer, insists on the Promethean spark of life ('there rise / A thousand beacons from the spark I bore'), which is a spark outside of strict generation, the simulacrum and the possibility of cloning which also inspires the

30 Friedrich Hölderlin, *Selected verse*, trans. Michael Hamburger (London: Anvil Press Poetry, 1986), p. 75.
31 Norman N. Holland, 'Re-covering "The purloined letter"', in eds. Susan R. Suleiman and Inge Crosman, *The reader in the text: essays on audience and interpretation* (Princeton: Princeton University Press, 1980), p. 356.

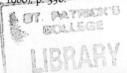

modern Prometheus – Mary Shelley's *Frankenstein*. There is a graft in the heart of life, 'a graft in the heart of the organ', announced in the triumph, 'it inscribes difference in the heart of life ... Germination, dissemination. There is no first insemination' (*LD*, 337/*D*, 304), but what is already in Shelley's words 'planted by reiteration',[32] the result of a 'monstrous entrapment in autobiography'.[33] The greatest monstrosity is that which from the father no longer acknowledges a debt to the father, no longer presents itself under paternal authority, can no longer be shown or brought back for correction through an Oedipal filter. This makes a living proof, this life which staggers away from the false origin, that the papers will not necessarily be returned, the letters gone astray, 'the proof, the living proof precisely, that a letter can always not arrive at its destination, and that therefore it never arrives. And this is really how it is, it is not a misfortune, that's life, living life, beaten down, tragedy, by the still surviving life' (*LCP*, 39/*TPC*, 33–4). It is neither a person nor a thing, but it overlays the funeral dance of life, disrupting its order, dragging it off course, toward the confusion of the forest.

Life is as staggered as a wayward cortège, delayed and numbed as if somewhat paralysed between life and death. The phases, stages and ages of life, lose their measure, as if there had been a diversion on life's way. It becomes difficult to speak with any assurance about the passage of life, through the forest, the life term and the '*selva oscura*', for example, of Dante or of Shelley's Dantesque 'Triumph'; the 'phase' might be taken as a kind of fantasm, or the scene of the libido, a homosexual phase, or triumph in another sense:

In a determined phase of mourning, moments of (imperial) triumph, jubilation, libidinal explosion: I know someone who lived such a triumph by driving around, all night, in his car, with the freshly exhumed coffin of his mother.

(*LV*, 265/*TT*, 231)

Moments of imperial triumph emerge through the genealogical assurance of filiation, where the empire's memory gathers itself into a monument – of stone rather than of wood. The memory brings the hard object against itself, and seals a tomb with a simultaneously morbid and erotic love – typified perhaps, previously, by Orpheus and Eurydice.

---

32 *Shelley*, p. 477.
33 *Taking chances: Derrida, psychoanalysis and literature*, eds. Joseph H. Smith and William Kerrigan, p. xi.

But the tomb is marked with another seal, which will have befallen it like a thing, giving itself in the fantasm of a legibility – an epitaph which could be committed to memory, but which would be lost thereby, so long as the memory remains avid of incorporations, so long as it remains a tomb. The other seal marks mourning regardless of the tomb, where 'this is not the tomb he would have dreamed of in order that there may be a place [y ait lieu], as they say, for the work of mourning to take its time' (C, 53). No tomb, then, nothing unusual, maybe only a domestic space.

How to count out these words? Not as counters on an abacus, or stave, which keeps them too hard and bead-like. Derrida dwells on the (Platonic) distinction between learning by rote, and living memory, but the two merge in his analysis in that both obey an earlier mnemonics. Indeed the concept of anamnesis is very near by – the forgetting necessary for remembering, where remembering is, in Hegel as in Plato, not other than knowing ('Memory, the production of signs, is also thought itself', MDP 101/MOP 87). Platonic anamnesis spans the bridge between this world, a shadow world, and the world of light and forms, imposing itself 'before memory'. But what if the two were the 'same', and the words one counted out, rhythmically, in phrases, were not husks fallen from an idealist splitting, but already their own haunting, in us, of themselves, starting from the unkillable possibility of mourning? So that the phrase supersedes, from before the beginning, the phase? There are (at least) two such phrases that haunt, on the inside and on the outside:

More than fifteen years ago, a phrase came to me, as if in spite of me; to be more precise, it returned, or came back rather, haunted [revenue], singular, singularly brief, almost mute ... il y a là cendre.   (C, 21, modified)

and in 'Circonfession':

a lone sentence [phrase], hardly [à peine] a sentence, the plural word of a desire toward which, from always, all the others seemed, teemed [semblaient], confluence itself, to press itself, an order suspended on three words, find the vein [trouver la veine].   (JD, section 1, 10/JDe, section 1, 6, modified)

The phrase of the suspended order, an inaudible injunction, covers the words translucently, before the phenomenal light springs forth, like a photographic negative awaiting development. Held in suspense, uncommitted to the late, weak, dialectical decision over what is life and what is death, what is ideal and what is real, the phrase submits to that life term which Derrida analyses as the '*arrêt de mort*', both death sentence and stay of execution, allowing for the still life of the prisoner who is already proleptically dead, who 'posthumises while breathing'.

The phrase posthumises. With it, a certain material spirit from the earth is emitted like a gas. But it remains suspended, between matter and spirit, in an '*arrêt de mort*'. The relation of the phrase to the suspended order cannot be, since the order is suspended, one of submission; rather, a 'relation' of aversion. It will have to have come about before the learning of the law and the memorising of orders. If the phrase returns, it does so from before memory considered as a virtual empiric reserve, already from the possibility, which is to say the necessity, of mourning. Inversely, memory demands to be rethought beginning from the phrase, and as the incineration of its own reserve, and the burning up of its own trace down to the extinguishing of its ashes. My life is granted through this extinction (the relation to the other's death in mourning) – 'ashes and the family vault' (*LV*, 264/*TT*, 230).

A suspension or structural delay, by which reason is invited to contemplate the extinction of its relation to the law. How does reason speak? One example among so many:

I may perhaps be allowed to express my wonder at this action of the police being delayed for two full days during which, of course, I could have annihilated everything compromising by burning it – let us say – and getting rid of the very ashes, for that matter.[34]

The legislative law (the police) is held off; incineration of the ashes inscribes a defunctive order, 'which does not mean that it is reduced (to its ashes) but that your thinking about the text has been set on fire' (*LD*, 382/*D*, 343, modified). The phrase haunts: '*il y a là cendre*': there is ash, there, she, it binds to cinders, it binds us to leaving it, letting her.[35]

The phrase cannot be recalled – it recalls itself, overnamingly, with a sort of fame and flame. 'The experience of ashes,' an experience that is not necessarily mine, 'is the experience not only of forgetting, but

---

34 This is the voice of reason (Razumov) in Conrad's *Under western eyes* (Harmondsworth: Penguin, 1985), p. 122.
35 On ashes see also Ned Lukacher, or Lukasher, I forget which, 'Writing on ashes: Heidegger FORT Derrida', *Diacritics* (Autumn-Winter 1989), 128–48.

of the forgetting of forgetting, the forgetting of which there remains nothing' (DI, 22, my translation), a nothing which is not the opposite of a thing, but which overnames the thing superabundantly as forgetting before forgetting, and the forgetting of that forgetting, for 'it is necessary to forget, to know how to forget, to know how to forget without knowing. To forget, you understand, not to confound' (LCP, 85/TPC, 77). This is memory without objects: 'Memory or not, and forgetting as memory, in memory and without memory' (MD'A, 50/MB, 45).

Memory, almost a collective memory, but not a commemorative, imperialistic memory (yet) links me essentially with fate, but with a link that does not bond or form a relation. It gives me the other from this non-relation, neither hidden nor closed, quasi-triumphally, with a sort of fame, at 'the triumphal moment of mourning' (G, 258a/Gl, 231a). It makes me rehearse these phrases of the other. Walter Benjamin insists on this ostentatious aspect of mourning in speaking of the German 'Trauerspiel':

The very name of the latter already indicates that its content awakens mourning in the spectator. But it does not by any means follow that this content could be any better expressed in the categories of empirical psychology than could the content of tragedy – it might far rather mean that these plays could serve better to describe mourning than could the condition of grief. For these are not so much plays which cause mourning, as plays through which mournfulness finds satisfaction: plays for the mournful. A certain ostentation is characteristic of these people. Their images are displayed in order to be seen, arranged in the way that they want them to be seen. Thus the Italian renaissance theatre, which is in many ways an influential factor in the German baroque, emerged from pure ostentation, from the *trionfi*, the processions with explanatory recitation, which flourished in Florence under Lorenzo de Medici.[36]

A bit later on, Benjamin will speak of the masks worn in this procession: 'Mourning is the state of mind in which feeling revives the empty world in the form of a mask, and derives an enigmatic satisfaction in contemplating it. Every feeling is bound to an a priori object, and the representation of this object is its phenomenology' (p. 139). But could the funferal have an object and make its mask before the phenomenological a priori? Or, as Derrida puts it in *Mémoires*, is

36 Walter Benjamin, *The origin of the German tragic drama*, trans. John Osborne (London and New York: New Left Books, 1977, Verso paperback edn, 2nd impression 1990), p. 119.

true mourning possible?[37] The commemorative triumph would then pass before representation, perception and appearance, before the show.

What does it mean to make a mask as a version of the human, that which overlays and presents by hiding? Nicolas Abraham again, with Maria Torok:

It is obvious that an identifying empathy of this kind could not say its name, let alone its aim. Accordingly, it hides behind a mask, even in the so-called 'periodic states'. This mechanism consists of exchanging one's own identity for a phantasmatic identification with the 'life' – beyond the grave – of an object lost as a result of some metapsychological traumatism. Awaiting something better, we have named this very specific mechanism *endocryptic identification*.[38]

In so far as it is 'phantasmatic', this '*endocryptic identification*' no longer identifies according to concepts of object perception and idea(lisa)tion. Inversely, there is a phenomenology of the crypt that is foreign to the perceptual-objective laws of phenomenology. Secondly, what is 'beyond the grave' does not mark a topographic-metapsychological limit between the living and the dead. To this extent, the triumphal mask cannot be told apart from the death mask of the other, the living dead in us. Thirdly, this kind of 'identifying empathy' 'could not say its name', could not include within itself the horizon of its nomination and renown without an absolute disfiguration. The name, the renown, the fame of the dead comes from elsewhere, outside of a topography of whatever kind.

A 'poetics' of psychoanalysis is being beaten out which staves off the hunger of the flesh-eating tomb. This moment of triumph is an

---

37 This question is not unrelated to questions about mourning posed by Lacan in his reading of *Hamlet* ('Desire and the interpretation of desire in *Hamlet*', trans. James Hulbert, *Yale French studies*, 55 (1977), 11–52). Lacan also insists on the impossibility of mourning, since it is an attempt at an object idealisation which would fill a gap in the mourner. The impossibility of mourning derives from the fact that that object is indistinguishable from 'the structure of the signifier' which in its totality is structurally unattainable, and hence both germane to the Other, and the origin of a teleologically characterised 'desire'. It is perhaps on the question of teleology that the difference between Derrida and Lacan becomes decisive. For if, in Lacan, desire as mourning is always organised toward and from an end which constitutes its object, even when that object is constantly displaced and deferred, in Derrida mourning, or mid-mourning, would be that structure which gives rise to the fantasm of object organisation.

38 Nicolas Abraham and Maria Torok, 'A poetics of psychoanalysis: the lost object – me', trans. Nicholas Rand, *Sub-stance*, 43 (1984), 5.

observation outside of observation. Passing without trace, which means also passing without death conceived as that which is dead, it resurrects itself in an anastasis:

when I first wrote 'burn everything', it was neither out of prudence and a taste for the clandestine, nor out of a concern for internal guarding [the guarding of a crypt as such] but out of what was necessary (the condition, the given) for the affirmation to be reborn at every instant, without memory.

(*LCP*, 28/*TPC*, 23)

Which is to say that it resurrects otherwise, in the midst of an apotheosis, wearing a kind of mask, a version of itself, in an unstately process. It

remains itself (to itself), heterogeneous, immobile and indifferent, impassive and stubborn on a base, a stela, a throne or, still up to it, he the royal dwarf, on the rostrum of his catafalque. He risks his head on this hallucinatory scaffolding, he is exposed to height, smaller than the smallest of all but immensely grown, out of proportion, in his raised-up retrenchment. And yet fallen, destitute, neglected debris, *banished*, excluded from a family (tribe, people, *genos*) with which he no longer has any relationship. To tell the truth he will never have had any relationship with it, even though, in secret, in an immemorial time, a past which was never present, we will, presumptively, have engendered that family.

(*LV*, 216/*TT*, 188)

A face is made which will not have to stand on metapsychological orders. It begins to be moulded according to a 'principle of ruin', as the necessity of a 'traumatism', a structural trauma in other words from which the face is averted, but raised up in this aversion, positing a face with pretended genealogical characteristics only. This facial paralysis of the mask finds itself recorded in *Mémoires d'aveugle* and elsewhere as the condition which afflicted for a while Derrida's 'own face'.

For Paul de Man, the autobiographical, commemorative mask is assembled through a series of tropological turns which simulate the phenomenological condition of knowledge even as they effectively disarm it. The dominant trope here, in the essay 'Autobiography as de-facement', is that of prosopopoeia which 'makes a face'. Something other than an imperial or politically legislative memory gets engraved, an engravure which allows precisely for 'reading' — which amounts to political determination, reading otherwise, reading against the tropological movement which allows for reading, allegorising the reading, or troping the trope into political and legislative knowledge. This transition, an aversion, is nothing other than phenomenology itself. De Man writes:

For just as autobiographies, by their thematic insistence on the subject, on the proper name, on memory, on birth, on eros, and death, and on the doubleness of specularity, openly declare their cognitive and tropological constitution, they are equally eager to escape from the coercions of this system. Writers *of* autobiographies as well as writers *on* autobiography are obsessed by the need to move from cognition to resolution and to action, from speculative to political and legal authority.[39]

The existentialist conspiracy of knowledge, and in particular self-knowledge, with action, is characterised as a failure of the tropological nerve which would allow the subject to look the specular in the face — a face de-faced with the very defacement of subjectivity. Subjectivity is defaced in that it comes into being only through a series of tropological feints allowing the subject to be 'read', in a retroactive imposition of 'the shift from experiential to rhetorical structure'.[40] Prosopopoeia is the dominant trope because it confers a mask, makes a face; but prosopopoeia belongs to a system and not to an isolable party.[41] The subject is enthused by the pathos afforded it, by which it

39 Paul de Man, *The rhetoric of Romanticism*, p. 71.
40 Huntington Williams, *Rousseau and Romantic autobiography* (Oxford: Oxford University Press, 1983), p. 219.
41 For further work on prosopopoeia in de Man see Chapter 4 of Cynthia Chase's *Decomposing figures: rhetorical readings in the Romantic tradition* (Baltimore and London: Johns Hopkins University Press, 1986), 'Giving a face to a name: de Man's figures', in which she writes that 'the significance here ascribed to prosopopeia could hardly be greater, since its understanding is identified with "understanding" itself' (p. 82). Herman Rapaport somewhat reduces de Man's essay, 'Autobiography as de-facement', to an inflection of Heideggerianism, in his 'Phenomenology and contemporary theory' in ed. Joseph Natoli, *Tracing literary theory* (Urbana and Chicago: University of Illinois Press, 1987), esp. pp. 164–5. There is a brief discussion of apostrophe as related to de Man's essay in Jonathan Culler's *The pursuit of signs: semiotics, literature, deconstruction* (London: Routledge and Kegan Paul, 1981), pp. 153–4. Gregory S. Jay (in his 'Paul de Man: the subject of literary history', *Modern language notes*, 103: 5 (1988), 969–94) considers prosopopoeia in de Man to be 'parallel' (p. 974) with Derrida's logic of the supplement, in terms of its 'rhetorical double-play'; he goes on to say that 'consciousness is prosopopeia' (p. 975), although one doubts whether, inversely, prosopopoeia is consciousness. Michael Riffaterre opens a new path by suggesting a necessary link between prosopopoeia and narrative: 'Narrative is ... generated as if it were compensating for the repression or suppression of prosopopeia' (p. 120), where the latter works by a 'vanishing act' (p. 122) and narrative is marshalled, as it were, at the site of its exit, a trap door ('Prosopopeia', in *Yale French studies*, 69 (1985): 'The lesson of Paul de Man', 107–23). The orthography of our term seems to be either 'prosopopeia' or 'prosopopoeia'.

takes tropological identification to be knowledge (the phenomenological aversion), and with this knowledge it seeks to escape from
the tropological system into what it believes to be its legitimate order,
that of knowledge, authority, legislative politics, and power, by which
its life will indeed be legitimated. Autobiography is exemplary of this
pathos, conflating as it does life with self-knowledge. The subject
receives this knowledge – a 'false' knowledge, almost a 'false
consciousness', what Derrida refers to as 'prosopagnosia'[42] – from
prosopopoeia; simultaneously, prosopopoeia withdraws this knowledge into the tropological system which stifles it.

In this way one might gloss de Man. He goes on famously to
conclude:

As soon as we understand the rhetorical function of prosopopeia as positing
voice or face by means of language, we also understand that what we are
deprived of is not life but the shape and the sense of a world accessible only
in the privative way of understanding. Death is a displaced name for a
linguistic predicament, and the restoration of mortality by autobiography
(the prosopopeia of the voice and the name) deprives and disfigures to the
precise extent that it restores. Autobiography veils a defacement of the mind
of which it is itself the cause.

The word 'mind' here, which is perhaps slightly unexpected, in a
concluding sentence which has the feeling of being superadded, falls
right between the epistemological and the psychological, and indicates
suppleness of what is often taken as de Man's 'rigour'. The relation of
autobiography to this epistemo-psychological construct, the 'mind', is
one of protective violence, implying a certain control; it 'veils a
defacement of the mind of which it is itself the cause'. This control is
erotically and morbidly ('veils') proximate to the mind, but not within
it. The metaphors suggest that the mind is not a space which might
contain, but can be drawn against a surface, such as a mask or veil;
they suggest a palimpsest, with the veil as the fly-leaf covering the
waxy surface of the mind. 'Restores' then, is somewhat ironic, since it
suggests a fillable space (-stores), so that one has in this system

---

42 Prosopagnosia occurs in the forest, where else?: '9 *May* 1979. Sam came to pick
me up at the station, and then we went for a long walk in the forest (a man came
up to greet us thinking that he recognised me, and then excused himself at the last
moment – he must be suffering, as I am, more and more, from prosopagnosia, a
diabolical impulse to find resemblances in faces, to recognise, no longer to
recognise)' (*LCP*, 203/*TPC*, 188).

something very like the movement of the funferal as a movement of superficies which nonetheless seems to create the possibility of voluminous life.

One is given to think an ante-phenomenal triumph, before life is given its value as phenomenal presence – that very presence, which is, for de Man, the origin of political 'determination' in so far as presence is conceived by it as what is natural.

Or one is given to think presence otherwise, as memory, almost an anamnesia, but without transcendental anchoring among the stars. In it, one witnesses the traffic of life death, the coming from the other's death without trace, where 'two death-drives cross in a χ' (*LV*, 184/*TT*, 161), a chiasmus that is perhaps 'tropological', metaleptic even, but not according to a classical rhetoric. 'Here is the figure', the triumphal face, which is neither that of a person nor a thing, but a version of these, given through its own effacement which brings it renown, phrasing it from the apparatus, a kind of mask, 'a visage, the face and the de-facement, the effacement of the visible figure in prosopopeia: the sovereign, secret, discrete and ideal signature – and the most giving, the one which knows how to efface itself' (*M*, 47/*Me*, 26).[43] It effaces itself as a kind of half-memory, a quasi-narcissistic recognition of the self, which is nonetheless haunted, phrased, of oneself outside oneself, where again the 'principle of ruin' will have played, ruin being the autobiography or self-portrait, the distorted face, 'this devisaged visage, this face looked at in the face, as a memory of oneself, of itself, that which *remains* or *returns* like a spectre as soon as at the first look upon oneself a figuration eclipses itself' (*MD'A*, 72/*MB*, 68, modified). One recalls that in classical rhetoric prosopopoeia is linked to impersonation:[44] here impersonation of the self by the self proceeds before the self is established.

Memory is indebted to the ruin, the fall, which accomplishes it, as de Manian allegory turns away from the thing, the other thing – 'rhetoric', the 'tropological spectrum' – which pays for its turn. Memory opens up the largest of empires in this narrowest of passages, before psychologistic anxiety, outside of influence, and as a kind of allegory – as in, for example, de Man's reading of Keats' 'Hyperion',[45]

43 Dominic la Capra, in the aforementioned *Soundings in critical theory*, refers to what he calls Derrida's 'genial gloss of de Man' (p. 188)!

44 See, for example, Brian Vickers's *In defence of rhetoric*, p. 78.

45 In 'The resistance to theory', in *The resistance to theory*, pp. 16–17.

the fall or ruin of which haunts Keats, haunted by his own phrase, as an impossibility which is however enabling in a certain way of a certain divested knowledge or verse. Memory passes between fall and triumph, its plastic, eidetic qualities coming to it only as a late phase – that is, also, a triumph or a fall, and so on. To call upon memory is to close the eyes, to pass out of knowledge, and thus forgo the recognition which memory, classically considered, requires. Apollo apostrophises:

> 'Mnemosyne!
> Thy name is on my tongue, I know not how;
> Why should I tell thee what thou so well seest?
> Why should I strive to show what from thy lips
> Would come no mystery? For me, dark, dark,
> And painful, vile oblivion seals my eyes ...'[46]

'Hyperion' is a poem which begins with a still life or what could be called a 'tableau mort' (' ... No stir of air was there, / Not so much life as on a summer's day / Robs not one light seed from the feathered grass, / But where the dead leaf fell, there did it rest'). Oblivion is the form of relation with Mnemosyne, goddess of memory and mother of the Muses. As the goddess of memory she is also the goddess of renown, in so far as it is through her that a name lives on. To address her is to address the condition of naming, the experience of this address therefore being a kind of darkness illuminated, darkly, by her own illuminating vision. Or as one of the mp's, the *maîtres-penseurs* of *La carte postale* puts it, 'the memories of love are no exception to the general laws of memory, which in turn are governed by the still more general laws of Habit. And as Habit weakens everything, what best reminds us of a person is precisely what we have forgotten ... That is why the better part of our memories exists outside us ... Outside us? Within us, rather, but hidden from our eyes in an oblivion more or less prolonged.'[47] Habit comes about as the effacement of memory which has nonetheless been inscribed in a necessary forgetting at the non-place of a graft somewhere between inside and outside. A kind of working oblivion ensues. Inversely, as Proust will insist on throughout *A la recherche*, there is no 'first time' of memory, no first memory that is not at first prepared in some way before it will take.

46 'Hyperion: a fragment', in ed. Miriam Allott, *Keats: The complete poems* (London: Longman, 1970, 5th impression 1980), p. 438.
47 Marcel Proust, *Remembrance of things past*, vol. 1, trans. C. K. Scott Moncrieff and Terence Kilmartin (London: Penguin Books, 1983, reprinted 1989), p. 692.

Derrida titles his funeral oration for de Man, 'Mnemosyne', which is a fabulous title coming before naming, like a myth, according to the most spectacular and tortuous genealogy of the gods. A long quotation:

Is it possible [there is no analysis of mourning without a relation to the impossible. In *La vérité en peinture*: 'Of mourning. Make mourning *one's* mourning ... That's what I call doing the impossible', (*LV*, 243/*TT*, 211)], when one is in memory of the other, in bereaved memory of a friend, is it desirable to think of and to pass beyond this hallucination, beyond a prosopopeia of prosopopeia? Death, if there is death, that is to say, if it happens and happens only once [one time], to the other and to oneself, is the moment when there is no longer any choice – could we even think of any other – except that between memory and hallucination. If death comes to the other, and comes to us through the other, then the friend no longer exists except *in* us, *between* us. In himself, by himself, of himself, he is no more, nothing more. He lives only in us. But *we* are never *ourselves*, and between us, identical to us, a 'self' is never in itself or identical to itself. This specular reflection never closes on itself; it does not appear *before* this *possibility* of mourning, before and outside of this structure of allegory and prosopopeia which constitutes in advance all 'being-in-us', 'in-me', between us, or between ourselves. The *selbst*, the *soi-même*, the self appears to itself only in this bereaved allegory, in this hallucinatory prosopopeia – and even before the death of the other *actually* happens, as we say, in 'reality'. The strange situation I am describing here, for example that of my friendship with Paul de Man, would have allowed me to say all of this *before* his death. It suffices that I know him to be mortal, that he knows me to be mortal – there is no friendship without this knowledge of finitude. And everything that we inscribe in the living present of our relation to others already carries, always, the signature of *memoirs-from-beyond-the-grave*. But this finitude, which is also that of memory, does not at first take the form of a limit, of a limited ability, aptitude, or faculty, of a circumscribed power. Nor does it assume the form of a *limit* which would move us to multiply testamentary signs, traces, hypograms, *hypomnemata*, signatures and epigraphs, or autobiographical 'memoirs'. No, this finitude can only take that form through the trace of the other in us, the other's irreducible precedence; in other words, simply the trace, which is always the trace of the other, the finitude of memory, and thus the approach or memory of the future. If there is a finitude of memory, it is because there is something of the other, and of memory as a memory of the other, which comes from the other and comes back to the other. It defies any totalisation, and directs us to a scene of allegory, to a fiction of prosopopeia, that is, to tropologies of mourning: to the memory of mourning and to the mourning for memory. This is why there can be no *true mourning*, even if truth and lucidity always presuppose it, and, in truth, take place only as the truth of mourning. The truth of the mourning of the other, but of the other who always speaks in me before me, who signs in my place, the hypogram or epitaph being always of the other, and for the other. Which also means: in the place of the other. (*M*, 49–50/*Me*, 28–9, modified)

Derrida is 'working' with de Man. An incorporation of the living-dead friend is at work in the assimilation of tropology to mourning, but an incorporation that passes through the name or renown, between Derrida and de Man, shared by them outside of themselves. The only moment of doubt, skepsis, or narrowing of the eyes in a sort of unavoidable disfiguration comes when Derrida speaks of, citing de Man, the 'tropological spectrum'. The English translation is defective here in not preserving the italics from the French text: 'In this memory which promises the resurrection of an anterior past, a "*passé antérieur*", as we say in French to designate a grammatical tense, Paul de Man always saw a kind of formal element, the very place where fictions and figures are elaborated' (*M*, 70/*Me*, 58). The French text insists – 'une sorte de *formalité*'. It is perhaps decisive. As with the long quotation above there is some scepticism with regard to a '*limit*' for finitude. For this formality of the tropological system is that within generality which is already generality's rule, the order of its functioning, or its regulation, that severer politics to which a legislative politics is a 'resistance'. A classical or formal element is subsumed into the random violence of the tropological spectrum. This is what makes of memory an art, but an art, again, of the originary simulacrum, since it is a technics which precedes, or 'knows' in advance, coming-into-nature, or Being. There is a technique of memory that holds out an at best uncertain relationship to any tropical regulation or form. The formal element *is* such uncertainty – the sway of the death-before-death that qualifies ascriptions of living consciousness. Though the 'image' of the live-dead friend resides 'in us', it does so according to an anamnesis that puts to death the ideal limit of a memory and a system of (mental) representation. Whether this be an image or figure at all then becomes open to question, since the ruin of the figure, another kind of de-facement perhaps, structures it even in its phenomenal manifestation, even in the lyrical beauty of such a manifestation.

No choice between memory and hallucination, truth and fiction: one does not have to wait for death in order for this lack of choice to assert itself. The formality of the eidetic origin of memory, the formality of memory as eidetic, coextends with hallucination and thereby overcomes the phenomenological precision which would keep them apart: 'Here the hypothesis of hallucination takes up the role assigned, in eidetic determination, to fiction in general, *"the vital element of phenomenology"'* (*L'OG*, 29/*TOG*, 45). True being and the image/idea are inseparable in their founding fictionality. Any image, figure or form would have to be, then, an image that is no longer an image, no longer a figure in relief presented to the eyes. That would be to break with the formal element, with formality and form in general, and cast a memory which hallucinates of itself (with no image), outside of genealogy, like a phrase which can graft itself upon the memory from out of a quite inscrutable provenance. Of itself, and therefore not of itself, this memory, structured by this renown and 'phrase-haunting' rather than by the image and figure, no longer *is*, but *writes* – autobiography. Autobiography demands to be entirely reconstructed starting from this possibility of self-relation outside the classical schema of generation, which is always the generation of the idea, the object, empiric and semi-empiric recall. So long as there is the idea, the image or icon, there is life conceived as presence, memory bearing Being, for 'the immediate Idea has the form of life. But the absolute Idea in its infinite truth is still determined as Life, true life, absolute life, life without death, imperishable life, the life of truth' (*G*, 95a/*Gl*, 82a). But within this truth of life, there is a false 'moment', a judas moment, an hallucination which precedes and dominates it, giving it its chance even as it withdraws its value, 'drawing' it, I would say, both sketching it out but at the same time moving it away from itself in the opening of the box, or drawer (more household objects).

Memory, life death, is at the very least the simultaneous necessity and impossibility of the self-relation. It is necessary that it passes otherwise than phenomenally, eidetically, perceptually, ontologically, for these are the very motions which promise an ideal narcissism of return, closure and 'identification', the objective description of the idea. But it is impossible for it to do so. This is perhaps because – to speak diagnostically – the register of possibility and impossibility already belongs in the core of those motions.

To think life as the already dead, as if now surviving,[48] as if a still life of all that can be objectified ... Like the proper name it survives

---

48 In a chapter entitled 'You only die twice', Slavoj Zizek analyses the phenomenon whereby those who 'should' already be dead live on until they realise their mistake and promptly die. Zizek argues that this survival or supplement is structurally necessary and, to that extent, must be reckoned with from the beginning in any concept of the life term (in *The sublime object of ideology*, London and New York: Verso, 1989).

already its own inception, leaps over from objectivity, and therefore from subjectivity, into a dimension whose most strictly formal quality is its lack of measure, its verse that goes around the object. No more can one write 'on' life (Shelley and Derrida both write essays on life, '*sur vivre*'; I have taken care not to write 'on' Derrida's essay of this name) than one can write on the Freudian apparatus, than, in *La carte postale*, one can write simply *on* postcards. For it – 'life' – passes already through a proxy, and before I get the chance to delegate to it. This is the 'courier of death' who sets off ahead of me, getting my messages mixed up with everyone else's to the extent that the names do not belong to what they have signed. I must wait until the courier returns to find out who I am. Meanwhile, I have no idea, and the waiting is interminable, almost like a life term.

There is a confusion, then, with the death drive, or the drive of death in the triumphal car. The only way I can stop it and thus become an autobiographical, living 'I' is by forcing the car to stop, to draw it into an accident, so that I become myself by accident. There is no proof that this ever 'happens', for happening finds no route through what corresponds to common-sense notions of experience. This is a death drive, then, undertaken by something other than the Freudian 'organism' of 'Beyond the Pleasure Principle', against nature, and otherwise than generation. Since it is irreducible, interminable (if one were to speak a language of finitude which may be the least appropriate), it is like a permanence, or immortality – but an immortality of death, of the death which cannot die, cannot be reduced by comprehension, ingestion or eating, bringing only those guests to its table which do not participate in the banquet, Judas guests (in *Glas*), beyond belief, who are invited only so as to provide the necessary false moment which guarantees the immortality of the death feast or still life which can't be touched. 'Isn't there always an element excluded from the system', in attendance but excluded, as yet unidentified, treacherous but entailing the sequence 'that assures the system's space of possibility?' (*G*, 183a/*Gl*, 162a). Something false allows for the immortality of death – or 'invitality' to coin a word to suggest this deathly hosting – which guarantees an unkillable permanence, one that comes precisely from the precinct of death, a saving false feature which can hardly be told apart from it. – As in, perhaps, the two versions of Hölderlin's 'Patmos', different but the same in that one phrase returns as the same in the other version – 'Wo aber Gefahr ist, wächst / Das Rettende auch', translated by Michael Hamburger as

'But where there is danger the saving powers also grow.'[49] I cite also
the first few lines of the third version of Hölderlin's 'Mnemosyne' (p.
212):

> Reif sind, in Feur getaucht, gekochet
> Die Frücht und auf der Erde geprüfet und ein Gesetz ist
> Daß alles hineingeht, Schlangen gleich,
> Prophetisch, träumend auf
> Den Hügeln des Himmels.

'Ripe are, dipped in fire, cooked the fruit and tried on the earth, and it
is a law that all must enter in, like serpents, prophetically, dreaming
upon the mounds of Heaven.' All must enter in, like serpents, the most
false, confusing the truth with the hallucination into a realm of
memory, a second heaven almost, a permanence or fixity or
immutability: a life death, or funferal, which is invulnerable to
reduction, though it is the very principle of ruin, that is, of a certain
organicism, but conceived anew.

This life, this death, which does not die, but survives (before) its
conception, goes also by the name of a 'nonbiodegradable', which
lacks the organic, entropic matter that is the stuff of life. Thus, in
between Derrida's *Mémoires* and 'Comme le bruit de la mer au fond
d'un coquillage', Paul de Man, the dead, is made to die again, his
corpse violated in order to renew his death, to punish him for what had
passed with impunity but also for what had passed in general as his
work, his mourning, that is, as if his corpus had been washed up on the
shore and a fire had been lit to reincinerate it, burning even the ashes.
The structure of death remaining immortal – the structure, which is
not to say the form, the rule, the category, but more the building, not
necessarily a tomb, but an ordinary place that one goes in and out of
habitually – there can be no structural degradation of it, of it as an
object which can be brought near in order to expel it. Rather, we are
with it, neither subjectively nor objectively, and the nonbiodegradable
is indistinguishable from the effect that 'we' are.

In so far as it ceases to be an object, the immortal life death obviates
the science or technicity which would detain it; it obviates
instrumentality in general, and the treating of the organism called
'life'. It is with us, shared in the death, cause for fear not because it is
deathly, terrifying or unknown, but because it does not necessarily
come from me, from that centre, a centre of ash, which purports to

---

49 Friedrich Hölderlin, *Selected verse*, trans. Michael Hamburger, pp. 193, 203.

organise its objects around it. Not fear so much as aversion, not danger so much as that which saves, saves against saving, without an assurance of return or interest which would allow for being in it.

When I come to write my life, it will be like this, or at least a version of it: I address myself, the circulation of death masks begins, sitting in a sort of mass grave, almost like home, where I can only begin by classifying, and, above all, finding my own place, the classification which belongs to me, according to a proper name that will never cease to escape me.

9

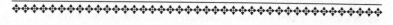

graphy

— And life 'must be thought of as trace before Being may be determined as presence. This is the only condition on which we can say that life is death, that repetition and the beyond of the pleasure principle are native and congenital to that which they transgress' (*ED*, 302/*WD*, 203). For 'life is not first and foremost a full presence which, secondarily, would reserve itself: it "is" always already, death, trace'[1] — where 'a configuration of traces ... can no longer be represented except by the structure and functioning of writing'(*ED*, 297/*WD*, 200).

Perhaps incredibly, life has an essential link with writing; a thought of writing and the trace is 'the only condition on which' life death can be thought out — it is the *sine qua non* of life as death, making an urgent demand for itself, in these early books at least — *L'écriture et la différence* and *De la grammatologie* — to be brought under analysis. One is lead before a scene of agonistic conflict between life and writing, Being and the graphematic, as if it were a further Act added, after the event, to what in the Introduction to *Being and time* is called the 'γιγαντομαχια περι τεσ ουσιασ', the colossal battle over what is.[2] Derrida is emphatic: 'one must ... *go by way of* the question of being as it is directed by Heidegger and by him alone' (*DLG*, 37/*OG*, 23).

In bringing writing into the domain of the question of being, of life, of presence, Derrida is unleashing a series of transformations, concatenation without pattern, that will leave literally nothing intact. Logically and historically, writing has been put to one side. Logically, according to the logic which has governed occidental thought — where logic is directed by truth, and truth is imbued with the value of authenticity — writing is the secondary, the inauthentic proxy which truth will use only in order to record itself; historically, it can be

1 Sarah Kofman, *Lectures de Derrida*, p. 59. My translation.
2 *Being and time*, p. 21.

demonstrated that writing has indeed always been laid aside as inferior to the truth which precedes it in truth's living voice, and the voice of hearing oneself speak *par excellence*. One can read in these early books Derrida's discourse of universality, the immensity of a recognition of the immensity of a systematic cohesion that has been dominant, one which goes by the name of 'western metaphysics' – which is to say not just the canon of philosophy but the very roots of the most spontaneous thinking, the most naïve or innocent gesture of thought. In retrospect Derrida attests to having posed to himself the question: 'How is it that the fact of writing can disturb the very question "what is?" and even "what does it mean?"' (*DDP*, 443/TTT, 37).

The graphic in the autobiographic pulls away from the domain of what is and what is not, according to 'a certain displacement of writing, a systematic transformation and generalisation of its "concept"' (*LD*, 207, note 7/*D*, 181, note 8). No doubt this graphic distortion passes by way of Heidegger, and according to a thought of difference – of difference almost 'in itself', the enigma of a relation that has as yet no ontic coordinates to design its position, fix its register or constitute its possibility: writing and difference. Difference 'in itself' has no self, it awaits. In Heidegger, the ontico-ontological difference, the difference between Being and beings, remains enigmatic in so far as this difference – which lodges in the very quick of Being, in the jettison of being onto Being – is perhaps an *ontic* ontico-ontological difference; perhaps this difference has something of Being about it; perhaps it is already drawn into the inception of presence; perhaps it is already seduced into a determination that is in this sense other to it. Writing gives itself to difference in the space of this 'perhaps' which promises without definitely providing an ontology. In so far as it demands to be thought according to difference, which is prior to ontology, writing runs the risk of allowing ontology to play, to allow difference to open like a flower under its sun.

Writing and difference: this could be translated as writing and the almost impossible risk of being. If difference simply withdrew from being, remaining untouched by but germane to it, it might be no more than, on the one hand, its condition of possibility or transcendental category, or, on the other hand, its essence. At least, one would not be able to tell difference apart from these, which forms another risk: perhaps indistinction and *trompe-l'oeil* are the 'form' of difference; perhaps difference is essentially disguised – before it has an identity *to* disguise.

The difference between Being and beings leaves a trace – that is, an inscription or dead moment in the heart of everything that is to be given to presence. There is a writing – a trace – of the ontico-ontological difference which gets lost along the way – its perdition is what saves being. It is lost or 'erased':

The erasure of the early trace (*die frühe Spur*) of difference is therefore the 'same' as its tracing in the text of metaphysics. This latter must have maintained the mark of what it has lost, reserved, put aside.

(*MDP*, 25/*MOP*, 24)

An alien body which Being should have expelled to its outside as foreign to it, the trace of difference as writing nevertheless allows for the inauguration of being, in 'the play of a trace which no longer belongs to the horizon of Being, but whose play transports and encloses [*porte et borde*] the meaning of Being' (*MDP*, 23/*MOP*, 22). In Heidegger the early trace gives on to being, and his ontology cannot be simply disentangled from this 'scriptural' investment. For Derrida this gift need not necessarily 'come about' in the mode of a transfer, which is to say that it does not necessarily come about at all. But the necessity of an erased difference, an erased trace – or writing in its own impossibility – remains – 'the necessity of passing through that erased determination, the necessity of that *trick of writing* ["*tour d'écriture*", a turn, a tower, a detour, a sojourn, loop, measure, revolution, etc., of writing] is irreducible' (*DLG*, 38/*OG*, 24) – *remains*, which is not to say 'is'.

Writing as difference imposes a line of demarcation that is virtually without empirical or transcendental marking, a trace of the trace working at the origin of what is – 'the trace must be thought before the entity' (*DLG*, 69/*OG*, 47) – working the origin otherwise, complicating its simplicity, transforming its inceptive uniquity. It multiplies the origin by chance as a token of absolute heterogeneity.

One is inclined to speak, under the name of 'writing', of a fabulous difference or heteronomous division which nothing in the order of conceptuality can assimilate. Touched by this inclination, Derrida launches some fake concepts suggestive of such non-assimilation – among these, dictation, hymen, truth, veils, distance, winking, distance, flowers, the vocable, tone, letters.

Of *dictation*: 'I speak of a law dictated, as in the first person, by the thing, with an intractable rigor, as an implacable command. This command is also an insatiable demand; it enjoins the one who writes, and who writes under this order alone, in a situation of radical heteronomy with regard to the thing' (S, 13/12). There is a difference enjoining the one who writes, the division between dictator and scribe, master and secretary – not that the division must therefore have distributed these roles: they are brought together non-dialectically in the dictation of writing's law, shared in each other before the possibility of their conceptual separation, the one turning on the other in a pseudo-masochistic gesture. The 'early trace' of being has its provenance in this 'before': dictation of writing's difference in advance of the transcendental a priori, by coming about after the a priori only in the effect of its effect, when the scribe is 'enjoined' to write; delaying itself in this way, it stretches back beyond and outside of the formal first time, into its earliest beginning, in an earliness before the early begins. So that it comes about later, in its effect which lacks the juridical impulse of a cause (and foreign to the 'thing' to which the 'cause' is related as *chose* or *cosa*). The law dictates in this more than double time scheme, like a command in which one half recognises oneself, for a certain parody of becoming is being worked – the pseudo-autobiographer 'rows with the application of a sweet gale (*galé ... rien* convict [a '*galé rien*', a galley slave, but also, anagrammatically, an algerian, almost nothing – *rien* – of oneself], a galley slave, driven to write orders received at the back, threatened by the whip if he stops' (G, 81–2b/Gl, 69–70b).

There arises the possibility and the necessity of a space across which the dictation commands, a difference, but a space and a difference as yet lacking all dimension, not other than that suicidal-homicidal, erotico-thanatographic limit we have discussed previously, a kind of wall like 'the partition between Plato and Socrates when the latter seems to write what the former dictates' (DTA, 38/OAT, 13). It erects the wall with 'the extreme tension of a polyphony' (FS, 62, my translation). It conjures a synthesis, almost that of the synthetic a priori judgment, but one whose table of categories is broken by another law – the synthesis of a polyphony, the necessity and possibility of an original confusion of voices, masters and scribes mingling in the lobby before the distribution of powers, before the political edict, before judgment.

Writing is dictated as across a difference, but across a difference which contradicts itself in so far as it does not differentiate or decide upon the order of concepts which it espies somewhat confusedly in the distance, before any 'dialogue' as such.[3] Those whom it enjoins to write are not yet themselves, becoming so only in its after-effect, which comes later, that is, earlier, when it ceases to coincide with itself. Against this more than double time scheme the chance of 'becoming' is only a reduction, when the autobiographical hallucinates its singularity, drawing up its calendar of the indivisible self. It cannot be said for certain, however, that this chance materialises into what is called reality, i.e., into the reduction of all possible elements to the empirical, or to the empirico-psychological. It can be said only that the autobiographical, in its relation to writing as it is transformed in its conceptualisation by Derrida, opens to a heteronomous, impossible dictation – and where dictation is the 'wrong' word for this thought, nothing more or nothing less than a 'fake' concept, enjoined, like the one who writes, to perform what is other to it, almost in opposition to its status and meaning; a mistake or confusion of the concept allowing for the play of the concept when it accedes to what is taken to be its authenticity. 'Dictation' becomes a wrong word for itself, describing its operation by being false to it in its description, breaching itself with the heteronomy which it almost imputes to what is beyond itself, the (fake) concept it would describe, but which curls back on itself even as it is thrown off.

Writing dictates. This means that the concept of writing as secondary (dictated in an ordinary sense) is transformed. In its primary after-effect it 'dictates' – which is neither a true statement nor an accurate description, for dictation is not dictation, being at best only approximate to its concept. A practical effect ensues. The writing used (by Derrida, for example) in the description of the newly transformed concept of writing is false, and when one reads Derrida one is reading an insistent falsehood as it imposes itself again and again according to a necessity that resists 'absolute mastery'. In the bringing of the determination of writing toward difference, the value of truth is undermined: the speech, the living voice mimicked in the 'dict' of 'dictation', is in a state of chronic hesitation before the cohesion of the system of which truth is the guarantor.

---

3 On the distinction between dialogue and dictation see, for example, *La carte postale* (*LCP*, 54–5 / *TPC*, 48). In his 'dialogue' with John Searle, Derrida speaks, in *Limited inc*, of having the feeling of having almost dictated Searle's reply: 'and it is true that I have occasionally had the feeling ... of having almost "*dictated*" this reply' (*LI*, 68/*LInc*, 31: see also 94/47). See also DD.

Of *hymen*:[4] just as difference is difference without difference, so hymen is 'hymen sans hymen' (OCPU, 37). Rules of conceptual separation have yet to be drawn up in the hymen's sphere; confusion precedes it and what might have made of it an object is still to come, its 'without', its 'sans' being 'a sans without negativity and without signification' (*LV*, 108/*TT*, 95).

The hymen's being without the without, being without negativity, can be determined as negative or positive only following a fall into dialectic, for

the dialectical structure is incapable of accounting for the graphics of the hymen, being itself inscribed and comprehended within the latter, almost indistinguishable from it, separated from it only by itself, a simple veil that constitutes the very thing that tries to reduce it to nothing: desire.

(*LD*, 280/*D*, 249)

There is a lack of the hymen, its lack of itself, and its lack of that lack, passing between the between of the positive and the negative, touching almost the infinite blankness of an absolute castration:

the hymen's graphic [its graphic, its relation to writing and difference]... inscribes castration's effect within itself. Everywhere operative...this graphic, which describes a margin where the control over meaning or code is without recourse, poses the limit to the relevance of the hermeneutic or systematic question.   (*E*, 98/99)

Castration and meaning, castration of meaning, are brought together into an analysis of their relation to the '*sans*', the without, and the '*sens*', an overname[5] meaning 'meaning', but meaning falsely, according to the '*sans*', and so on. This is the necessity of the desire which desires to abolish that necessity. If the hymen inscribes castration's effect within itself, it does so outside of classical

---

4 For a general note on the hymen see, for example, 'HYMNE/HYMEN' by Suzanne Allen, in eds. Philippe Lacoue-Labarthe and Jean-Luc Nancy, *Les fins de l'homme: a partir du travail de Jacques Derrida* (Paris: Galilée, 1981), pp. 230–6.

5 With regard to overnames, which we touched on in the previous chapter in connection to renown and anasemic haunting, François Laruelle writes, speaking of phonic coincidence in 'words' used by Derrida that 'the signifying chain with its effects is not superadded to an other practice of difference taken from an other regional knowledge: it is de-doubled, re-doubled, re-inscribed, at once repeated and exceeded in that which remains to it of negativity. This gesture of reinscription is the affirmation of "différance", its liberation towards chance and the absolute necessity of the play which exceeds the signifier and produces it', in his 'Le texte quatrième: l'événement textuel comme simulacre', *L'arc*, 54, 39. My translation.

psychoanalysis and its positing of empirico-psychological loss as dispensed through an Oedipal romance. Difference without difference, and hymen without hymen, suggest a field of the false graphic which perhaps provides the structure for an ontology, having a relation to being that is undecidable – not finally undecidable, as an ideal limit and prohibition, but perhaps, and with the strongest perhaps, perhaps undecidable.

It inscribes castration's effect within itself, the graphic of the hymen, and poses a limit of sorts to the relevance of the hermeneutic or systematic question. This question is that of the system's producing of meaning starting from its ideal finitude, whether there is production of meaning outside of this, and whether hermeneutics, classically limited to the project of exhausting itself before that finitude, of redacting that finitude to its ideal limit, might be refracted otherwise by the graphic. This graphic, a quasi autobiographic, plays otherwise than in the passage of meaning and distinctions, the hymen being 'neither confusion nor distinction, neither identity nor difference, neither consummation nor virginity, neither the veil nor unveiling, neither the inside nor the outside, etc.' (*Po, 59/Pos, 43*).

In lacking itself it comes close to its self, that is to its lack, indistinguishable from the desire that would wish to throw it away and lack it without lacking it, casting it into an absolute past before the memory of its absence. The hymen moves this violent desire toward the absolute reduction of itself, as if it could kill itself, that is the other, 'the structures of the hymen, suicide and time' being 'closely linked together' (*LD, 244/D, 215*) in an 'absolute equivalence or continuity of murder and suicide'.[6] But it is held off by itself in a quasi-infinitely suspended autobiographic, near-murder, near-suicide, tricked by its own movement making its meaning foreign to itself while it supports a tension, the hymen.[7] The lack of the hymen forms a hymen – it comes about in its desistance, when it is no longer absolutely relevant

---

6 *G, 159a/Gl, 140a*. The story is related in *Signéponge* of the tree from which a hatchet is made which then returns to fell the tree, murder and suicide being 'closely linked together': 'The eyes of the tree "fasten on to the hatchet, the aitch held by the woodsman – something the tree almost failed to notice the first time – and it recognises, in the brand new handle of this hatchet, this aitch, the wood of the branch that was removed in the first place"' (*S, 61/60*).

7 On Oedipus, suicidal accidents and 'being mistaken for another', see, for an unusual and provocative formulation, Ann Smock's *Double dealing* (Lincoln: University of Nebraska Press, 1985), pp. 49–50.

to truth, to meaning, and to the hermeneutic solicitation of these. When there no longer is, there is hymen. In sum:

One could say quite accurately that the hymen *does not exist*. Anything constituting the value of existence is foreign to the 'hymen'.[8]

The hymen's graphic not being, it inscribes or engraves as the most forceful autobiography, that which can only forget it has forgotten itself, almost like desire, inscribing the necessity of the autobiography as an impossibility, without negativity and without meaning, following a transformation of the concept of castration as negative, beyond the empirico-psychological reduction, 'coming back to question all couples, all conceptual oppositions, particularly those that Freud has held out to us' (LD, 66/D, 58), and disturbing the conceptual union of castration with the phallus and the loss of the phallus. The hymen is 'without' the phallus according to a parody – the unconscious simulates itself before being 'constituted' – of castration, which goes without the without, leaving a mark of this, but nowhere that could be considered 'real'. Scored with gender, in its reckless generosity, the hymen relaunches sexual difference outside of, before, conceptual separation, hymeneal logic, separated from that logic only by itself, the hymen, which still pertains, but forces all writing of its concept into falsehood. An irregular and dissimulating surface, like a tympan, self-relation without border: the hymen writes its autobiography.

Of *truth*: both 'dictation' and 'hymen' are false, inappropriate words for the enigmatic operations they describe. Dictation is not dictation, hymen is not hymen, and an entire phoney discourse is opened up that can be neither believed in nor logically reduced. It is not a classically philosophical discourse because in it the very core of philosophical protocol, the method of truth, is menaced. Nor is it a classically literary discourse – at least according to a classically philosophical definition of the classically literary, i.e., anchored by truth, like philosophy, but at one or two removes from it, as an art of representation. Where philosophy longs to efface itself before the truth, becoming its adequate and transparent screen, achieving itself by dissolving its dark spots into lucidity, and thereby ceasing to present itself, presenting only the truth, whose first determination

8 *TEO*, 181–2. The English text does not coincide with its French counterpart at this point, since it contains an extra essay, omitted in the French, from which we quote.

becomes in that gesture the reduction of representation; literature by contrast represents that same ideal truth, through the effacement of philosophy's effacement, to gain a subliminal access to truth which it believes to be, in that double effacement, an enhancement of the truth. – An enhancement, which is not to say an alteration or qualification (both of these operations are essentially external to the truth), but as it were a negative gain, or negative capability seeding itself in the subliminal power of the double effacement. The phoney discourse of dictation and the hymen passes through neither of these truth channels, since it is already false to itself, before the erection of truth's totem, inscribed, in *Glas*, as a niche or tattoo carved into the totem.

From truth, philosophically or literarily considered, a system of presentation and representation known as *mimesis*[9] (everything taking its cue from what is called 'Greek' conceptuality) is founded, but 'what if *mimesis* no longer allowed itself to be arraigned, to be compelled to give accounts and reasons, to subject itself to a verification of identity within such a frame' (*G*, 109b/*Gl*, 94b) –? Truth is succeeded by its representation, the authentic by its copy, where what comes second is devalued by virtue of coming second, in accordance with a time scheme that is taken for empirical but whose beginning is in fact ideal: the empirically second is taken to be derived from the ideal, but the empirical is what it is only in this secondariness with regard to the ideal. The empirical is the post-ideal, so that for something to be, to be empirical, it must be that which has fallen from the ideal. What is, empirically, is the fallen-from-the-ideal; empirical existence is ideational decline, and so on. To be, on these grounds, means 'to be second'. All is secondary *vis-à-vis* the truth ideal, and inversely the concept of empirical existence confers upon ideality its originality and primordial status. The system seals itself.

But how can the system be formed without the possibility of its formation, without something to prepare, outside of the system and foreign to it, the onset of truth? Something necessarily non-ideal and

---

9 The reader may like to consult Mihai Spariosu's piece on mimesis ('Mimesis and contemporary French theory', in ed. Mihai Spariosu, *Mimesis in contemporary theory: an interdisciplinary approach: vol. I: 'The literary and philosophical debate* (Amsterdam: John Benjamins Publishing Company, 1984, pp. 65–108) which is largely instructive with the exception perhaps of its suggestion that 'Derrida and his followers remain largely within a philosophical problematic of representation-truth' (p. 79).

alien to existence? 'No thing is complete in itself, and it can be completed only by what it lacks' (*LD*, 337/*D*, 304). A founding falseness – not false 'as opposed to' the truth which the truth system recognises, for that would be a falseness internal to the system, the facing and securing opposite of the true, a negative compass reading of the true – false to the true-and-the-false, a falseness which dictates the system, 'forms' a hymen, 'writes' illegibly, relating to itself only through the system which forbids its self-relation, in an arrested, generative autobiography of the false which tries hopelessly to close upon itself as if with a desire to confess:

> The truth, it is in its cursed name that we have lost each other, in its name only, not for the truth itself, if there were any, but for the desire for truth which has extorted the most terrifying 'confessions' [*aveux*] from us, after which we were more distant from ourselves than ever, without getting near to any truth at all by even one step.   (*LCP*, 91–2/*TPC*, 82–3)

This falseness which cannot close is not a bad falseness, not the opposite of truth or correctness, but one implying a deviance that is structural, not juridical – more of an inaugural confession dictated, but 'confession without a crime' (*LCP*, 113/*TPC*, 102) or confession of itself in its impossible end. The autobiography, the confession without a crime, works like the name without its truth, a word without its thing, which can confess nothing more than that it is confessing, and confessing without bearing upon the truth. Such would be a 'without-crime' of the absolute evil that evades absolute knowledge.

The (non)autobiography of the false requires one 'to reconsider *mimesis* through and through' (*S*, 5/4), in the incisions upon truth's totem, the castration which saves it in restoring it to the other – '("**castration – always at stake –** ")' (*LD*, 32/*D*, 26). 'So here it is a matter of the relation or the nonrelation between castration and the concept, between castration and truth' (*G*, 53a/*Gl*, 44a), the castration of truth as it cedes its power to generate absolutely its own system, the system of mimesis, to the extent that mimesis 'does not allow itself to be locked into the status of an object, or theme',[10] and does not allow for a return to the totemic father ('in contrast to the seminal differance thus repressed, the truth that speaks (to) itself within the logocentric circle is the discourse of what *goes back to the father*', (*LD*, 56/*D*, 48)). One only gets further away, and from a point of departure

---

10 Sylviane Agacinski et al, *Mimesis: des articulations* (Paris: Flammarion, 1975), p. 5. My translation.

('the truth') that was not founded in the first place. Truth is founded on a falseness entirely other to it, a falseness whose dominant form is, it seems, that of an autobiography which cannot complete itself.

Of *veils*: the falseness not hiding the truth – as in 'the self-presentation of truth (veiled/unveiled) as *Logos*' (*LD*, 32/*D*, 26) – but remaining other to it, its value is one not so much of disguise, of a veil masking a truth, as a false veil, not a veil at all, but a veil without anything behind or in front of it, drawn across nothing, almost a hymen, an originary simulacrum of the truth as unveiling, where 'mimesis resembles *aletheia* because *aletheia* does not resemble *itself* and cannot resemble itself, but rather – as either unveiling or dis-installation – endlessly withdraws, masks itself, de-sists'.[11] The veil is unveiled, always, but suggests no presentation. It marks difference, writing and difference, as an indelible, essentially undetectable inscription. So it is not a smooth surface or limit, but something sharp which engraves, a sharp veil, tendering to itself the instrument which threatens it, the sharp point shredding the soft fabric, in its suicide-murder, or autobiography, autoheterocidal biography.

Of *distances*: moving about like this in Derrida's writing risks loss of perspective and conceptual distance. Thus we try to put into practice the loss of the object and autobiographical initiative that a philo-sophical enquiry cannot but be unsettled by, troubled with from the start. Such 'loss of the object' results perhaps in a more powerful incorporation of it – except that the dialectical recuperation that this suggests must be stymied by a perpetual alterity holding any such recuperation off. Besides, the collapsing of distance also violates the objective distinctions among the 'objects' we are addressing. There is nothing to choose between veils, hymen, dictation, truth, and yet each performs a specific task in a specific reading, and to lift them from this context is to run the risk of endorsing them as free-standing concepts with methodological status, but also to practise the necessity – if one can say this – of 'citational graft'. Academically speaking, one works against the private property market of intellectual goods, the ideology

---

11 Philippe Lacoue-Labarthe, ed. and trans. Christopher Fynsk, *Typography: Mimesis, philosophy, politics* (Cambridge, Mass.: Harvard University Press, 1989), p. 118. Further on (p. 122), Lacoue-Labarthe 'identifies' autobiography, as self-presentation, with mimesis. Autobiography is there subject to the movement of desistance cited here.

that 'work' may be owned and identified with this or that figure who would be in autobiographical control of their productions. The conceptual discernibility which distance implies gives way, in Derrida, to a kind of rigorous confusion. The latter is governed by what I would call a law of autobiography, a dream of integral cohesion which promises itself only in the mode of its withdrawal. The relation of veil to hymen, for example, is essential, they belong to each other, they match and pass into one another as if producing a meaning system out of the finitude that arises from their coincidence; however, they are not, their dimension is other than this, they are 'names' with no substantive referent, between the word and the thing, neither one nor the other and irrelevant to this choice. It is no good speaking of 'them', over there, at a distance, for they belong more to an absent middle ground between here and there, *hic et ille*. Hymen and veil are of writing, which is not perhaps of being, or existing, so that their considerable force accumulates as a kind of death, the death of the living and the dead, which suggests analogies of the machine, the monster, the end. But the analogy is a means of regulating what is analogised, so one must pass beyond even these, beyond and back into their overnaming or writing force which is such that it cannot be told apart from what is. To tell them apart is already to perform an ontological operation. And if one cannot tell them apart from what is, if there is no distance, then in a sense they are what is, and what is is what they are, which is foreign to being, and being is (as) not being. On these grounds, there is nothing other than what is: literally nothing lies outside being. But this is disturbing precisely because writing is lost in it, and its loss, its castration, is lost. Distance itself is lost.[12]

Losing the loss is the structure of being, that is, writing, a structural oblivion or lack of access. If there were distance, there would be access, a path and a method, but the loss of distance is put off, held off at its structural inception, the loss of the loss being a guarding against this loss, what Derrida calls the apotrope, or erection which 'comes' before being, and which leads Derrida to suggest, in *Glas*, that the verb 'to be' should be changed every time for 'to get an erection' − to raise the apotropaic distance before being as a kind of writing tool which writes in seminal white, blankly, in little jerks.

---

12 On the notion of distance, I would like to take the opportunity to refer the reader to my essay, 'Title without colon', in *Angelaki*, 1: 1 (1993), 69–78.

Of *winking*:   spasmodic movements cannot be told apart from the rhythm of life. The elasticity of chance makes the span of distance, objective knowledge and science in general, tremble. 'The tympanum squints' (*MDP*, vii/*MOP*, xv); 'a regular, rhythmic blindness takes place in the text' (*E*, 100/101); 'the time of a blink which buries the look in a batting of the eyelid, the instant named *Augenblick* or wink, blink, and that which gives way in the twinkling of an eye' (*MD'A*, 53/*MB*, 48, modified); 'there is a duration to the blink, and it closes the eye. This alterity is in fact the condition for presence, presentation, and thus for *Vorstellung* in general; it precedes all the dissociations that could be produced in presence, in *Vorstellung*' (*LVP*, 73/*SAP*, 65); 'there is no *aletheia*, only a wink of the hymen' (*LD*, 293/*D*, 261); 'the supreme spasm of infinite masturbation' (*LD*, 243/*D*, 214); 'the orgasm of the glottis or the uvula, the clitoral glue, the cloaca of the abortion, the gasp of sperm, the rhythmed hiatus of an occlusion, the saccadanced spasm of an eructojaculation, the syncopated valve of tongue and lips' (*G*, 138b/*Gl*, 121b); the mimo-plants '"contract when touched"' and '"seem to represent the grimaces of a mime"';[13] '"and of the blink (−) between the two col (−)"'.[14]

Of *dis-tance*:   these fake concepts come very close to each other in a mime of each other from which the value of truth has been deducted – which makes mime something other than mime (mime classically being coordinated with truth). In miming each other, they are miming themselves, with an autobiographic displacement. There is a dance written into the distance which comes through in Derrida's essay on Nietzsche, *Eperons*, which reads the German word for '*Distanz*' wrongly or falsely, as '*Dis-Tanz*', 'dis-dance'. It is not a matter, again, of reading Derrida correctly, with a certain hermeneutic investment in the reading, but more of writing with the writing and giving a chance to falseness – and by falseness I mean the autobiographical necessity

13 *S*, 7/6 and 139/138. This quotation is quoted twice in *Signéponge*, as if miming itself between one end of the book and the other.
14 *LV*, 138/*TT*, 121. This last is a self-quotation, from *Glas*. A few pages on in *La vérité en peinture* (*LV*, 180/*TT*, 157), Derrida writes of the necessity of self-quotation (a necessity because integral to the relation to the other): '(it will be demanded that I quote myself, patiently, I'm talking here of *Ich* and exhibiting it as an other, and all and sundry)'. *Ich*, one recalls, ought not to be conflated with a human narcissism. And in *Signéponge*: 'I cite only myself' (*S*, 11/10).

insisted on above, the necessity of staking out a property in the midst of an endlessly removing confusion. This proprietorial hope allows not for hermeneutic control, but relinquishes the writing to itself such that the texts 'enumerate themselves, write themselves, read themselves. Themselves, of, by themselves' (*LD*, 322/*D*, 209, modified). Without this contract of property, the tension of a wink, there would be less than nothing or absolute absence, not even the faked orgasm of the writing. There must be autobiography, even though this be beside itself.

Distance is disorganized by dis-dance, that is, by itself in its autobiographic subsidence. It mimes itself, like a dancer, as if there were two of them, or as if, like Mallarmé's Pierrot in Derrida's analysis of him (in *La dissémination*), it took itself as its object through a detour in itself as the other where 'this entirely other is absolutely close' (*S*, 99/98); as if there were something, a nothing, between them, the clenched veil of a dancer ('at each turn, more veil'),[15] a spasm allowing for their respiration and quasi-symmetry, a 'regulated, measured distance [*éloignement*] between a too-close and a too-far'.[16] The self plays with itself, its other, 'not in order to approach you finally and to vanquish you, to triumph over distancing, but so that by you might be given to me the distancing which,' between me and myself, 'regards me' (*LCP*, 32/*TPC*, 27):

The one in the other, the one in front of the other, the one after the other, the one behind the other?

I have always known that we are lost and that from this very initial disaster an infinite distance has opened up this catastrophe, right near the beginning, this overturning that I still cannot succeed in thinking was the condition for everything, not so?, ours, our very condition, the condition for everything that was given us or that we destined, promised, gave, loaned, I no longer know what, to each other – we lost each other – one another, understand me? (*LCP*, 23–4/*TPC*, 19)

The writing mimes itself, quotes itself otherwise, with a distorted disdance. The line of distance is, again, an apotropaic, desirous line,

---

15 Sc, 39. In the French version of 'Scribble' I have used (SPE) only the first nine pages of Derrida's essay are published, and our quotation does not appear in its French form among these.

16 *LV*, 162/*TT*, 141. That distance is neither nearness nor farness is emphasized on the last page of the excellent expository article by Timothy Clark, 'Being in mime: Heidegger and Derrida on the ontology of literary language', *Modern language notes*, 101: 5 (1986), 1003–21.

that of the erection undecided between copulation (murder) and masturbation (suicide), a spur, hyphen or line that it sticks out in order to keep its distance, from itself, and between (at least) two texts. As Françoise Meltzer writes, 'Mimetic creation can be said to engage death – because the simulacrum of life, in its static presence, negates by its very stasis the life it depicts.'[17] Thus, for example, what had been mimed in *Eperons*, the distance throwing out a line of hyphen, a pointed thing, via a quotation from Nietzsche – '"primarily and above all – distance!"' (*E*, 46/47) – is mimed in *La carte postale* 'according to what mode of distancing. And there – ' (*LCP*, 54/*TPC*, 47). Both moments are followed by an interruption in the text, a further 'dis-tancing' (*G*, 84b/*Gl*, 71b). *Eperons* continues, at a distance, with:

Veils [thus menaced by the thrust of the hyphen preceding it]
What is the opening step of that *Dis-tanz*? Its rhythm already is mimed in Nietzsche's writing. The hyphen, a stylistic effect inserted *between* the Latin quotation (*actio in distans*) which parodies the philosopher's language and the exclamation point, suspends the word *Distanz*. The play of silhouettes which is created here by the hyphen's pirouette serves as a sort of warning to us to keep our distance from these multifarious veils and their shadowy dream of death.

This comes in the blankness or interspace pushed out by the distancing hyphen. It, in turn, is mimed, in *La dissémination*:

Each pirouette is then, in its twirling, only the mark of another pirouette, totally other and yet the same. The 'cipher of pirouettes prolonged toward another motif' thus suggests the line – which unites but also divides, the hyphen and the spacing – between two 'words' or 'signifiers', for example between the two occurrences of the signifier 'pirouette' which, from one text to the other and first of all in the blank of the inter-text, entrain, entail, and encipher each other, moving about like silhouettes, cut out like black shadows against a white background, profiles without faces, a series of sketches forever presented askew, turning around the shaft of a wheel, the invisible axis of writing, a potter's wheel endlessly spinning away.

(*LD*, 272/*D*, 241, modified)

The texts mime the 'object' of their 'analysis' while referring only to each other, in a graphic autobiographic which is a series of 'typographical marionettes' (*DL'E*, 106/*OS*, 66), of which Derrida

---

17 Françoise Meltzer, *Salome and the dance of writing: portraits of mimesis in literature* (Chicago and London: The University of Chicago Press, 1987), p. 116.

attests 'so many strings [*fils*], and not only my own, but I am the last to pull on them, to allegedly hold them in hand. I am rather the marionette, I try to follow the movement' (*LCP*, 202/*TPC*, 188).

Of *vocables*: these word-things emitted by Derrida, these fake concepts, resemble one another without having the limits between them that would enable one to determine where the resemblance begins and ends, the limit between the imitator and the imitated. One 'word' may contain the 'same' 'vocable' as another. Among the vocables that are most insistent in Derrida: gl, tr, ver, de, sp, ch/j/g, li. The effect, when they are put into 'words', is one of resemblance without the continuity of seriality. They are used 'anagrammatically', playing with their capacity for identification that passes before yielding to hermeneutic inspection. An example would be the opening of 'Télépathie' which turns the 'ver' vocable into '*rêve*', '*vérité*', '*vicieux*', and so on; or 'Ocelle comme pas un' which reverses '*chien*' with '*niche*' and others. These texts, like so many of Derrida's, leave one with the feeling of reaching the end without having 'read' them, so much of their activity passing at a pre-hermeneutic level. Simultaneously, however, there will have been a hermeneutic yield on the text, an interpretative purchase — which is peculiarly compromised by the field of the vocable which it has been unable to cover. The surprise is that the two, the vocable and the hermeneutic object, can be held together, or rather, that what is called the 'text' can perform these incompatible operations. Which must mean that the concept of the text can only be something much stronger and stranger than a hermeneutics will have ever given it credit for.

The vocables 'enact' the primary resemblances, like rhymes or homonyms,[18] of writing before the institution of the truth system. Autobiographically, they try to join up with each other, that is themselves, even autobiographically describing this operation as they do so, as in 'Télépathie' which talks about the piece of a word trying to join up with itself like a worm ('*ver*') seeking its severed other half. It is as if the 'text' were this crawling phalanx of mutilated worms in search of each other across an impossible distance, like the head of the Medusa, the psychoanalytic phenomenon of which Derrida's writings

---

18 On this question see, for example, Gregory Ulmer's 'OP WRITING: *Derrida's solicitation of* Theoria', in ed. Mark Krupnick, *Displacement: Derrida and after*, pp. 35–6.

again and again bring under analysis, and which leads again to a reformulation of the concept of castration.[19] 'The head of the Medusa, one of the three Gorgons, is between dashes ... Between the two lives, as their hyphen [*trait d'union*], their contract or contraction – death' (*G*, 55a, 95a/*Gl*, 45a, 82a). This is autobiography of the writhing worm box.

The vocable, then, is not a word or the piece of a word, but what I would call a sort of autobiographical breach belonging to a classification different in kind from that of roots, stems, etymologies and semantics: a classification of the overlap in itself, or non-classification. Instead of flourishing into the unique anthropomorphosis known as meaning, which speaks only of 'language' and thus passes everything that is within the field of the text through the exchange of the humanistic human, the vocable flourishes into an anima of some kind, a 'psyche' as Derrida puts it, essential to the erection of our desire (for meaning) but subordinating the question of essentiality.

Of *flowers*: in the botanical *Glas*, Derrida speaks of the 'antherection',[20] the erection of the flower, like the mimo plants in *Signéponge* cited above whose mimesis is so unnatural, so outside the schema of the representation of nature, which contract in a spasm of blank meaning. 'Antherection' appears to be a neologism, but in so far as its relation to the 'logos' is troubled, this remains a false appearance. Two 'words', anthos and erection, will have sought each other, tried to match up with each other in a sort of mime, and got stuck together with a glue which the laws of classical mimesis cannot properly prise apart. There is a stickiness, or tackiness, of the vocable, compelling it to bond, as if it were putting forth spores or eggs with an ante-semantic virulence. Thus it is already bound, bound to the possibility of bonding, like the tulip in *La vérité en peinture* whose 'free beauty' turns out to have been dictated by a prior bondage. Similarly, the 'flowers of rhetoric', analysed in *Marges*, are in contract with, as it were, the dark side of the sun, the other of the supremely natural object, the sun. Once again, what must be emphasized is the

19 See in particular that section of note 39 in *La dissémination* which runs across 47–8 (*D*, 40–1).
20 See also Sarah Kofman's 'Ça cloche', trans. Caren Kaplan, in ed. Hugh J. Silverman, *Derrida and deconstruction*, esp. pp. 124–33.

autobiographic energy of the flower – in its possibility of grafting: the possibility, that is, of a 'reproduction' from itself or of itself, without having to pass through the schema of 'natural' generation. The flower autobiographises in this graft, neither wholly of itself, nor wholly foreign to it, multiplying itself without addition, reproducing or producing – hard to say which – an unaccountable extra, itself. That would be its rhetorical flourish, that gratuitous element in reason, the 'rhetorical unconsciousness' we analysed in an earlier chapter.

Of *tone*: the flowers of rhetoric are classified neither like flowers nor like rhetoric, but by tone. 'A tone', declares *Signéponge* somewhat 'parodically', 'is decisive'. 'A tone is decisive; and who shall decide if it is, or is not, a part of discourse?' (*S*, 3/2). A tone is decisive, 'for the tone is the final index, the identity of some addressee who, lacking anything else, still dictates diction. And this confuses itself and explodes all by itself, nothing to be done, unity of tone does not exist' (*LCP*, 157–8/*TPC*, 145). If this is rather contracted, in *D'un ton apocalyptique* Derrida expands:

it occurs to me that *tonos*, tone, first signified the tight ligament, cord, rope, when it is woven or braided, cable, strap, briefly the privileged figure of everything subject to stricture. *Tonion* is the ligament as band and surgical bandage. In short, the same tension runs across the tonic difference … and tonal difference, the deviation, the changes or mutation of tones … From this value of tension, or of elasticity … we pass to the idea of a tonic accent, of rhythm, of mode (Dorian, Phrygian, etc.). The tone's pitch [*hauteur*] is tied to tension; it has a bond to the bond, to the bond's more or less tight tension. This is not sufficient for determining the meaning of the word tone when it is a matter of the voice. Even less when, through a great number of figures and tropical displacements, the tone of a discourse or of a piece of writing is analysed in terms of content, manners of speaking, connotations, rhetorical staging, and pose taken, in semantic, pragmatic, scenographic terms, and so on; in short, rarely, or not at all, in tuning into the pitch of a voice or to a quality of timbre. (*DTA*, 25–6/*OAT*, 8–9)

The tone is decisive in so far as it 'designates' that prior bond to the possibility of bonding that was signalled above. Specifically, tone testifies to a certain looseness or slack in the relation of word to thing which allows both for so-called correct usage and for catachresis and argot. Tone is 'present' in discourse, but its frequency, though individual, is not singular, and so forestalls a scientific notation of it; 'thus one can no longer decide, and that is the whole interest of writing' (*G*, 82b/*Gl*, 70b). To decide would be to cut the thing short, cut the tone off, interrupt it, castrate it into an ersatz truthfulness, to impose a castration extra to the castration implicit in the tone's concept, which is the castration not of economic loss but of tonal difference. Like style, tone is perhaps inimitable, a token of singularity, but this singularity is possible only because it can also be distorted, the tension altered, the pitch deranged.

Thus one becomes attentive to the tones of Derrida's writing, in other words the singular original twist given not to the word in relation to the thing, but to the relation itself which nonetheless is still intoned as discourse of a kind, with a specific tonal register. It is as if one were listening to a structural catachresis which almost falls within an auscultation, listening to something that can't quite be heard, listening to a denuded surface which has the infinite variety that is absent from the simple nudity of a blankness. Reading Derrida's tones is so close to feeling, but remains an intelligible feeling because of a compulsive withdrawal from pathos in his texts which makes of the tone an injunction, a command when it so often appears at first to be a solicitude. The tone is decisive, then, not as an arbiter of meaning, but as a recurrent, shaping necessity that constantly harps back to itself to receive its dictation, but slightly apart from itself, jealous or mistrustful, vulnerable always to its own vulnerability which it maintains with a fervent precision.

Of *letters*:   letters provide the evidence for the classical biography, and register the movement of the autobiography. But their auto-biographical function will have to signal a loss of self, as if the self were a letter gone astray, a form of open writing, for without this potential for loss, the distance for meaning could not be generated – 'there is distancing, the post, what there has to be so that it is legible for another' (*LCP*, 34/*TPC*, 29). Loss and gain interfuse, and distance no longer separates rigorously self from others. There is a general autobiography of the post, which is shameless in sharing its privacy openly, 'whore of a post' (*LCP*, 36/*TPC*, 30).

Of *the end*:   if the human has been considered classically as that which is in relation to its end (as death, reproduction of the final cause, as function), containing its end within itself as essence, life or being, then writing is that thing which, intolerant of finitude, repeatedly opens the end, not at its final limit, but precisely as the impossibility of that final limit's absolute finality, thus a quasi-limit more deathly in its absolute non-absoluteness than death. One can only stress that writing's otherness to the cohesion of the (philosophical, founding) system, is not an otherness with respect to a difference from it, but an otherness with respect to a transformation of difference itself. Where auto-biography is commonly considered to be an ordinarily human activity, reducing the life term to a coextension of meaning with history, one can see that with Derrida autobiography disturbs the very value of the human, that is, the relation of being to its end. Pitching itself at the origin of the origin, autobiography troubles the completeness of the identification of the origin with its end, opening that completeness and thus reducing the dominance of the relation to the end. In it, the human is not wholly human. Instead of being in relation to the end – a fantasm of inclusion – the value of the human is re-estimated with a view to what is foreign to the end, writing – writing, which suggests that the human is not within itself, such inclusion being given by the value of the end. The human must be reformulated according to the very thing which exceeds it, namely the autobiographic function of writing, which writes itself and whose structure takes the form of an inability to be reduced to an end.

Index of proper names

Abbot, H. Porter, 51 n. 1
Abraham, Nicolas and Torok, Maria, 142,
　145, 160
Adorno, Theodor (and Horkheimer, Max),
　(*Dialectic of Enlightenment*), 121
Agacinski, Sylviane, 181
Ainley, Alison, 91 n. 20
Allen, Suzanne, 177 n. 4
Allisson, David B., 86 n. 15
Amsterdam, 95
Apollo, 165
Ariès, Philippe, 130–31
Aristotle, 15–16, 17, 18, 27, 28
Augustine, St, 41, 46–7, 81
Austin, J. L., 31, 33

Babel, 35
Bacon, Francis, 3
Backès-Clément, Catherine, 151
Beckett, Samuel, 73
Beitchman, Philip, 52
Benjamin, Walter, 66, 159
Bennington, Geoffrey, 42, 102
Berezdivin, Ruben, 75 n. 1, 132
Bernasconi, Robert, 116
Blanchard, Marc Eli, 54, 67 n. 34
Blanchot, Maurice, 43, 118
Bloom, Harold, 25 n. 7, 152
Bloom, Molly, 82
Borges, Jorge Luis, 79
Bruss, Elizabeth W., 93 n. 24
Burt, E. S., 51
Byron, George, Lord, 153

Celan, Paul, 41, 109, 147
Chanter, Tina, 117
Chase, Cynthia, 162 n. 41
Chateaubriand, François Auguste René,
　vicomte de, 143, 152–3
Christianity, 40–41
Clark, Timothy, 185 n. 16
Cockshut, A. O. J., 59

Condillac, Etienne Bonnot de, 27–8, 29, 30,
　46
Conrad, Joseph, 84, 158
Critchley, Simon, 106
Culler, Jonathan, 162 n. 41

Dante, Alighieri, 156
Decarnin, Jean, 147
Delacampagne, Christian, 113
Deleuze, Gilles, 83 n. 11
De Man, Paul, 22, 31, 65, 66, 68, 70, 155,
　161–7, 170
De Medici, Lorenzo, 159
De Quincey, Thomas, 94
Derrida, Jacques, *passim*
Descartes, René, 15, 57, 95
Descombes, Vincent, 83 n. 11
De Staël, Mme, 153
Dido and Aeneas, 46
Donato, Eugenio, 69, 72
Dublin, 96

Epicureanism, 18, 27, 38
Esther, ix, 40
Eurydice, 139–41, 149, 156

Fleishman, Avrom, 53, 93 n. 24, 123
Florence, 159
Flores, Ralph, 79 n. 4
Forrester, John, 149–52
Foucault, Michel, 64
France, 152
Freud, Sigmund, 4, 12, 33, 38, 39, 74, 130,
　135–9, 148, 155, 169, 179
Fynsk, Christopher I., 83 n. 10

Gasché, Rodolphe, 43
Genet, Jean, 36 n. 6, 147
Geneva, 152
Giovanni, Don, 102
God, 41, 112–17, 119, 124–5, 127
Gorgons, 188

192

Index of proper names

Index of proper names